FANON'S WARNING

A Civil Society Reader on the New Partnership for Africa's Development

Second Edition

Edited By

Patrick Bond

Africa World Press, Inc.

P.O. Box 1892
Trenton, NJ 08607

P.O. Box 48
Asmara, ERITREA

Africa World Press, Inc.

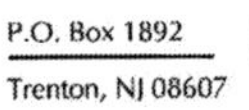

P.O. Box 1892
Trenton, NJ 08607

P.O. Box 48
Asmara, ERITREA

Book design: Sam Saverance
Cover design: Roger Dormann

Cataloging-in-Publication data is available from Library of Congress.

ISBN: 1-59221-008-2 (hb)
ISBN: 1-59221-009-0 (pb)

Table of Contents

1

Introduction

The national middle class discovers its historic mission: that of intermediary. Seen through its eyes, its mission has nothing to do with transforming the nation; it consists, prosaically, of being the transmission line between the nation and a capitalism, rampant though camouflaged, which today puts on the mask of neocolonialism. The national bourgeoisie will be quite content with the role of the Western bourgeoisie's business agent, and it will play its part without any complexes in a most dignified manner. But this same lucrative role, this cheap-Jack's function, this meanness of outlook and this absence of all ambition symbolise the incapability of the middle class to fulfill its historic role of bourgeoisie. Here, the dynamic, pioneer aspect, the characteristics of the inventor and of the discoverer of new worlds which are found in all national bourgeoisies are lamentably absent. In the colonial countries, the spirit of indulgence is dominant at the core of the bourgeoisie; and this is because the national bourgeoisie identifies itself with the Western bourgeoisie, from whom it has learnt its lessons...

In its beginnings, the national bourgeoisie of the colonial country identifies itself with the decadence of the bourgeoisie of the West. We need not think that it is jumping ahead; it is in fact beginning at the end. It is already senile before it has come to know the petulance, the fearlessness, or the will to succeed of youth.[1]

Frantz Fanon, *The Wretched of the Earth*

1. Fanon, F. (1963)[1961], *The Wretched of the Earth*, New York, Grove Press, pp.152-153.

INTRODUCTION

What can Africans and their supporters do about what is being termed 'global apartheid' - especially the chains represented by international economic processes and institutions?

To answer, this guide to the *New Partnership for Africa's Development* (Nepad) attempts to capture some of the spirit of the analyst, strategist and activist Frantz Fanon, whose work still best represents the radical spirit of political liberation and critical 'civil society' that emerged in Africa's anti-colonial struggle. (During the late 1950s and early 1960s, Fanon wrote glowingly of the Algerian revolution's liberated zones and celebrated the self-activity of ordinary people, organised in their communities, labour, youth and women's groups, in a manner similar to the style of progressives today.)

What Fanon unveils as 'the decadence of the West' - or, in our contemporary language, 'globalisation' - and the 'lucrative role, this cheap-Jack's function, this meanness of outlook and this absence of all ambition' come together, many contributors to this book believe, in elite-Africa's new response to the continent's crisis: Nepad.

This is a harsh way to begin. No doubt, such charges would be rejected by South African president Thabo Mbeki and his two main internationally-oriented cabinet colleagues, finance minister Trevor Manuel and trade/industry minister Alec Erwin. They deserve an introduction that highlights their impressive *positionality*, for probably no other African rulers have had such systematic influence at home and abroad:

- Since succeeding Nelson Mandela in 1999, Mbeki has chaired or hosted the Non-Aligned Movement, the Commonwealth, the World Conference Against Racism, and (in 2002-03) the African Union.
- Manuel was chair of the IMF/World Bank board of governors in 1999-2000, chair of the IMF/World Bank Development Committee in 2001-02, and co-chair of the March 2002 UN Financing for Development conference in Monterrey.
- Erwin held the presidency of the UN Conference on Trade and Development from 1996-2000, and helped broker the November 2001 Doha deal.

Contrary to Fanon's implicit accusation, these men locate not only their own (national) ambition but also the continent's potential transformation not in lucrative personal accomplishments or Western-style bourgeois decadence, but rather in the further integration of Africa into a world economy, they would also concede, that is itself in need of better regulation and fairer economic rules. Their project is to reform interstate relations and the embryonic world-state system. As Nepad explains,

> While globalisation has increased the cost of Africa's ability to compete, we hold that the advantages of an effectively managed integration present the best prospects for future economic prosperity and poverty reduction... The case for the role of national authorities and private institutions in guiding the globalisation agenda along a sustainable path and, therefore, one in which its benefits are more equally spread, remains strong.[2]

The reform strategy will fail, although not because of Pretoria's lack of international-elite credibility. Instead, the failure is already emanating from the very project of global-reformism itself, namely, Mbeki's underlying philosophy and incorrect analysis, ineffectual practical strategies, uncreative and inappropriate demands and counterproductive alliances. These problems are explored below.

Rather than leading the world, Mbeki and his Pretoria colleagues will more likely tread a well-known, dusty path: a post-colonial, neoliberal cul-de-sac of predictable direction and duration. Moreover, notwithstanding mixed rhetorical signals, Mbeki and Nepad for all effective purposes exclude (indeed, most often reject) alliances with civil society movements – local and international social, labour and environmental groups – which, in their struggles for socio-environmental and economic justice, *are the main agents of progressive global change.*

Thus South Africa's post-apartheid government leadership will not achieve its own limited objectives, much less the further-reaching transformation required under current excruciating global conditions, and in the process will continue alienating the poor and working-class base of Mbeki's African National Congress (ANC). In concluding that Thabo Mbeki *cannot* establish a new framework of

2. *New Partnership for Africa's Development*, 23 October 2001, http://www.nepad.org, p. 28, 40.

interaction with the rest of the world, but can instead merely front for a slightly modified residual version of 'global apartheid,' more hopeful analyses, strategies, demands, and alliances necessarily arise as alternatives.

WHAT IS DRIVING THE 'GLOBALISATION OF APARTHEID'?

It is quite evident that economic globalisation - by which is generally meant free flows of trade, finance and direct investment, under conditions of overwhelming transnational corporate power, underpinned by a system of global embryonic-state institutions based mainly in Washington - *simply doesn't work for South Africa, or Africa.*

South Africa is perhaps the best case: the economy with the most durable 'home-grown' (settler-based) capital accumulation process in Africa's history. Yet post-apartheid South Africa exists within an extremely unfavourable balance of global forces; to point this out had, by the turn of the 21st century, become pedestrian. As one trivial illustration, in July 2000 just after Germany had won the 2006 soccer World Cup hosting role by one vote, he bitterly remarked to his party's National General Council: 'As the ANC, we therefore understand very well what is meant by what one writer has described as the globalisation of apartheid.'[3]

It is with such phraseology that Mbeki accomplishes a dual elision: on the one hand a displacement of the South's problems from the (untouchable) economic to the moral-political terrain, which in turn evokes calls for reform (not dismantling) of existing economic systems and institutions; but on the other, as noted above, a relentless campaign to persuade his constituents that 'There Is No Alternative' to globalisation. For here, with Mbeki addressing the ANC National General Council, we locate a striking difference in Mbeki's rhetorics regarding racial apartheid - which the ANC always insisted should be 'abolished' not reformed - and global apartheid:

> [T]here is nobody in the world who formed a secret committee to conspire to impose globalisation on an unsuspecting humanity. The process of globalisation is an objective outcome of the development of the productive forces that create wealth, including their continuous improvement and

3. Mbeki, T. (2000), 'Keynote Address to the ANC National General Council,' Port Elizabeth, 12 July.

> expansion through the impact on them of advances in science, technology and engineering.[4]

Thus even though, *symptomatically* perhaps, power relations are skewed, the driving force of globalisation boils down, in Mbeki's neutral story, to little more than technological determinism. According to Nepad, 'The current economic revolution has, in part, been made possible by advances in information and communications technology (ICT)... We readily admit that globalisation is a product of scientific and technological advances, many of which have been market-driven.'[5]

The technology-centric 'admission' is fundamentally apolitical, and disguises the reality of dramatic changes in class relations, especially the resurgent power of US and EU capital in relation to working classes there and across the world (as reflected in stronger state-corporate 'partnerships' and the decline of the social wage during the Reagan, Thatcher and Kohl administrations). Ironically, in contrast, a far more insightful explanation of globalisation came from the ruling party of South Africa in October 1998, at a time when it needed to engage in leftwing rhetoric so as to pull its political Alliance (with trade unions and communists) together in preparation for a forthcoming national election:

> The present crisis is, in fact, a global capitalist crisis, rooted in a classical crisis of overaccumulation and declining profitability. Declining profitability has been a general feature of the most developed economies over the last 25 years. It is precisely declining profitability in the most advanced economies that has spurred the last quarter of a century of intensified globalisation. These trends have resulted in the greatly increased dominance (and exponential growth in the sheer quantity) of speculative finance capital, ranging uncontrolled over the globe in pursuit of higher returns.[6]

If this assessment is valid, then in addition to technological change – which *facilitated* but did not cause or catalyse globalisation – the more fundamental factors would include

4. Mbeki, 'Keynote Address.'

5. Nepad, p. 29, 39, 31.

6. ANC Alliance (1998), 'The Global Economic Crisis and its Implications for South Africa,' ANC Alliance Discussion Document, Johannesburg, reprinted in *The African Communist*, Fourth Quarter 1998.

- profound changes in the incentive structure of investments, especially the decline in manufacturing profits during the late 1960s and, consequently, the geographical search for new markets and cheaper inputs, and a switch by many major firms of productive reinvestment into financial assets;
- institutional factors associated with financial sector deregulation, concentration and centralisation, which permitted banks and other financiers to escape national boundaries and search out far-flung borrowers;
- the decaying power of nation-states and increased power of the Bretton Woods institutions and trade agencies; and
- shortened investor time horizons.

All of these factors can, and should be, reversed. Most are cyclical in nature. None are inevitable. None are even mentioned in Nepad. The analysis, thus is wanting - and so too are the mildly-reformist strategies that Mbeki subsequently endorses.

DRAWING OUT THE STRATEGIC IMPLICATIONS

Nepad's public reading of globalisation is blinkered and unrealistic, and so too are Mbeki's plans for reform. Here, South Africa's own experience is instructive, both in relation to lessons learned and actions taken to combat the excesses of global apartheid.

For post-apartheid South Africa, the mood of liberation shifted quickly to despair during three periods of powerful international financial discipline, currency crashes and capital flight, in early 1996, mid-1998 and 2000-01. The prime culprits in making South Africa so vulnerable were, firstly, the government's March 1995 decision, under intense pressure from local and international financiers, to discard the 'financial rand' dual-rate exchange control mechanism, and secondly the permissions granted from 1999-2001 to allow the largest South African firms to relocate (or delist entirely) their financial headquarters from Johannesburg to London.[7]

As the key decision-maker even under Nelson Mandela's presidency, Mbeki authorised both neo-liberal strategies. The initial effect of financial liberalisation was to attract enormous speculative financial inflows in 1995, which in turn fled rapidly as conditions changed and the investor-herd turned. All efforts to reverse the

7. *Mail & Guardian*, 6 and 13 December 2001.

flows failed in 1996, including much higher interest rates, the announcement of partial privatisation of the telephone company Telkom, and the adoption - without consultation and at the risk of ongoing, intensive political turmoil amongst Mbeki's Alliance partners - of the misnamed *Growth, Employment and Redistribution* (*Gear*) programme. All of that programme's targets failed from year one, with the exception of extremely low annual budget deficits and inflation rates, by recent historical standards.

Although widely acclaimed by South African capital, *Gear* did not change capitalist minds, and net disinvestment continued. To illustrate the capital strike, Pretoria's permission to grant the largest firms offshore status ensures South Africa's permanent decline. Dividends and profit repatriation were the main reason for the crash of the currency during 2000-01 (from R6.1/$ to R10.3/$), prior to the dramatic run in December 2001 (down to R13.8/$) by several major speculators.

Even aside from damage done by both major financial liberalisations, the country's allegedly 'sound economic fundamentals' had deteriorated markedly during the late 1990s. Growing foreign imports amplified local deindustrialisation and job loss, while trade with Africa became extremely biased, contributing to geopolitical tensions and economic refugees from neighbouring lands (and resulting world-class xenophobia by South African workers). Notwithstanding the battered currency, the consequent rapid rise in exports did not trickle through the rest of the economy. There was, moreover, a net outflow of international direct investment from South Africa during the first five years of democracy, while the uneven dribs and drabs of incoming foreign investment were largely of the merger/acquisition variety rather than for new fixed-investment ('greenfield') projects.

Simultaneously, economic advice poured in from international financial centres, based upon persistent demands not only for macroeconomic policies conducive to South Africa's increased global vulnerability, but also for social policies and even political outcomes that weakened the state, the working-class, the poor and the environment. The country's per capita living standards sunk to levels last seen during the early 1960s, while the world's worst inequality intensified. By 1998, real interest rates had reached their highest-ever levels in modern South African history, and the Johannesburg Stock Exchange crashed further than ever before in its history. At grassroots level, other manifestations of neo-liberalism during the late 1990s included unprecedented municipal bankruptcies (which forced cuts in water and electricity to the poorest citizens and exacerbated apartheid geographical segregation), the failure of the highest-profile microcredit schemes and most small banks, and, in the wake of a million jobs lost under ANC rule, the rise of the unemployment rate to 45%, higher than at any other time in the country's recorded history. Under these conditions, a host of diseases - cholera, diarrhoea, TB, Aids - flourished as never before, with five million South Africans HIV+ by 2002.

Mbeki could have learned from such homegrown problems, in considering how to implement an Africa-wide plan that also entailed reform of global economic institutions and processes. His ambitious lobbying schedule of world leaders during 2000-01 suggests he had all the access he required. However, what he said and wrote during this period confirms that instead of identifying how to uproot the causes of worsening global apartheid, Mbeki preferred to prune only the symptoms.

MBEKI'S SELF-MANDATE

The world was becoming an increasingly brutal place when Mbeki assumed the South African presidency in May 1999, as testified to by rising levels of mass-popular protest, both at meetings of the global elites and in numerous Southern settings, from Argentina to Zimbabwe, where neo-liberalism was generating intense pain.[8] In 1999, the main Northern protests occurred in London (June), at the G-8 Cologne meeting (July) and WTO Summit in Seattle (1999). In 2000, demonstrations against corporate globalisation and the Bretton Woods institutions were held in Davos (January), Washington (April), Windsor (July), Okinawa (July), Melbourne (September), Prague (October), and Nice (November). During 2001, the main protest sites were Gothenburg (March), Quebec City (April), London (May), Genoa (July) and Brussels (December). Momentum picked up in 2002 when protests targeted the World Economic Forum in New York (February) and EU leadership meeting in Barcelona (March).

South Africa, too, witnessed mass protests against neo-liberalism: by the Congress of South African Trade Unions in May 2000 and August 2001, at the World Conference Against Racism in September 2001, and in repeated local settings (against, for example, water/

8. For details, see Bond, P. (2003), *Against Global Apartheid: South Africa meets the World Bank, IMF and International Finance*, Cape Town, UCT Press and London, Zed Press, Chapters 8-12, and documentation by the World Development Movement: http://www.wdm.org.uk/cambriefs/DEBT/unrest.htm, and at *GreenLeft Weekly* newspaper.

electricity cutoffs and evictions due to poverty and in favour of land reform) in Soweto, Chatsworth, Mpumalanga, Bredell, Tafelsig and many other sites. Yet rather than responding by changing the local policies which were causing such grievances, Mbeki and his colleagues claimed a unique noblesse oblige, namely that Pretoria could help bridge the gap between the world's rich and poor.

For example, Mbeki explained to his party's National General Council in July 2000 that, in the wake of defeating apartheid, the ANC must dramatically expand its objectives:

> When we decided to address the critical question of the ANC as an agent of change, the central subject of this National General Council, we sought to examine ourselves as an agent of change to end the apartheid legacy in our own country. We also sought to examine the question of what contribution we could make to the struggle to end apartheid globally.[9]

Mbeki had earlier embarked upon a late 1990s' 'African Renaissance' branding exercise, which he endowed with poignant poetics but not much else. The contentless form was somewhat remedied in the secretive *Millennium Africa Recovery Plan,* whose powerpoint skeleton was unveiled to select elites in 2000, during Mbeki's meetings with Bill Clinton in May, the Okinawa G-8 meeting in July, the UN Millennium Summit in September, and a subsequent European Union gathering in Portugal. The skeleton was fleshed out in November 2000 with the assistance of several economists and was immediately ratified during a special South African visit by World Bank president James Wolfensohn 'at an undisclosed location,' due presumably to fears of the disruptive protests which had soured a Johannesburg trip by new IMF czar Horst Koehler a few months earlier.

By this stage, Mbeki managed to sign on as partners two additional rulers from the crucial North and West of the continent: Abdelaziz Bouteflika and Olusegun Obasanjo from Nigeria. But these allies came under mass protests and oversaw various civil, military, religious and ethnic disturbances at home, diminishing their utility as model African leaders. (Obasanjo, for example, spent February 2002 coddling the Mugabe dictatorship in Zimbabwe, jailing his trade union leaders when they engaged in a national strike against him, and saying, on CNN, 'Shut up!' to angry mourners whose family

9. Mbeki, 'Keynote Address.'

members had been amongst at least 2000 people killed by a Nigerian military arms depot explosion in a residential neighbourhood.)

That incident aside, 2001 was a successful year for selling Nepad. Another pro-Western ruler with a deplorable recent human rights record, Tanzania's Benjamin Mkapa, joined the New Africa leadership group in January at the World Economic Forum in Davos, Switzerland. There, Mbeki gave the world's leading capitalists and state elites a briefing, which was very poorly-attended. A few days later, an effort was made in Mali to sell West Africans to the plan, alongside Wolfensohn and Koehler. The July 2001 meeting of the African Union in Lusaka gave Mbeki the opportunity for a continent-wide leadership endorsement, once his plan was merged with an infrastructure-project initiative – the 'Omega Plan' – offered by the neo-liberal Senegalese president, Abdoulaye Wade, to become the *New African Initiative*. Next, the Genoa G-8 summit provided soothing encouragement, as 300,000 protesters gathered outside the conference accusing the world's main political leaders of running a destructive, elitist club.

Likewise, Mbeki's October 2001 visits to Japan and Brussels confirmed his elite popularity, perhaps because there was no apparent demand for formal monetary commitments. The same month, enthusiastic endorsements of Mbeki were published in the *Financial Times* by lead representatives of Johannesburg capital (Anglo American/DeBeers) and Washington multilateral banks.[10] After another name change, Nepad was publicly launched in Abuja, Nigeria, by several African heads of state on October 23, 2001. In February 2002, global elites celebrated Nepad in sites ranging from the World Economic Forum meeting in New York City to the summit of self-described 'progressive' national leaders (but including the neo-liberal Tony Blair) who gathered in Stockholm to forge a global Third Way. All elite eyes were turning to the world's 'scar' (Blair's description of Africa), hoping that Nepad would serve as a large enough bandaid.

OPTIMISM OF THE WILL, AND THE INTELLECT

'There are already signs of progress and hope,' Nepad asserts. 'Democratic regimes that are committed to the protection of human rights, people-centred development and market-oriented economies are on the increase.'[11] Set aside, for the moment, the 2001-02 elections

10. See the articles, reproduced in Chapter Two, below. See also South African Institute of International Affairs (2001), *Breaking the Cycle* (video), Johannesburg.

11. Nepad, p.7.

stolen by ruling parties in Tanzania, Madagascar, Zambia and Zimbabwe, thanks in part to the lethargy of all Africa's leaders, including Mbeki. The discursive strategy, here, is to uncritically posit the (untenable) neo-liberal conflation of free markets and free societies - a presumption that typically came unstuck in Africa during the 1990s during the course of repeated IMF Riots.

To this end, Nepad's core elements include:

- more privatisation, especially of infrastructure - no matter its failure, especially in South Africa;
- more insertion of Africa into the world economy - in spite of the even more rapid decline in terms of trade since the late 1990s;
- more multi-party elections - typically, though, between variants of neo-liberal parties, as in the US, which serves as a veil for the lack of thorough-going participatory democracy;
- grand visions of information and communications technology - hopelessly unrealistic considering the lack of simple reliable electricity across the continent; and
- a self-mandate for peace-keeping - which South Africa has subsequently taken for its soldiers stationed in the Democratic Republic of the Congo and Burundi.

Most importantly, Nepad fits into the globalisers' modified neo-liberal project, by which it is vigorously asserted, ever more incongruously, that integration into global markets solves poverty. To understand the damage associated with this ideological assumption, it is time to turn from Mbeki's analysis and strategic process to the specific content of his vision.

Making demands

As head of the Non-Aligned Movement, Mbeki addressed the Group of 77's April 2000 South Summit in Havana, and argued for reforming global apartheid on at least five fronts:

a) the alleviation of the debt burden carried by many of our countries, including its cancellation;
b) an effective mechanism to ensure a substantial increase in capital flows into the developing economies as this is a prerequisite for development;

c) the reversal of the trend resulting in a sharp drop in official development assistance;
d) the opening of the markets of the developed countries to our products, including agricultural products; and
e) the transfer of technology.[12]

Although Nepad only rarely ventures into detailed demands - which the document says are to be worked out later, by technical teams - we can consider these one by one, using the crucial issue of HIV/Aids treatment to exemplify the challenge of technology transfer.

DEBT DEBACLE

It is arguable that Mbeki's approach to the first, debt relief, has already done incalculable damage, mainly by virtue of his failure to endorse the Jubilee movement's campaign against 'Odious Debt,' including apartheid debt. Numerous vitriolic debates between civil society and Pretoria have occurred on this issue since 1996, and do not bear repeating in full here. Suffice to say, Jubilee critics argue, had Mbeki and his predecessor Nelson Mandela been truly serious about the debt issue, they would not have

- agreed to repay the apartheid foreign debt to commercial banks when it was last rescheduled in October 1993;
- claimed, repeatedly, that there *is no* foreign debt owed by the South African government (by ignoring roughly US$25 billion parastatal and private sector debt, for which the South African state inherited repayment and guarantor responsibilities);
- negated the possibility of demanding reparations for previous foreign credits to the apartheid regime; and
- endorsed, repeatedly, the Highly Indebted Poor Countries initiative of the G-8, IMF and World Bank, which proved such a distraction from the cause of debt cancellation.[13]

By October 2001, this latter point was more widely recognised, so Nepad contains the observation that HIPC 'still leaves many countries within its scope with very high debt burdens... In addition, there are countries not included in the HIPC that also require debt relief to

12. Mbeki, T. (2000), 'Address at the Opening of the South Summit,' Havana, 12 April.
13. http://www.aidc.org.za

release resources for poverty reduction.' (Presumably Nigeria is the main country in mind, since post-apartheid South Africa has always aimed to avoid lowering its credit rating by questioning its own debt repayment.)

Yet rather than attempting to challenge HIPC forthrightly, the Nepad strategy is to:

> support existing poverty reduction initiatives at the multilateral level, such as the Comprehensive Development Framework of the World Bank and the Poverty Reduction Strategy approach linked to the HIPC debt relief initiative... Countries would engage with existing debt relief mechanisms - the HIPC and the Paris Club - before seeking recourse through the New Partnership for Africa's Development.[14]

Only later will Nepad 'establish a forum in which African countries may share experiences and mobilise for the improvement of debt relief strategies' with the aim of ending 'the process of reform and qualification in the HIPC process.'[15] To be sure, the idea of sharing experiences and mobilising to improve 'debt relief strategies' is portentous. But HIPC is already widely derided - especially in the Jubilee South movement - as 'a cruel hoax.'[16] Along with the IMF/World Bank Comprehensive Development Frameworks and the Poverty Reduction Strategy Programmes, HIPC deals are fundamentally committed to maintaining existing power relations and the neo-liberal economic philosophy because they entail only very slight adjustments to debt loads, and in return require lowest-income countries to further liberalise.

To illustrate, in the main Southern African pilot HIPC, Mozambique's conditionality requirements included quintupling cost-recovery charges (user fees) at public health clinics, privatisation of urban and rural water supply systems, and the simultaneous liberalisation and privatisation of its largest agro-industry, cashew-nut processing, which destroyed the industry. President Chissano publicly complained about the low levels of debt cancellation and the pressure he was under to inappropriately liberalise the economy by the Bretton Woods institutions.

---

14. Nepad, p.118,149.
15. Nepad, p.150.
16. http://www.jubileesouth.net

Nepad takes the African debate on HIPC backwards. Its proposed course of action - namely, prioritising HIPC and the Paris Club where structural adjustment loans are negotiated - will initially cement African debt-peonage. When Africa is further weakened by further slides down the HIPC slope, as more wretched countries sign up, only then will experiences be shared and the programme's neo-liberal conditions (perhaps) be contested. At the very time that Argentina was forced to default, a much more profound questioning of the ethics of foreign debt repayment would have been welcome.

REVERSING CAPITAL FLOWS

Regarding the second issue, inflows of capital, there are two kinds worth considering: financial and foreign direct investment. It hardly needs arguing that 'hot-money' speculative inflows to emerging markets such as South Africa do not by any stretch qualify as 'a prerequisite for development.'

Nor do the vast majority of foreign loans granted to Third World governments over the past thirty years, including concessional (0.75% interest rate) loans through the World Bank's International Development Association and African Development Bank. Those loans serve as the leverage for gaining neo-liberal conditions from borrowers. Repayment of even concessional hard-currency loans is extremely expensive once a country's currency collapses, as happens regularly to Africa. Yet Nepad calls for more such loans in one of its mandates to signatories:

> Work with the African Development Bank and other development finance institutions on the continent to mobilise sustainable financing especially through multilateral processes, institutions and donor governments, with a view to securing grant and concessional finance to mitigate medium term risks.[17]

Financing is one of Nepad's Achilles Heels, because existing institutions and processes are so destructive. Most importantly, there is no logic to the African Development Bank and World Bank process of lending in *hard currency* for developmental goods and services - e.g., rural education - whose components are nearly entirely based on locally-sourced inputs (not requiring hard currency repayment). The loans are repayable with high effective interest rates, as the value

17. Nepad, p.106.

of African currencies falls. The uses of the hard currency are rarely in the interests of the majority of Africans.

A more appropriate self-mandate in relation to foreign financiers is readily available in the ANC's 1994 *Reconstruction and Development Programme* (*RDP*):

> [Southern African countries] were pressured into implementing [IMF and World Bank] programmes with adverse effects on employment and standards of living... The RDP must use foreign debt financing only for those elements of the programme that can potentially increase our capacity for earning foreign exchange. Relationships with international financial institutions such as the World Bank and International Monetary Fund must be conducted in such a way as to protect the integrity of domestic policy formulation and promote the interests of the South African population and the economy. Above all, we must pursue policies that enhance national self-sufficiency and enable us to reduce dependence on international financial institutions.[18]

Regrettably, Mbeki and Manuel ignored this provision, amongst many other progressive *RDP* mandates.

Even if attracting further financial flows of the hot-money and multilateral types is a questionable objective, the second kind of potential capital inflow – plant, equipment and machinery through foreign direct investment – is typically understood as an essential ingredient in any Washington-approved development strategy. But after having done all in his power to attract foreign direct investment (FDI), not even Mbeki has succeeded. Good governance and political stability are not the key factors, Africa has learned, *otherwise oil-rich Angola and Nigeria would not be the continent's main beneficiaries of FDI inflows*.

Nepad's main solution to the foreign investment drought appears to be the promotion of a foreign stake via 'Public-Private Partnerships' in privatised infrastructure, an extremely controversial strategy that is discussed at length in the *Annotated Critique*.

Instead of foreign portfolio or even FDI flows, the more important financing challenges for Africa are establishing scrupulous, publicly-owned development finance institutions and tough financial-sector

18. African National Congress (1994), *The Reconstruction and Development Programme*, Johannesburg, Umanyano Publications, s.1.4.17,6.5.16.

regulations, including effective exchange controls, that would allow for the circulation and reinvestment of the continent's existing financial resources, too many of which are frittered away in debt repayments, speculative projects, luxury real estate development, and capital flight via African branches of foreign banks (typically headquartered in London and Paris) and by corrupt, *comprador* local banks. Nepad offers little or nothing to help Africa become more self-reliant in financing using such strategies, which were the basis of, for example, Korea's success. One reason is that active state intermediation in financial markets remains out of favour in Washington.

AID FATIGUE

Third, regarding foreign aid, Mbeki calls for 'more and better managed aid so as to deal with the basic needs that will have to precede any form of development in certain areas.'[19] One problem is that Mbeki did very little in practice to dissuade Clinton and other international leaders of the classically neo-liberal trend known as 'trade, not aid' (the 1990s value of North-South aid fell by a third).[20]

What lessons does South Africa itself have to offer? Were foreign donors encouraged, under post-apartheid rule, to turn aid pledges into real programmes; sustainably provide for basic needs; promote civil society; and support good aid-management (e.g., monitoring and evaluation, and regular collective consultations with government)? There is a strong case that the Mandela and Mbeki governments were disastrous models in all these respects.

As one example, donor pledges of nearly $5 billion were made to Pretoria between 1994 and 1999. But just as government failed to disburse much of its own domestic-sourced development funding (80% annual *RDP*-related budget 'rollovers' were typical in the early years, but even during the late 1990s, inability to spend poverty relief funding became a national scandal), the record of South Africa's largest donor (the European Union) was also appalling. Thus in making the case for more aid internationally, Mbeki has not yet provided a convincing case that such aid won't exacerbate well-known problems of bureaucratic capture and non-sustainability.

---

19. Mbeki, 'Address by President Thabo Mbeki to the Commonwealth Club, World Affairs Council and US/SA Business Council Conference.'

20. *Financial Times*, 11 November 1998.

Trade rules

Fourth, Mbeki wants to correct what he calls the 'rules and regulations that make the world trading system unbalanced and biased against the very countries that need a fair trading system so that these countries, which represent the majority of humanity, benefit from international rules of trade.'[21] Even if the South African economy is on the margins of world trade, Pretoria won a high profile in global circuits for at least three institutional reasons: Alec Erwin's 1996-2000 presidency of the UN Conference on Trade and Development; his controversial role in the 1999 WTO Summit in Seattle; and his subsequent attempt to bring together both a new middle-income bloc and African countries to restart WTO negotiations. The latter two functions - particularly Erwin's distaste for the Seattle social-movement protesters and his near-refusal to join the Africa bloc of trade ministers protesting abominable treatment by US trade negotiator Charlene Barchefsky - have been addressed by other experts.[22]

Throughout, Erwin argued for less Northern protectionism for 'dinosaur industries' like manufacturing and agriculture, but he has done so meekly: 'In addressing the challenge of trade and development in Unctad IX, we were attempting to break with a conception of contestation by stressing partnership.'[23] The effectiveness of 'partnership' was made explicit in 1998-1999, when US vice president Al Gore lobbied Erwin, health minister Nkosazana Dlamini-Zuma and Mbeki himself, to roll back the 1997 *Medicines Act*, which promoted the parallel import and generic production of anti-retroviral drugs essential in fighting HIV/Aids. The transnational pharmaceutical corporations threatened a constitutional lawsuit against the *Act*, which they actively pursued for a month in March 2001 before international protest forced them to withdraw. This life-and-death case of technology transfer - blocked by corporations whose billions of dollars in profits overrode access to drugs that would save millions of lives - is instructive about the nature of alliances.

21. Mbeki, 'Address to the Commonwealth Club, World Affairs Council and US/SA Business Council Conference.'

22. See, e.g., Tandon, Y. (1999), 'A Blip or a Turnaround?,' *Journal on Social Change and Development*, 49, December; Keet, D. (2000), 'South Africa's Role in the WTO,' Alternative Information and Development Centre Occasional Paper, Cape Town.

23. Erwin, A. (2000), 'Opening Address to the Tenth Session of Unctad,' Bangkok, 12 February.

BLOCKING ACCESS TO DRUGS

Fifth and finally, what do we learn about the struggle for technology transfer in the case of Aids drugs? It was not Erwin's philosophy of a fair and just trade partnership that persuaded the US leader to halt his campaign against HIV+ Africans. A vibrant 'Treatment Action Campaign' of grassroots militants emerged in South Africa during 1999, embarked on protests at US consulates in Johannesburg and Cape Town, and began networking with the Philadelphia, New York and Paris chapters of the advocacy group ACT UP (Aids Coalition to Unleash Power). Gore was confronted repeatedly and aggressively by protests in Tennessee, New Hampshire, California and Pennsylvania at the very outset of his presidential election campaign in mid-1999. Numerous newspapers carried front-page stories on Gore's quandary.

Within weeks, the vice president's own cost-benefit analysis began to reveal the danger of siding with the pharmaceutical firms, whose millions in campaign contributions would not offset sustained damage to the politician's image. In a September 1999 meeting with Mbeki in New York, Gore conceded the validity of the SA *Medicines Act*. With Thailand, Brazil and India also taking strong non-partnership positions by establishing generic production facilities, and with tens of thousands of protesters in the streets, President Clinton agreed at the Seattle WTO summit not to push for harder-line patent protection for US pharmaceutical companies. (The firms reacted with promises of cheaper, though not free, drugs, which in turn were spurned by activists as too little, too late. When faced with the prospect of local production, drug companies changed the subject by announcing offers of free medicine, which subsequently did not materialise.)

The South African government then failed to take advantage of the space won by the activists, as Mbeki searched for excuses – such as a controversial investigation into whether HIV is indeed associated with Aids, the alleged toxicity of anti-retrovirals and (artificial) fiscal constraints (which did not prevent Mbeki authorising tens of billions of rands worth of arms expenditures) – to *not* implement the parallel importation or generic production options. By the time Nepad was launched, Mbeki's HIV/Aids policies were routinely described as 'genocidal' in the local and international press, and Mbeki seemed to amplify his extraordinary image as South Africa's 'undertaker-in-chief' in December 2001 by authorising the Constitutional Court appeal of a hostile court judgment that required the state to begin widescale anti-retroviral mother-to-child-transmission treatment. Nelson Mandela had demanded the same of Mbeki, very publicly at the July 2000 Durban international Aids conference, but notwithstanding Nepad's brief mentions of a 'high priority given to tackling HIV/Aids' and leadership in a 'campaign for increased international financial support for the struggle against HIV/Aids,'[24] Mbeki continued to make arguments and policy that classified him as an Aids-dissident.

Even if in retrospect it was pyrrhic, the joint struggle by the South African government and the activists over Gore and the pharmaceutical corporations was instructive. In short, the David-v-Goliath battle against pharmaceutical companies - and the White House - was won. Yet Mbeki quickly grabbed defeat from the jaws of victory, and the broader war against Aids took a quick turn for the worse.

In sum, progress on any of the five key issues Mbeki listed in Havana depends on whom he is in partnership with. Before considering the question of alliances, a sixth major problem has suddenly found its way to the agenda of South African elites: environment.

African ecological modernisation

On environmental issues, in preparation for the August-September 2002 World Summit on Sustainable Development (WSSD) in Sandton, Johannesburg, much the same will be expected of Mbeki: putting a bandaid on global ecological crisis on behalf of the Northern polluters. The environmental analysis that Nepad promotes combines bland sustainable-development rhetoric with faith in global eco-reform processes (like the WSSD) based on market mechanisms, augmented by an implicit and sometimes explicit Malthusianism. Thus 'The expansion of industrial production and the growth in poverty contribute to environmental degradation of our oceans, atmosphere and natural vegetation.'[25]

Several contradictory processes are conflated in this pop-environmental reading of the relationship between poverty and ecological degradation. Africa's main economic problem is not excessive pollution-intensive industrialisation, but insufficient industrialisation, which in turn leads to greater reliance for export earnings upon ecologically-destructive raw material extraction (e.g., the rain-forests and strip-mines, or the substitution of cash crops

24. Nepad, p. 49, 127.

25. Nepad, p. 37.

for food crops). Globalisation has exacerbated these processes, because the 'environmental degradation of our oceans, atmosphere and natural vegetation' is mainly a function of transnational and local corporate irresponsibility: e.g., over-exploitative EU and East Asian fishing trawlers, pollution-intensive South African mines and metal companies which defile the air and water without paying the externality costs, and forestry companies whose alien-timber plantations destroy the integrity of African soils.

In some cases, obviously, the colonial/apartheid displacement of large populations from good farms to infertile areas led to worsening soil degradation, for which the solution is a thorough-going land reform and rural development programme – i.e., the opposite of the extremely meagre efforts the South African government is making (less than 1% arable land redistribution during the first term of ANC rule, 1994-99, and an even slower pace since). But more generally, to ascribe environmental destruction to 'growth in poverty' is to blame the victims: the masses whose poverty has worsened in part because of corporate-led globalisation.

Again, by way of distorting complex socio-environmental processes, Nepad announces, 'It is obvious that, unless the communities in the vicinity of the tropical forests are given alternative means of earning a living, they will co-operate in the destruction of the forests.'[26] Here would have been an opportunity to target the transnational corporations and banks involved in rainforest destruction,[27] as well as mercenary armies from Zimbabwe, Angola, Uganda, Rwanda and other countries which are presently stripping timber and raw materials from the DRC, but Nepad fails to do so.

Another crucial example of Nepad ducking the issue is its two-sentence note on how the Environmental Initiative will tackle global warming: 'The initial focus will be on monitoring and regulating the impact of climate change. Labour-intensive work is essential and critical to integrated fire management projects.'[28] Starting at home, if Mbeki was serious about offering strong leadership, he would address the fast-growing contribution of South Africa to greenhouse gas emissions. Pretoria's industrial policy is premised upon minerals beneficiation which requires vast amounts of electricity, for the sake of glutting already-saturated metals markets. South Africa, as a result, ranks amongst countries with the most greenhouse gas

26. Nepad, p.13.
27. http://www.ran.org
28. Nepad, p.141.

emissions per person, corrected for income levels.[29] (The alternative would be to demand far stronger treaties and agreements on the need to reduce in absolute terms the production of global warming gasses by moving to genuinely sustainable development strategies - which is off Mbeki's agenda in South Africa.)

Nepad's overarching ideology of market-led growth with sustainable development comes together in this paragraph:

> While growth rates are important, they are not by themselves sufficient to enable African countries achieve the goal of poverty reduction. The challenge for Africa, therefore, is to develop the capacity to sustain growth at levels required to achieve poverty reduction and sustainable development. This, in turn depends on other factors such as infrastructure, capital accumulation, human capital, institutions, structural diversification, competitiveness, health and good stewardship of the environment.[30]

There is, here, an annoying combination of progressive and neo-liberal objectives: infrastructure, human capital, institutions, structural diversification, health and good stewardship of the environment in the first category, and capital accumulation and competitiveness in the second. Objectively, neo-liberal policies have, during the past two decades, destroyed Africa's infrastructure, human capital, institutions, structural diversification, health and stewardship of the environment. The failure to come to grips with this contradiction is emblematic of Nepad's double-talk, and helps explain why the programme's core strategies and demands are so

---

29. As a palliative, Mbeki has authorised the development of a Clean Development Mechanism (CDM) prototype, mainly designed by the World Bank, so that South Africa can help to pilot the idea of carbon trading in the Third World. Consistent with the most questionable characteristic of the Kyoto Protocol, the CDM effectively means that wealthy countries and transnational corporations can *buy* the right to continue destroying the environment. Pretoria has also confused its own environmental community by accepting the use of appallingly destructive alien-invasive forest plantations as alleged Kyoto carbon 'sinks,' and is also firmly promoting the Pebble Bed Nuclear Reactor concept which industry advocates also hope to make a Kyoto sink as part of the Protocol's weakening, in order to bring the US back in.

30. Nepad, p.64.

weak. But 'talking Left, acting Right' is a more general feature of Mbeki's rule, as we see from his outreach to internationalists.

'GLOBAL SOLIDARITY'

At one point in his May 2000 US trip, speaking to an African-American congregation at the venerable Ebenezer Church in Atlanta, Mbeki invoked the forces of social progress:

> In a world where no country can insulate itself from other parts of the same world, our success is highly dependent on your concrete support. This global solidarity between ourselves was part of the vocabulary of the civil rights movement, and some of us will remember that Dr King was one of the first world leaders to call for a boycott of South Africa as part of the struggle for democracy. This kind of solidarity amongst those who work for the same objectives, has been the hallmark of our own movement and struggle for democracy. We are therefore saying that we should continue with this struggle of working together and striving for social and economic justice for the poor, for countries of the South, and come with practical ways of assisting Africa to pull herself out of the quagmire of poverty. I can assure you that you will find many amongst Africans who are ready to work in honest partnership with yourselves.[31]

But with whom in the world does Thabo Mbeki really have an honest partnership, and with whom is he building genuine solidarity? Notwithstanding the eloquence of his Atlanta speech, the answers are not obvious.

To illustrate, under Mbeki's influence, post-apartheid foreign policy examples of areas where solidarity was *not* extended to democrats include the Indonesian and East Timorese people suffering under Suharto (recipient of a 1997 Cape of Good Hope medal), Nigerian opposition activists who in 1995 were denied a visa to meet in Johannesburg, the Burmese people (given the junta-controlled 'Myanmar's' unusual diplomatic relations with Pretoria), the Polisario Liberation Front struggling for self-determination in the Western Sahara (until Mbeki ended his allegiance with Morocco in 2002), and victims of murderous central African regimes which were SA arms recipients. The National Conventional Arms Control Committee reported that from 1996-98 alone, undemocratic regimes

31. Mbeki, T. (2000), 'Address at the Ebenezer Baptist Church,' Atlanta, 26 May.

like Colombia, Algeria and Peru purchased more than R300 million rand worth of arms from South Africa.[32]

Is there scope for an honest partnership between Mbeki and the world's progressive social movements? One problem immediately arises and must be openly confronted. In controversies surrounding Africa's relation to imperialism, as witnessed in numerous campaigns by South African labour and social-justice movements, Mbeki and the ANC repeatedly unveiled repressive tendencies: against millions of anti-privatisation strikers in the trade union movements, against thousands of community residents in Soweto suffering from unaffordable services because of privatisation pressure, and against leading opponents of Mbeki's Aids policies, who during 2000 were reportedly labeled by Mbeki as 'infiltrators' of the trade union movement and agents of pharmaceutical corporations and the CIA.

Thus on the eve of the 29-30 August 2001 anti-privatisation stayaway, as insults flew between leaders of the ANC and the SACP/ Cosatu, the front page of *Business Day* carried the following report:

> Cabinet ministers were subsequently dispatched to influential radio and television programmes first to 'clarify' government positions, but also to 'show Cosatu members they are being urged to commit suicide', according to an official involved in the spin-doctoring offensive. Also part of the strategy - championed by Trade and Industry Minister Alec Erwin, Transport Minister Dullah Omar and Public Enterprises Minister Jeff Radebe - was to seek to caution Cosatu members against the possible hijacking of their strike by outside elements such as those protesting at World Bank and International Monetary Fund meetings.[33]

Bizarre as it sounded at first blush, the same newspaper demonstrated the valid underlying rationale for Pretoria's hijack-phobia on the following day:

> SA needs to cut import tariffs aggressively, privatise faster and more extensively, promote small business effectively and change labour laws to achieve far faster growth and job creation. This is according to a World Bank report that

32. Batchelor, P. (1999), 'South Africa: An Irresponsible Arms Trader?,' in *Global Dialogue*, 4, 2, p.17.

33. *Business Day*, 27 August 2001.

will soon be released publicly and has been circulating in government.[34]

EMPOWERMENT?

Under such circumstances, what kind of role did Nepad envisage for civil society, aside from 'asking the African peoples to take up the challenge of mobilising in support of the implementation of this initiative by setting up, at all levels, structures for organisation, mobilisation and action'?[35] Nepad contains no concrete actions to be taken by the African peoples, no offer of organisational resources, and no civil-society implementation plan. The document itself was available to African civil society only through internet websites (very obscurely). There were no leadership-catalysed discussions of Nepad within civil-society organisations in South Africa itself - which is perhaps explained by the fact that Mbeki's Alliance partners in the trade unions and the SA Communist Party firmly opposed central neo-liberal Nepad economic and infrastructure provisions via mass protests and stayaways, simultaneous to Mbeki's attempt to sell these in international and a few continental venues.

Instead, the spirit of grassroots partnerships envisaged is captured in the vague mandate to 'Promote community and user involvement in infrastructure construction, maintenance and management, especially in poor urban and rural areas, in collaboration with the *New Partnership for Africa's Development* Governance Initiatives.'[36] This is, in principle, a useful strategy. But in practice, it has had the effect of placing financial and technical obligations that are the responsibility of the state in most civilised societies, onto the shoulders of Africa's most impoverished communities.

In South Africa, for instance, the effect of requiring a greater role for communities in administering full cost-recovery rural water schemes, was to leave most of them broken due to lack of community affordability. More than 43,000 children die of diarrhoea each year in South Africa as a function, mainly, of inadequate water and sanitation, which in turn is mainly an affordability problem. Similarly, the disconnection of (existing free) water supplies due to unaffordability occurred at the epicentre of the 2000-01 cholera epidemic, which affected more than 200,000 low-income people,

34. *Business Day*, 28 August 2001.

35. Nepad, p.56.

36. Nepad, p.106.

killing more than 200. Similar 'full cost-recovery' mandates come from the World Bank in its African water programme manuals, as discussed in the *Annotated Critique*.

It hardly needs saying that the implications of cutting off water, electricity and access to other vital services is most harmful to African women. That should be no surprise, as at least one impressive feminist analysis of Nepad has shown. Lusaka gender researcher Sara Longwe argues that,

> Nepad is deeply and comprehensively gender blind. It fails almost completely to recognise or address the major issues of gender inequality and discrimination, and the oppression of women that lie hidden and unacknowledged within Nepad goals and objectives, and which must be revealed and addressed if the participating governments are to meet its commitments under various international agreements and conventions.

What is revealed by such demands of African societies - made by both Mbeki and his Washington partners - is not only the counterproductive and illusory establishment of alliances and partnerships with the forces promoting global apartheid, but also the contradictory character of Mbeki's rhetoric concerning international social change. Notwithstanding the practical hostility Mbeki often shows when dealing with civil-society opposition to his neo-liberal policies, he often makes rhetorical gestures to the enormously important role of social-change activists. And as in Mbeki's own speeches, there is a high degree of empowerment rhetoric in Nepad:

> The New Partnership for Africa's Development seeks to build on and celebrate the achievements of the past, as well as reflect on the lessons learned through painful experience, so as to establish a partnership that is both credible and capable of implementation. In doing so, the challenge is for the peoples and governments of Africa to understand that development is a process of empowerment and self-reliance. Accordingly, Africans must not be wards of benevolent guardians; rather they must be the architects of their own sustained upliftment.[37]

37. Nepad, p.27.

This is inspiring rhetoric. But Nepad, in reality, shuns 'self-reliance' and the self-upliftment of Africans. To illustrate, none of the social-justice 'achievements' that cut against the grain of then-prevailing features of globalisation - especially mass civil-society protests that threw off the yokes of slavery, colonialism and apartheid - are specifically mentioned in Nepad. And Nepad asks readers to 'reflect' - but only in a blinkered way, so as to avoid a more thorough-going analysis and set of policy options. Thus none of the anti-imperialist ideas of the most progressive architects and analysts of 20th century African political and socio-economic liberation - e.g., Ake, Amin, Biko, Cabral, Fanon, First, Kadalie, Lumumba, Machel, Mamdani, Mkandawire, Nabudere, Nkrumah, Nyerere, Odinga, Onimode, Rodney, Sankara, Shivji - are considered worthy of reference, much less engagement and endorsement.[38]

Yet radical rhetoric still characterised some of Mbeki's speeches during 2000-01, as if to substitute for the top-down, elite-centred, non-consultative nature of Nepad. For example, to one audience of social-democratic activists in mid-2000, Mbeki was resolute in his commitment to nurture challenges from the grassroots:

> All of us, but most certainly those of us who come from Africa, are very conscious of the importance that all tyrants attach to the demobilisation of the masses of the people. At all times, these tyrants seek to incite, bribe or intimidate the people into a state of quiescence and submissiveness. As the movement all of us present here represent, surely our task must be to encourage these masses, where they are oppressed, to rebellion, to assert the vision fundamental to all progressive movements that - the people shall govern![39]

Mbeki, in reality, discourages rebellion - notably in Zimbabwe, where he repeatedly sided with the repressive Mugabe regime against the masses. Indeed, to understand how far the ANC government has gone to downgrade alliances with the Left, consider a 1996 ANC discussion document, which concluded with these lines:

> The democratic movement must resist the illusion that a democratic South Africa can be insulated from the processes

38. We know from Mbeki's August 2000 Oliver Tambo lecture that he is well acquainted with the ideas of radical Africans. His failure to invoke these in Nepad is revealing.

39. Mbeki, T. (2000), 'Vox Populi - Is it Real?: Speech at the IUSY Festival,' Stockholm, 28 July.

> which characterise world development. It must resist the thinking that this gives South Africa a possibility to elaborate solutions which are in discord with the rest of the world, but which can be sustained by virtue of a voluntarist South African experiment of a special type, a world of anti-Apartheid campaigners, who, out of loyalty to us, would support and sustain such voluntarism.[40]

The 1997 *Medicines Act* was, activists insist, precisely such a 'voluntarist experiment.' It was, indeed, *only* sustained by virtue of appeal, by local activists, to 'a world of anti-Apartheid campaigners' who 'out of loyalty,' militantly demonstrated in favour of the Act.

Conclusion: Shining or breaking global apartheid's chains?

This is where, finally, the argument comes to a head. So far, we have taken seriously the extent to which Mbeki says he *wants* to change the world, even if the analysis is wanting, the rhetoric often confuses listeners, the strategy is dubious and the tactics ineffective. Central to this problem, is whom Mbeki most comfortably allies with. The social forces represented in the Aids-treatment example are emblematic of the challenge, for they evoke enormous potential for real solidarity, *for changing the balance of forces.*

Nepad could – but doesn't – document 'the deep popular will' to build a new Africa. That ambition certainly does exist in various civil society initiatives, most of which stand in explicit opposition to Nepad. Across the continent, varied grassroots organisations – community-based groups, HIV/Aids support organisations, traditional and ethnic-based movements, progressive churches, women's and youth clubs, environmental groups and many others – have joined trade unionists and radical intellectuals in diverse struggles against neo-liberalism, for democracy and humanity. Many of the strongest expressions of popular will exist in South Africa, and involve Mbeki's Alliance partners who fundamentally reject the same policies of alleged 'macroeconomic stability' (fiscal and monetary austerity) and privatisation which Nepad axiomatically promotes.

The same deep philosophical rejection of Nepad and promotion of a genuine human-rights culture exists across Africa. In the political sphere, this led to mass demonstrations against unfree, unfair

40. ANC (1996), 'The State and Social Transformation,' Discussion document reprinted in *African Communist*, 4.

elections in Tanzania, Madagascar, Zambia and Zimbabwe, amongst other sites. In the economic sphere, trade unions regularly protest structural adjustment, and are joined by diverse citizen's movements. For example, Jubilee Africa branches motivate strongly for full debt repudiation, cancellation and reparations across the continent, and fundamentally reject Washington's debt relief strategies. African initiatives are also evident in the grassroots campaign for the return of Nigerian dictator Sani Abacha's billions in looted funds in Swiss and London banks. Early success helped to break open bank secrecy, following similar campaigns over fifteen years waged by citizens' groups and governments in the Philippines and Haiti in relation to the Marcos and Duvallier hoards.

In addition, specific World Bank projects in Africa have come under attack by progressive local and international groups, including the Chad-Cameroon pipeline, the Lesotho Highlands Water Project, Namibia's Epupa Dam and Uganda's Bujagali Dam, as well as various Bank attempts to commercialise national water management and privatise urban water/sanitation systems. Other growing campaigns that link African and international civil society organisations include the environmental debt that the industrial North owes the South, and the campaign to ban 'conflict-diamond' trade that contributes to civil war in Sierra Leone, Liberia and Angola.

Across Africa, such solidarity is being discussed in relation to concrete and potential linkages between social-justice movements of the North and South. An 'African People's Consensus' campaign was catalysed by Jubilee anti-debt, other church, labour, NGO and community groups in Lusaka in May 1999 and then taken forward at a major Dakar gathering in December 2000 that for the first time linked progressive grassroots and shopfloor activists from English, French and Portuguese-speaking areas of Africa. And likewise, while Thabo Mbeki was gathering international elite support for Nepad and only later checking in on African capitals, a 'Southern African People's Solidarity Network' headquartered in Cape Town held regular workshops across the region to generate analysis, establish positions and coordinate campaigns against neo-liberalism and political repression.

Inevitably, Nepad itself would be subject to criticism by progressives across Africa (as explained at greater length in Chapter Two, below):

- According to the African Social Forum meeting in Mali in January, 2002, Nepad is 'inspired by the IMF-WB strategies of structural adjustment programmes, trade liberalisation that continues to subject Africa to an unequal exchange, and strictures on governance borrowed from the practices of Western countries and not rooted in the culture and history of the peoples of Africa.'
- A fortnight later, at a New York meeting of the most active African NGOs in international financial matters, 'apprehension' was expressed over 'the prominence given to Nepad... We oppose any attempt to use it to deepen Africa's external dependence and the exploitation of its resources.'
- In February, trade unionists met in Dakar and complained that Nepad 'pretends to pave the way for Africa's development [yet] seems to have been painted on the very neo-liberal canvass which ignores demands for social insurance.'
- In April, African intellectuals met in Accra under the auspices of the Council for the Development of Social Science Research in Africa and Third World Network-Africa. Their finding was that Nepad 'will reinforce the hostile external environment and the internal weaknesses that constitute the major obstacles to Africa's development. Indeed, in certain areas like debt, Nepad steps back from international goals that have been won through global mobilisation and struggle.'
- In South Africa, the Congress of South African Trade Unions 'raised concerns about the economic proposals in Nepad. In particular, we need to ensure that macro-economic governance does not stray too far towards stabilisation, at the cost of growth and employment creation. Moreover, the emphasis on privatisation in the section on infrastructure ignores the reality: that privatised services will not serve the poor on our continent.'
- Also in South Africa, the Civil Society Indaba argued that Nepad 'will push Africa and her people further into poverty, ill-health, hunger and marginalisation.'

What kind of alternatives are being suggested? Generally, the African networks of social-justice movements push for what might be termed economic 'deglobalisation' by their nation-states (e.g., more exchange controls, protection of vital infant industries, debt repudiation), and for greater regional cooperation and mobility of people across Africa's artificial colonial-era borders, with the aim of reorienting domestic political economies away from the financial and trade circuitry which has been so disempowering these past two decades.

Ultimately, a 'rights-based' philosophy is emerging that stresses decommodification and destratification in the material sphere, women's rights, and social-environmental harmony. The largest deficits are in the spheres of democracy and basic needs, particularly in relation to rural women, and particularly in areas whose production basis should be easy to expand - rural water/sanitation and small-scale irrigation systems, electricity, public works - without debilitating import requirements. By stressing a for-profit orientation in the supply of infrastructure and services, Nepad moves in the opposite direction from Africa's leading popular forces.

Mbeki is moving against the progressive movements in numerous ways. To summarise the analytical, strategic, tactical and alliance-building differences between Mbeki and African social movements, consider a bumper-sticker slogan that translates demands often heard in the international social justice movements: *'The Globalisation of People, not of Capital!'* It is that edict which says so much more about social progress than can Thabo Mbeki, and in turn hints more profoundly about why his initiatives, including Nepad, reflect Fanon's warning so disturbingly. In sum, if international capital and its various institutional foundations, including the Bretton Woods institutions and WTO, represent the 'chains' of global apartheid, it is evident in what we have seen above that Mbeki's project has been reduced to shining, not breaking those chains.

2

Organisational Statements

Statement by Civil Society Participants in the Canadian International Development Administration meeting on Nepad

Montreal, 5 May 2002

We, the undersigned participants in the May 4-5, 02 Cida meeting on the *New Partnership for Africa's Development* (Nepad) make the following observations:

1. We welcome the opportunity provided by Cida to exchange views on the Nepad programme, because that programme has serious implications for Africa's development.
2. We underline our conviction that while Nepad is well intentioned, it suffers from many serious flaws which have been pointed out in various meetings in Africa at the national and continental levels. Two of the most fundamental limitations are:

   (i) the economic strategy at the heart of Nepad is based on the discredited package of IMF/World Bank inspired economic policies that have been implemented by African countries for the past two decades with disastrous effects for their economies. The continued pursuit of this economic and developmental strategy will undermine any positive contribution that Nepad can make to Africa's development;

   (ii) the programme did not sufficiently engage the diversity of African people in its conception and formulation and it remains largely unknown to most Africans.

3. While Nepad offers an opportunity for wide discussion of the issues of Africa's development, such discussion needs to engage with the African people, and incorporate their own experiences and views on development strategy over and beyond the visions of development contained in the Nepad. Forums such as the current one hosted by Cida can contribute to this discussion, but they are not sufficient. Indeed, these forums may be counter-productive if they create the impression that they offer sufficient basis for subsequent implementation of Nepad.
4. We therefore call for sufficient time and space to be allowed for Africans to engage with their own governments over the issues and strategies of development raised by Nepad, before its further implementation, in order to elaborate more appropriate strategies for development, including action to redress the imbalanced and inequitable international economic regime which negatively affects Africa's development.

• • •

CIVIL SOCIETY INDABA (SOUTH AFRICA), JOHANNESBURG

RESOLUTION ON NEPAD

4 May 2002

The Civil Society Indaba met in full session on the 2nd to 4th May 2002 at the NUM Training Centre in Johannesburg. Delegates from various civil society formation, including rural communities, urban communities, youth, women, First Nations Indigenous people, Non-governmental organisations, provinces and others, attended the meeting and deliberated on various issues concerning the World Summit on Sustainable Development.

After extensive deliberations on the *New Partnership for Africa's Development* (Nepad), the Civil Society Indaba agreed on the following resolution:

Noting

- That Africa and her people face daunting challenges. Among many challenges is the challenge of lifting its millions of sons and daughters out of poverty, and restoring Africa's dignity and self-respect.

- That this challenge is made all the more daunting because the forces of neo-liberal globalisation which now dominate the globe are the single most important cause of Africa's misery, poverty, marginalisation and exploitation.
- That Nepad is being widely promoted as a path of sustainable development for the African continent and its peoples.
- That Nepad is being presented as a programme that will lift Africa's people out of poverty, and thereby reverse centuries of impoverishment, marginalisation and exploitation.
- That African governments, and in particular the South African government, will be presenting Nepad as a platform of African governments at the World Summit for Sustainable Development to be held in Johannesburg in August 2002.
- That Nepad has been imposed on the continent by the few governments and elites, supported the countries of the North and the Bretton Woods institutions (World Bank, International Monetary Fund and the World Trade Organisation). Africa and her people have not been involved in devising this path of development.

Further Noting

- That Nepad embraces the forces of neo-liberal globalisation, and promotes these forces as a cure for Africa's ills.
- That Nepad embraces the World Bank, International Monetary Fund, the World Trade Organisation, and other international institutions of the process of neo-liberal globalisation, as partners in Africa's development. These institutions have a long history of plunder and exploitation of Africa's resources and her peoples.
- That Nepad and the strategies it adopts pose a grave danger to the preservation and rehabilitation of the environment. Africa and the world's environment have suffered profoundly from unhindered profit maximisation, and from the processes that have impoverished Africa and her people.
- That the development path adopted by Nepad will push Africa and her people further into poverty, ill-health, hunger and marginalisation. In this respect the following policies of Nepad deserve special mention:

♦ *The leading role of the private sector in development*

We believe that the private sector's drive for profit maximisation at all costs is one of major contributing factors to Africa's present condition.

- *Privatisation of the provision of infrastructure*

  We believe that privatisation of services and infrastructure provision has led to these services being inaccessible to the majority of the people, and to job loss and impoverishment.
- *Free Trade*

  We believe that the policies of so-called free trade, promoted by the World Trade Organisation and its associated institutions, has led to the destruction of Africa's industries and the livelihoods of its people.
- *Promotion of a market orientated agriculture*

  We believe that over the years Africa has been forced into cash crop production, and this has led to profound food insecurity on the continent. A further drive for cash crop production will accelerate impoverishment and food insecurity.
- *Increasing direct foreign investment*

  We believe that so-called foreign direct investment has only benefited the multinational corporations that extract Africa's wealth and exploit her people. Over many years foreign investment has failed to live up to the promise of more jobs and prosperity for the continent.
- *World Bank inspired 'poverty reduction strategies'*

  We believe that the World Bank and the other multilateral institutions that Nepad embraces have a dismal record of reducing poverty on the continent. If anything, through their structural adjustment programmes these institutions have deepened Africa's poverty.
- *Debt reduction strategies based on the HIPC initiative*

  Nepad embraces debt reduction strategies that have been set up by the International Monetary Fund. We believe that these strategies, like the Highly Indebted Poor Countries initiative that Nepad champions, are meant to perpetuate the enslavement of Africa and her people to the creditor nations and banks. Nepad fails to even call for the cancellation of Africa's debt.

We also note that

- The South African government has used Nepad as a way of extending and imposing its policies of *Growth, Employment and Redistribution* (*Gear*) onto the continent as a whole.
- That *Gear* has led to massive job loss and impoverishment in South Africa, and has been opposed by all progressive forces of civil society.

We therefore resolve:

- To reject Nepad as development path for the continent and its people.
- To join with other progressive forces to raise awareness about Nepad and the dangers it posses for Africa and her people.
- To join with other progressive forces on the continent to campaign against the adoption of Nepad as a development path for Africa.

• • •

Council for the Development of Social Science Research in Africa, Dakar and Third World Network-Africa, Accra

Declaration on Africa's development challenges

Adopted at the 'Joint Conference on Africa's Development Challenges in the Millennium,' Accra, 23-26 April 2002

1. From the 23 to 26 April, 2002, we, African scholars and activist intellectuals working in academic institutions, civil society organisations and policy institutions from 20 countries in Africa, as well as colleagues and friends from Asia, Europe, North America and South America, met at a conference jointly organised by the Council for the Development of Social Science Research in Africa (Codesria) and the Third World Network-Africa (TWN-Africa) to deliberate on Africa's developmental challenges in the new millennium.
2. Our deliberations covered such issues as Africa's initiatives for addressing development; Africa and the world trading system; mobilising financing for development in Africa; citizenship, democracy and development; education, health social services and development, and gender equity and equality in development.

Challenges to the space of Africa's own thinking on development

3. In our deliberations, we recalled the series of initiatives by Africans themselves aimed at addressing the developmental challenges of Africa, in particular the Lagos Plan of Action and

the companion African Alternative Framework for Structural Adjustment. Each time, these initiatives were counteracted and ultimately undermined by policy frameworks developed from outside the continent and imposed on African countries. Over the past decades, a false consensus has been generated around the neo-liberal paradigm promoted through the Bretton Woods institutions and the World Trade Organisation. This stands to crowd out the rich tradition of Africa's own alternative thinking on development. It is in this context that the proclaimed African initiative, the *New Partnership for Africa's Development* (Nepad), which was developed in the same period as the United Nations Economic Commission for Africa's *Compact for African Recovery*, as well as the World Bank's *Can Africa Claim the 21st Century?*, were discussed.

4. The meeting noted the uneven progress of democratisation and in particular of the expansion of space for citizen expression and participation. It also acknowledged the contribution of citizen's struggles and activism to this expansion of the political space, and for putting critical issues of development on the public agenda.

External and internal obstacles to Africa's economic development

5. The meeting noted that the challenges confronting Africa's development come from two inter-related sources: (a) constraints imposed by the hostile international economic and political order within which our economies operate; and (b) domestic weaknesses deriving from socio-economic and political structures and neo-liberal structural adjustment policies.
6. The main elements of the hostile global order include, first, the fact that African economies are integrated into the global economy as exporters of primary commodities and importers of manufactured products, leading to terms of trade losses. Reinforcing this, secondly, have been the policies of liberalisation, privatisation and deregulation as well as an unsound package of macro-economic policies imposed through structural adjustment conditionality by the World Bank and the IMF. These have now been institutionalised within the WTO through rules, agreements and procedures, which are biased against our countries. Finally, the just-mentioned external and internal policies and structures have combined to generate unsustainable and unjustifiable debt burden which has crippled Africa's economies and undermined the capacity of Africa's ownership of strategies for development.

7. The external difficulties have exacerbated the internal structural imbalances of our economies, and, together with neo-liberal structural adjustment policies, inequitable socio-economic and political structures, have led to the disintegration of our economies and increased social and gender inequity. In particular, our manufacturing industries have been destroyed; agricultural production (for food and other domestic needs) is in crisis; public services have been severely weakened; and the capacity of states and governments in Africa to make and implement policies in support of balanced and equitable national development emasculated. The costs associated with these have fallen disproportionately on marginalised and subordinated groups of our societies, including workers, peasants, small producers. The impact has been excessively severe on women and children.
8. Indeed, the developments noted above have reversed policies and programmes and have dismantled institutions in place since independence to create and expand integrated production across and between our economies in agriculture, industry, commerce, finance, and social services. These were programmes and institutions which have, in spite of their limitations, sought to address the problems of weak internal markets and fragmented production structures as well as economic imbalances and social inequities within and between nations inherited from colonialism, and to redress the inappropriate integration of our economies in the global order. The associated social and economic gains, generated over this period have been destroyed.
9. The above informed our reflections on Nepad. We concluded that, while many of its stated goals may be well-intentioned, the development vision and economic measures that it canvases for the realisation of these goals are flawed. As a result, Nepad will not contribute to addressing the developmental problems mentioned above. On the contrary, it will reinforce the hostile external environment and the internal weaknesses that constitute the major obstacles to Africa's development. Indeed, in certain areas like debt, Nepad steps back from international goals that have been won through global mobilisation and struggle.
10. The most fundamental flaws of Nepad, which reproduce the central elements of the World Bank's *Can Africa Claim the 21st Century?* and the ECA's *Compact for African Recovery*, include:

    (a) the neo-liberal economic policy framework at the heart of the plan, which repeats the structural adjustment policy packages of the preceding two decades and overlooks the disastrous effects of those policies;

(b) the fact that in spite of its proclaimed recognition of the central role of the African people to the plan, the African people have not played any part in the conception, design and formulation of Nepad;

(c) notwithstanding its stated concerns for social and gender equity, it adopts the social and economic measures that have contributed to the marginalisation of women;

(d) that in spite of claims of African origins, its main targets are foreign donors, particularly in the G8;

(e) its vision of democracy is defined by the needs of creating a functional market;

(f) it under-emphasises the external conditions fundamental to Africa's developmental crisis, and thereby does not promote any meaningful measure to manage and restrict the effects of this environment on Africa development efforts. On the contrary, the engagement that it seeks with institutions and processes like the World Bank, the IMF, the WTO, the United States Africa Growth and Opportunity Act, the Cotonou Agreement, will further lock Africa's economies disadvantageously into this environment;

(g) the means for mobilisation of resources will further the disintegration of African economies that we have witnessed at the hands of structural adjustment and WTO rules.

Call for action

11. To address the developmental problems and challenges identified above, we call for action at the national, continental and international levels to implement the measures described below.
12. In relation to the external environment, action must be taken towards stabilisation of commodity prices; reform of the international financial system (to prevent debt, exchange rate instability and capital flow volatility) as well as of the World Bank and the IMF; an end to IMF/World Bank structural adjustment programmes; fundamental changes to the existing agreements of the WTO regime, as well as a halt to attempts to expand the scope to this regime to new areas including investment, competition and government procurement. Most pressing of all, Africa's debt must be cancelled.
13. At the local, national and regional levels, development policy must promote agriculture, industry, services including health

and public education, and must be protected and supported through appropriate trade, investment and macro-economic policy measures. A strategy for financing must seek to mobilise and build on internal and intra-African resources through imaginative savings measures; reallocation of expenditure away from wasteful items including excessive military expenditure, corruption and mismanagement; creative use of remittances of Africans living abroad; corporate taxation; retention and re-investment of foreign profits; and the prevention of capital flight, and the leakage of resources through practices of tax evasion practised by foreign investors and local elites. Foreign investment while necessary, must be carefully balanced and selected to suit national objectives.

14. Above all, these measures require the reconstitution of the developmental state: a state for which social equity, social inclusion, national unity and respect for human rights form the basis of economic policy; a state which actively promotes, and nurtures the productive sectors of the economy; actively engages appropriately in the equitable and balanced allocation and distribution of resources among sectors and people; and most importantly a state that is democratic and which integrates people's control over decision making at all levels in the management, equitable use and distribution of social resources.

The challenge for African scholars and activist intellectuals

15. Recognising that, by raising anew the question of Africa's development as an Africa-wide concern, Nepad has brought to the fore the question of Africa's autonomous initiatives for development, we will engage with the issues raised in Nepad as part of our efforts to contribute to the debate and discussions on African development.

16. In support of our broader commitment to contribute to addressing Africa's development challenges, we undertake to work both collectively and individually, in line with our capacities, skills and institutional location, to promote a renewed continent-wide engagement on Africa's own development initiatives. To this end, we shall deploy our research, training and advocacy skills and capacities to contribute to the generation and dissemination of knowledge of the issues at stake; engage with and participate in the mobilisation of social groups around their interests and appropriate strategies of development; and engage with governments and policy institutions at local, national, regional

and continental levels. We shall continue our collaboration with our colleagues in the global movement.

17. Furthermore, we call:

    (a) for the reassertion of the primacy of the question and paradigm of national and regional development on the agenda of social discourse and intellectual engagement and advocacy;

    (b) on Africa's scholars and activist intellectuals within Africa and in the Diaspora, to join forces with social groups whose interests and needs are central to the development of Africa;

    (c) African scholars and activist intellectuals and organisations to direct their research and advocacy to some of the pressing questions that confront African policy and decision making at international levels (in particular negotiations in the WTO and under the Cotonou agreement), and domestically and regionally;

    (d) upon our colleagues in the global movement, to strengthen our common struggles, in solidarity. We ask our colleagues in the North to intervene with their governments on behalf of our struggles, and our colleagues in the South to strengthen South-South co-operation.

18. We pledge ourselves to carry forward the positions and conclusions of this conference. And we encourage Codesria and TWN-Africa to explore, together with other interested parties, mechanisms and processes for follow-up to the deliberations and conclusions of this conference.

• • •

THE CONGRESS OF SOUTH AFRICAN TRADE UNIONS, JOHANNESBURG

MEDIA STATEMENT ON THE COSATU CENTRAL EXECUTIVE COMMITTEE

25 April 2002

The Cosatu Central Executive Committee met from 23 to 25 April to discuss a set of organisational, political, socio-economic and international questions...

1. The CEC was addressed on Nepad and the African Union by Trade and Industry Minister, Alec Erwin, Nepad Secretariat member,

Professor Wiseman Nkuhlu, Government Communications Director, Joel Netshitenzhe and Wits University economist, Professor Patrick Bond.

2. After a very thorough discussion the CEC agreed that Cosatu should embrace the broad principle that there is a need for Africans to undertake an initiative to ensure better governance, end conflicts and embark on sustainable development. The continent needs to put an end to wars, coups, military dictatorships, and permanent indebtedness. Ways must be found for Africans to develop the continent's resources for the benefit of the African people and to strengthen the role of civil society.
3. The CEC believe that the transformation of Africa can only happen if it is driven by its people. There was a strong feeling that the Nepad plan has been developed only through discussions between governments and business organisations, leaving the people far behind.
4. The CEC decided to engage with government, in collaboration with our trade union colleagues in the rest of Africa, to bring about changes to Nepad which will address the needs of the workers and the poor of Africa. To begin this process Cosatu will be asking for Nepad to be put on the agenda of the Presidential Working Group. The federation will also look into the possibility of holding an all-Africa trade union conference at the same time as the inaugural meeting of the African Union.
5. The CEC raised concerns about the economic proposals in Nepad. In particular, we need to ensure that macro-economic governance does not stray too far towards stabilisation, at the cost of growth and employment creation. Moreover, the emphasis on privatisation in the section on infrastructure ignores the reality: that privatised services will not serve the poor on our continent.
6. The CEC decided that we should open a broader discussion on Nepad within the structures of the movement. The Executive Committee meeting towards the end of May has been given a mandate to pronounce the Cosatu stance on the contents of Nepad.

•••

AFRICAN FINANCING FOR DEVELOPMENT CAUCUS, MONTERREY, MEXICO

PRESS RELEASE AT THE UN INTERNATIONAL CONFERENCE ON FINANCING FOR DEVELOPMENT

18–22 March 2002

An Imposed Consensus

The African Caucus welcomes the initiative by the UN to reassert its role in social and economic development. It is about time that the 'great pretenders' of the Bretton Woods institutions are reminded that they are not accountable to themselves nor the G -7 countries, but to the global community, including the poor.

Sadly, the path the Monterrey Consensus pursues is a continuation of the old discredited neo-liberal model that has failed our people. This Consensus does not include us nor the poor of our continent. The core flaw of this path is its fundamental presumption that what development needs is more finance, and that the market can be relied upon to equitably distribute wealth and resources in a sustainable manner.

Staying engaged

We take note of the lack of effective measures for civil society's active involvement in the 'Staying Engaged' section of the Monterrey Consensus. That process appears to be confined only to consultations between the UN and the Bretton Woods institutions with the WTO. We protest the exclusion of civil society in the planning and implementation of the follow-up process, and demand to be fully included in any discussions on how the Monterrey process is move forward.

The New Economic Partnership for Africa's Development (Nepad)

The African civil society endorses the overall aim of the New African Initiative which is a commitment by African leaders to place the continent on an accelerated path of social, technological and economic development. The *Initiative* is unique, in that it is an African driven, African owned and African led renewal and development programme. As members of civil society, we commend our leaders for their courage and foresight. However, in its present form as the New Partnership, we need to caution the inherent dangers and strongly protest the manner in which the programme is being pursued.

Our first protest is against the marginalisation of civil society from the process. We are convinced that without popular participation, Nepad will suffer the same fate as other past initiatives. The development of Africa lies in the hands of its people, both its poor and rich, as well as its state leaders and civil society. Secondly we are concerned that our leaders are placing Africa's development in the hands of speculators, the gamblers of the global casino and the Bretton Woods institutions. The success of Nepad is being made contingent on the generosity and charity of wealthy nations. This is dangerous and should be reversed - it is never too late.

Furthermore, we wish to warn our leaders that Nepad's strategy of seeking foreign private capital to develop the service and infrastructure of Africa will subvert the human rights of our people; it would place basic social services and infrastructure in the hands of the private sector, which is dominated by foreign capital. We can not allow the practice of putting profits before human rights form the basis of Africa's development. To this end, we are pleased that at our invitation, President Wade of Senegal spent some of his valuable time to engage with the Africa Caucus on the issues of Nepad. He recognised that the lack of in-depth consultation with civil society was a mistake, but encouraged civil society to give their support to Nepad. It is crucial that the Nepad Implementation Secretariat formally extends an invitation to civil society to join the consultation process already taking place. This would enormously facilitate the active participation of African civil society.

Debt and ODA

On debt, we think it is immoral and scandalous that the debt burden prevails. We reiterate our demand for immediate and unconditional cancellation of the debt of the poorest countries. We reject any debt work-out mechanism that is accompanied by external conditionalities. We have lost confidence in Official Development Assistance (ODA) as a source of development for Africa. ODAs are not charitable handouts but the obligation of the rich countries, and they have failed miserably to keep their promise; hence any effort to increase ODAs with conditionalities is disingenuous.

•••

African Trade Union Conference, Dakar

The Dakar declaration on the role of African workers and trade unions in the New Partnership for Africa's Development

20 February 2002

We, the representatives of the Workers and Trade Unions of Africa met in Dakar, Senegal from February 18-20, 2002 and endorsed this Declaration.

Aware of the continued economic non-performance of African economies and therefore the need to design a framework for African economic emancipation;

Conscious of the continued marginalisation of the African continent in the global division of labour;

Determined to be torch bearers of the African economic emancipation struggle;

Entrusted with this mandate by the workers and trade unions of Africa;

Noting that the present stage of global development requires a holistic approach, and that Nepad seems to be premised on this philosophy;

Do therefore DECLARE:

1. That Africa's development landscape is nothing but a mirror-reflection of her trodden socio-historical path.
2. That there has been a consistent failure of African economies since the second decade of independence, a phenomenon that has led to the externalisation of Africa's economic management.
3. That this external management of African economies has been premised on the neo-liberal paradigm of free market economy, which paradigm has been responsible for the continued indebtedness, poverty, social, instability and marginalisation of the African countries. Here we quote Joseph Stiglitz to support our point. 'Today, it is without dispute that the Washington Consensus policies have pushed policies which enhance instability. Instability on the other hand is among the most important causes as well as manifestations of poverty'.

4. We demand therefore that Africa moves away from this neo-liberal economic paradigm and opt for a socially oriented economic paradigm.
5. That curiously, though Nepad pretends to pave the way for Africa's development, it seems to have been painted on the very neo-liberal canvas which ignores demands for social insurance, thus simultaneously constraining the ability of governments to respond effectively to any such demands.
6. Nepad failed to place itself on existing structures - the African Economic Community, the African Union, other regional groupings, etc. - and it is difficult to fathom how Nepad would effectively shoot off, totally divorced from the structures mentioned above. Indeed the basic objectives of Nepad can hardly be realised, save against the background of sub-regional and/or regional integration, which is only mentioned in passing in the Nepad document.
7. That Nepad also failed to be guided by history: A careful study of Nepad would reveal that most of the issues tackled therein have been confronted before and that the broader challenge for Africa therefore would have been to engineer a new balance between the market and society, one that would continue to unleash the creative energies of private entrepreneurship without eroding the social bases of cooperation, and which would also induce international acceptance and/or partnership.
8. That Nepad's claim of it being African-owned seems yet difficult to accept, since the socio-economic partners for its realisation have been ignored in its preparation. This is more evident not only from the up-down approach employed in the formulation of Nepad, but also in the fact that in Section Three of the Nepad document, vivid guidelines have been drawn for African leaders to follow, while a partial reference is made to the 'peoples of Africa'. Incidentally, no mention is made of the *African Charter for Popular Participation in Development and Transformation* (ACPPD), adopted in Arusha, Tanzania, February 1990 and by the OAU Summit in July 1990.
9. That Nepad seems to be preoccupied with strategies for rapid economic development without first adopting programmes for eliminating the bottlenecks that had helped in strangulating African economies for decades.
10. That while accepting the concept of, and the need for, partnership with Africa's Development partners, Nepad should have avoided

the asymmetrical relationship that has existed between Africa and her partners since independence.

Now therefore, we reiterate our commitment to programmes that would emancipate African economies from the doldrums of stagnation and decay, among them Nepad, and we recommend to the decision-makers the following:

i) Nepad should be regarded as a working platform that needs re-crafting and re-casting in order to avoid the pitfalls that earlier programmes had encountered. More importantly the need for mutually beneficial symmetry in the partnership concept cannot be ignored.

ii) Nepad should represent a paradigm shift in Africa's relationship with her international development partners. There are very strong moral and compelling economic reasons of common interest for Africa's development partners to buy into the new paradigm, since the continued economic non-performance of Africa has enormous impact on global progress. In this vein the need for commitment is paramount.

   Reference here may be made to the UN Programme of Action for Africa's Economic Recovery and Development (UN-PAAERD) - 1986-1990, and other programmes like the African Alternative Framework to Structural Adjustment for socio-economic Transformation (AAF-SAP), Africa's Priority Programmes for Economic Recovery (APPER), the Lagos Plan of Action, the Final Act of Lagos (FAL), the Treaty Establishing the African Economic Community and the Constitutive Act of the African Union, where either the African leaders failed to demonstrate the necessary political commitment needed for their implementation or the development partners also reneged on their part of the bargain.

iii) In close relation with what has just been said, we also call for the adoption of effective measures to provide free market access for African products. There is need therefore to redress the serious imbalances and discrimination against African countries as a result of prohibitive measures - barriers to trade and other unfair trade practices and rules.

iv) The structure of African economies vis-à-vis globalisation makes it imperative to devote attention to sub-regional and regional integration. The postulates of Nepad may hardly be realised under the present fragmented, weak African economies that virtually lack horizontal links to each other. We therefore recommend a fast-track, multiple geometry approach to sub-regional integration to serve as a platform on which Nepad may be anchored. Nepad should therefore be recast to take advantage of the socio-economic platforms of the African Economic Community and African Union; it cannot replace the latter, neither can they run parallel to each other.

v) A key component of the implicit post-war social bargain in the industrialised countries has been the provision of social insurance and/or safety nets at home (unemployment compensation, severance payments, etc.) in exchange for the adoption of liberal policies. The role of governments has thus increased (not diminished) in the industrialised countries. The prescriptions given to Africa, however, while espousing global capital and trade mobility, advocate at the same time, contraction of government and casualisation of labour and subject social protection and social justice to the vicissitudes of the market. This is unacceptable. We recommend therefore that Nepad should design a role for government that ensures a balance between the market and social sustainability, a balance that would ensure that social development becomes the foundation for economic development (and not the other way round).

vi) It is our firm belief that the realisation of Nepad is only possible against the background of the total absence of war and the crystallisation of popular democracy in Africa. The need therefore for the intensification of efforts towards peace, stability and transparency and participation in good governance in Africa cannot be over-emphasised.

vii) Closely tied with (vi) above is the question of the African debt. Nepad is simply meaningless unless it is linked up with the total elimination of the debt albatross. Estimated at well beyond 300% of exports, the African debt is simply not sustainable. What is worrisome is that quite a sizeable percentage of the African debt accrued as a result of factors not of Africa's making. It is against this background that we call for a total and unconditional cancellation of the African debt. Nepad should not be another preparatory programme for ensuring debt repayments.

viii) Lack of equity in international economic relations has been the bane of most African Development programmes. In the framework of Nepad equity is assumed. It does not exist. That is why we call for a realignment of the global division of labour.

ix) On the labour front we call for the incorporation of respect for core labour standards into the administration of Nepad, and the establishment of a formal structure (within Nepad) to address trade, development and core labour standards, with the full participation of the ICFTU-AFRO and OATUU. We equally call for the inclusion of social, labour, gender, environment and development concerns in Nepad's trade and development policy review mechanisms.

x) Finally, to recap, that attention should be concentrated on some basic areas, if the current endeavour is to succeed. These are:
   - ensuring the total absence of war on the continent and crystallising popular, transparent and participatory democracy;
   - fostering sub-regional and regional integration;
   - development and transformation of agriculture, not only as a means of ensuring food sufficiency and security, but also as a pivot for industrial take-off;
   - ensuring world market access for African products;
   - minimising the spread of HIV/Aids;
   - empowering women;
   - prioritising the creation of decent well-paid jobs as a basis for wealth-creation and poverty eradication;
   - development of human capital;
   - setting up an operational tripartite structure facilitating effective participation of African workers and employers;
   - including the representatives of African workers and employers in the Heads of State delegations negotiating Nepad's implementation with development partners.

xi) ICFTU-AFRO, OATUU and ODSTA and affiliated bodies should:
   - promote the wide dissemination of the Dakar Declaration among African workers and all segments of society;
   - raise public awareness in all Africa's regions demanding social dimension to be integrated in the economic orientations of Nepad;
   - set up large coalitions with NGOs, human rights and civil society associations and synergise to safeguard the interest of African populations in the implementation of Nepad.

These, it seems, are the pillars upon which should rest the other programmes envisaged under Nepad.

• • •

World Forum for Alternatives and Third World Forum, Dakar

The African Social Forum in Bamako

February 2002, Bulletin #3

The rising strength of the world social movement as the most important form of contesting the dominant order and the construction of alternatives is an unprecedented opportunity, for our continent, to realise the heavy tribute levied on it by the consensus of the rich, known as globalisation. If regions are to be considered part of the world in terms of trade, it is Africa that has paid the highest price five hundred years ago, when millions of Africans were torn from their community and put on cargo ships for the profit of the countries that are now industrialised.

Since then Africa has been the object of many, uninterrupted levies, which have been hidden by analysts suffering from amnesia. Of the 49 less advanced countries in the world, 34 of them are in Africa. The continent carries the heavy burden of an external debt that, over the last twenty years, is used to justify the arbitrary and destructive programmes of structural adjustment. The per capita income is lower than it was in 1970. The African population who, with the opening up to democracy, had expected to enjoy their rights to employment, education, health, housing and a clean environment, have been inflicted with so-called wars on poverty which are nothing else but a headlong rush into deceptive activities that will usher in liberal reforms.

The State, which has been dispossessed of most of its prerogatives, has been weakened and reduced to the role of salvage operations.

By subordinating the financing of development to neo-liberal economic regulations, the International Monetary Fund (IMF) and the World Bank have vitiated the democracies and rendered them vulnerable. They delegitimise the power that the people have given to their elected representatives and have created conflictual economic and social situations, which are the source of political instability and armed conflicts that the international community claims to prevent but without questioning the dominant order.

World trade, which is governed by the WTO regulations that are recognised as being inequitable, is put forward like a new religion, from which no country can withdraw without becoming marginalised. There is every sign however that Africa will have to submit to the new rules of the game and lose even more of its capabilities of exploiting its own resources and satisfying people's basic needs. Pretoria was a test case on access to medicines and it says much about the nature of the forces that Africa will have to face if it espouses the neo-liberal dogma. It seems already clear that the discourse on the benefits of globalisation is an ideological dressing to make the unacceptable acceptable.

Official Africa has genuinely tried to establish collective alternatives. The Lagos Action Plan was the first common framework, soon put aside for the Berg Plan and replaced by structural adjustment policies. The Lagos Plan was followed by an African Alternative to the adjustment plan, but it came up against the World Bank and IMF control over the continent's macro-economic policies.

The 1990s saw the announcement of the treaty of African Economic Unity (the Abuja Treaty), and finally the birth, in 2001, of the African Union and the New Partnership for Africa's Development.

The international financial institutions ignore the African initiatives when they do not reflect their own initiatives. The help given to the New Partnership shows its neo-liberal orientation. Elaborated by four African Heads of State without consultation with their population and institutions, it risks delivering a new instrument into the hands of the financial institutions and the multinationals to perpetuate their control over the African economies and macro-economic policies.

The economic and political confusion on the continent is so great that the classic opposition at the local and national levels and the headlong rush into elections, however free and transparent, have little meaning. As with the world economic system, resistance to arbitrariness and injustice must take on a world dimension.

The world social movement has transmitted new dynamism to the construction of African civil society which, in turn, enriches it and reinforces it through its own experience, aspirations and visions.

The African Social Forum is an offshoot of the World Social Forum and serves a double role in that it reinforces the organisations of the social movement in Africa and it consolidates the world social movement. As such, the Bamako Forum will pursue the following objectives:

- consolidation of the capacity to analyse, propose and mobilise the organisations of the African social movement so that they can play their full role in Africa and within the world social movement;
- construction of an African space for elaborating alternatives to neo-liberal globalisation, based on a diagnosis of its social, economic and political effects;
- elaboration of strategies of social, economic and political reconstruction, including a redefinition of the role of the State, the market and citizens' organisations;
- identification of ways in which citizens can exercise their control so that political alternation favours the expression and implementation of alternative, credible and viable solutions.

• • •

African Financing for Development Caucus, New York

Statement on the 4th PrepCom on Financing for Development

January 25, 2002

The African civil society representatives have looked forward to the FfD process as an unprecedented opportunity for the international community to implement the commitments made by the world's Head of States at the Millennium Summit 'to make every effort to ensure the success' of the FfD event, and to 'making the right to development a reality for everyone and to freeing the entire human race from want.'

We, members of the African Caucus, are deeply concerned by the developments in the negotiations, which are undermining the values and principles of equality, solidarity and shared responsibility of the Millennium Declaration. Instead of ensuring the availability of sufficient financial resources to reach the goals set by the major UN conferences and summits, the current process is likely to endanger the achievement of the development goals of African countries, thereby worsening the effects of globalisation on their peoples.

Although we welcome the innovative approach adopted by the PrepCom to involve all relevant stakeholders, including the civil society, in an inclusive and participatory manner, we have noted that this process has been perverted by the lack of clarity in procedure and the attempts by some stakeholders to go beyond the agreed-upon rules.

We affirm that the purpose of financing is for people-centred, gender-sensitive, equitable and sustainable development, as defined by the UN conferences of the last decade on social development, women, environment, population and development, human rights and racism. The Monterrey Consensus must re-affirm the rights-based approach to development, in order to ensure the realisation of economic, social and cultural rights, gender and racial equity and equality, and the right to sustainable development.

We note with apprehension the prominence given to the *New Partnership for Africa's Development* (Nepad) by the FFD process. We expect its implementation to respect the principles of transparency and participation of all the relevant stakeholders. We oppose any attempt to use it to deepen Africa's external dependence and the exploitation of its resources.

We are seriously concerned by the discussions on international trade. It is outrageous that attempts are being made by some developed countries, especially the European Union, to make use of the FfD process to advance their WTO objectives of getting new issues to be negotiated to produce new multilateral agreements in the WTO, especially on investment, competition, transparency in government procurement, and trade facilitation. Negotiations and new rules on these topics have been strongly objected to by hundreds of African NGOs, with many other NGOs worldwide. Most African governments have also rejected the start of negotiations. In Doha, in the closing ceremony, the Chairman of the Conference stated clearly that no negotiations could begin until there is an explicit consensus by all countries. Therefore, the developed countries must withdraw their attempts to go further than Doha. Such attempts are reprehensible.

Furthermore, we are concerned about the emphasis put on trade liberalisation in developing countries in the FfD process, regardless of its negative impact on the rights and livelihoods of African peoples, especially the poor, children and women. We affirm that the FfD process, as well as IMF and World Bank policies such as the PRSPs, must not be used to force African countries to assume new obligations in the WTO.

We remind delegations of the resolution of the Millennium Declaration 'to have halted, and begun to reverse the spread of HIV/Aids, the scourge of malaria and other major diseases that afflict humanity by the year 2015'. The failure to meet the internationally agreed targets set for ODA will greatly hamper the realisation of this resolution, especially in Africa, where the HIV/Aids pandemic has a devastating impact on human development.

The growing number of armed conflicts in Africa is strongly related to the control of international players over natural resources in Africa. The suffering of millions of innocent victims is going hand in hand with over-exploitation and trade of natural resources at an extremely low rate, and increased trade in arms. We call for the establishment of an international economic environment in which the trade of natural resources will support the development of African countries, instead of fuelling wars that destroy the livelihoods of their peoples. We also call for sanctions on companies contributing directly or indirectly to the financing of wars in Africa.

Many least developed countries, the majority of which are in Africa, are overburdened with unsustainable debts that compromise their human development. We reiterate our call for the immediate cancellation of the debts of all African countries. We support the establishment of an independent legal process of arbitration at the international level that will ensure shared responsibility between creditors and debtors, and enable future debt workout mechanisms to preserve the capacity of debtor countries to meet their national development objectives.

We urge the governments to expedite action to realise the proposed United Nations Comprehensive International Convention on Corruption, and the transfer of the illicitly acquired public funds to their countries of origin.

We call for the democratisation of global economic governance, and in this connection, for the World Bank, IMF, WTO, and ad hoc groupings to provide equitable access to African countries for decision-making. We call for the UN, through the General Assembly and ECOSOC, to be the fundamental pillar for the promotion of international cooperation on global economic policy and finance. In particular, the role of UNDP and UNCTAD needs to be strengthened for more coherent and coordinated approaches within the global financial architecture in order to achieve sustainable human development.

We express our strong determination to stay engaged in this process and beyond Monterrey in a constructive and open way, and to hold our governments accountable for their commitments.

• • •

AFRICAN SOCIAL FORUM

THE BAMAKO DECLARATION: ANOTHER AFRICA IS POSSIBLE!!

9 January 2002

From 5 to 9 January 2002, more than two hundred social movements, organisations and institutions from forty-three African countries met in Bamako, Mali, in an African Social Forum. We undertook serious analyses, shared experiences and heard testimonies on wide-ranging economic, social, political and cultural matters affecting African peoples. Our collective reflections and shared sentiments confirmed our conviction that another Africa is possible, and that we can create it.

We met at a time when the world order had not yet recovered from the tragic events of 11 September when America, for the first time, was physically attacked in its own territory. In counter action, the United States unleashed an asymmetric war against the ordinary civilians of Afghanistan, and has threatened to do the same in other countries such as Iraq, Yemen and Somalia. Those who attacked the symbols of American military and economic power within the US violated the rules of international relations. But the US went even further and has taken upon itself, together with its allies, to set aside all norms of international law, to violate the sovereignty of states, and to inflict massive sufferings on the innocent civilians. At the same time, wars in Africa are taking toll of the lives and livelihood or peoples in many parts of Africa, such as Rwanda, Somalia, Sierra Leone and Chad. The Forum noted that there can be no peace until the legitimate aspirations of people are respected, and that there can be no growth until there is peace.

We met at a time when AIDS and other eradicable diseases are decimating the population of Africa; when under the scourge of neo- liberal globalisation Africa's economies are being forced to open to further and intensified exploitation by multinational corporations; when under forced privatisation people are deprived of their basic human needs such as clean water, education, sanitation and housing, food security; and when under the IMF-imposed structural adjustment programmes and the regime of the World Trade Organisation the states in Africa are being deprived of all fiscal, monetary and economic policy options to intervene in the market to regulate it and to provide their peoples with their basic human needs.

The participants noted that the Bamako Forum is a continuation of the many initiatives taken in Africa to put right the historic injustices meted out to the people of Africa. These initiatives include the World Conference Against Racism in Durban, South Africa, in September 2001, when 6000 delegates from 153 countries gathered to expose the evil of racism, and the Goree Conference that condemned slavery inflicted on Africa as a crime against humanity.

A strong consensus emerged at the Bamako Forum that the values, practices, structures and institutions of the currently dominant neo-liberal order are inimical to and incompatible with the realisation of Africa's dignity, values and aspirations.

The Forum rejected neo-liberal globalisation and further integration of Africa into an unjust system as a basis for its growth and development. In this context, there was a strong consensus that initiatives such as Nepad (*New Partnership for Africa's Development*) are inspired by the IMF-World Bank strategies of structural adjustment programmes, trade liberalisation that continues to subject Africa to an unequal exchange, and strictures on governance borrowed from the practices of Western countries and not rooted in the culture and history of the peoples of Africa. The Forum further noted that the global architecture of financial and capital movements is seriously flawed and has led to repeated crises of the kind that happened in East Asia in August 1999, and more recently in Argentina. Africa too is exposed to the fragility of the system of global governance of the financial market.

The Forum, therefore, strongly recommended to African governments to develop and enforce national and regional regulatory systems to control capital movements. It also demanded that the developed countries take seriously their responsibility to control the capital market, and to create ways of increasing international liquidity to help finance the development of Africa and the other developing countries.

In this context, the Forum took note that the United Nations has organised a meeting at Monterrey in Mexico in March 2002 on Finance for Development. The Forum demands of its political leaders that they do not further inflict on Africa the unjust system of the Bretton Woods institutions in the name of financing Africa's development. Africa should, first and foremost, demand that its outstanding debts are cancelled forthwith. Africa has not only paid the financial debts many times over already, but it is the countries of the West that owe Africa debts arising from slavery and colonialism. Africa demands that the issue of reparations be addressed seriously at the Monterrey conference. On Overseas Development Aid (ODA), the Bamako Forum noted that this is used to impose economic and political conditionalities on the governments and peoples of Africa. As such, ODA as a basis for Africa's development should be rejected unless it is given on Africa's own needs and conditions.

In relation, furthermore, to the World Trade Organisation (WTO) the Bamako Forum noted its inherently undemocratic character. The Forum committed itself to struggle to delegitimise the outcome of the Doha Ministerial Conference, to ensure that the ongoing processes in Geneva and in Brussels (where the ACP-EU negotiations are taking place) do not further undermine Africa's legitimate interests. Africa must reject the attempt to launch a comprehensive new round of negotiations at the next meeting of the WTO in 2003. Africa must negotiate when it is ready; and it is not yet ready to negotiate. Promises of 'technical assistance' are welcome but they are not a sufficient basis for Africa to be lured into negotiations into a new round that will burden Africa with onerous obligations, even as many of the commitments made to Africa remain unimplemented.

The Bamako Forum expressed its dissatisfaction with the progress so far made on addressing issues of concern to the women of Africa. Very little progress has been made since the Beijing Conference. The Bamako Forum underlined the need to link women's continuing economic and social exclusion to neo-liberal globalisation that has made their situation even worse than before. The Forum emphasised the need to build on African women's culture of resistance, imagination and talents.

The Bamako Forum also noted that neo-liberal globalisation has further eroded the human rights of the people of Africa. When the basic needs of the people to food, shelter, clothing, housing and sources of energy are daily under threat because of forced privatisation and opening up of Africa to multinational corporations, then neither democracy nor human rights are possible. Western and the IMF-WB strictures on democracy, good governance and corruption are both hollow and hypocritical. In the 'other Africa' that the Bamako Forum had in its vision, development has to be based on the human being and not on the profit of corporations. Furthermore, it is only on the basis of the satisfaction of the basic material needs and the human rights of the people that genuine democracy can be built.

The future of Africa lies in the hands of African peoples. Africa has the human and natural resources to shape the destinies of its peoples, and we are determined to break out of the inherited and imposed dependency on external forces.

We value the richness of our diversity as a source of strength, and we resolve to act together with our peoples nationally, regionally and continentally. In this spirit we are in solidarity with all forces in Africa that are committed to the realisation of real alternatives. We are also part of the World Social Movement to build a different world. To this end, we endorse and adopt the Charter of the World Social Forum, and pledge to build the African Social Forum on the principles enunciated in the Charter.

The time to ponder over theoretical 'models' of development, such as those imposed on Africa, by the IMF, the World Bank, the WTO and the G7 countries is over. It is now time to act. Africa must seize its destiny in its own hands. The peoples of Africa - workers, farmers, trade unionists, women, students, the youth - must fight against all manifestations of injustices, and protect their human dignity by direct action.

ANOTHER AFRICA IS POSSIBLE !!

ANOTHER WORLD IS POSSIBLE !!!

3

Independent Analysis

Trevor Ngwane, AntiPrivatisation Forum, Johannesburg

Should African social movements support Nepad?

Notes from a speech to the African Social Forum's African Seminar, World Social Forum, Porto Alegre, Brazil, 2 February 2002

1. Introduction

How long must Africans suffer? After many years of plunder, robbery, slavery, colonialism, neo-colonialism and apartheid, we are now facing the ravages of neo-liberalism. We continue to suffer from disease, hunger, poverty and a lack of control over our resources and our destiny. How and when will it all end?

Three African leaders, namely, Thabo Mbeki of South Africa, Abdelaziz Bouteflika of Algeria and Olusegun Obasanjo of Nigeria, all presidents of their countries, have come up with a solution to Africa's problems called Nepad. Its aim is 'to eradicate poverty and to place African countries on a path of sustainable growth and development'.

Will this plan work? Should African social movements support this plan? This short paper looks at the underlying assumptions of Nepad and finds them very problematic because of the wrong strategic options they engender. My recommendation to the African Social Forum, in line with the position we took in Bamako, is that we should reject this plan and wage a vigorous campaign of education and denunciation against Nepad.

2. Political and economic context

Africa is locked in a debt trap and suffers from unequal terms of trade mainly as a result of structural adjustment programmes imposed upon it by the World Bank, IMF and the World Trade Organisation's policies. In order to attract foreign investment and qualify for loans and aid, our governments have been implementing austerity programmes based on a 'one size fits all' economic model of development which has led to tremendous deprivation and suffering in Africa. While our 'leaders' continue to live in luxury and opulence, millions of working class and peasant people live in abject poverty. African heads of state pay little heed to the wishes and plight of the masses, instead they do everything that they are told to do by the international bankers, multi-national corporations and bourgeois politicians. Even where they seem to do 'their own thing', it is self-serving and does not benefit the people. The ruling power elite in Africa has usurped the promise of people and workers' power that was the hallmark of the national liberation movement.

In January 2002, like a bolt out of the blue, the African Social Forum was formed. It is part of the gathering of popular forces and social movements in the world who have had enough and have decided to organise against a system that kills and robs ordinary people everywhere. In line with the World Social Forum we believe that 'another world, another Africa, is possible'.

3. Problems with Nepad

3.1 No consultation with the social movement

No civic society, church, political party, parliament or democratic body was consulted in Africa when Nepad was put together. Instead the first time we heard of it was when Thabo Mbeki presented it in Davos at the World Economic Forum in January 2001 to the likes of George Soros. At the time it was called the Millennium African Recovery Plan (MAP). Through a series of 'high-level' discussions, that is, discussions above the heads of the people, MAP changed into NAI (New Africa Initiative) and now to Nepad. Any changes to the plan have been in response to the international ruling class' comments on the plan, for example, during the G8 Summit in Genoa where Mbeki was told to include 'good governance' in his plan. The G8 treated him with utter contempt, giving him only five minutes to make his presentation before sending him off to do his homework.

3.2 Little credibility of Nepad authors

Mbeki is failing his own people in South Africa while busy trying to solve the continent's problems. He has failed miserably to respond to the HIV/Aids crisis, choosing instead to publicly entertain maverick views on the subject which question the very existence of the pandemic. But everyone knows that he does not want to spend money treating the disease because of fiscal discipline and similar neo-liberal considerations. Instead Mbeki is spending billions buying arms. Last year five million workers went on strike in South Africa against his government's policy of privatisation. This strike was led by COSATU (Congress of South African Trade Unions), the union federation which is in a political alliance with the South African Communist Party (SACP) and the African National Congress (ANC), Mbeki's party. For their part, Obasanjo and Bouteflika are well-known violators of human rights in their own countries, stoking religious, ethnic and military conflict leading to the death of many people. Recently Obasanjo sent to jail worker leaders for calling a general strike in Nigeria.

3.3 Nepad fails to call a spade a spade

The document uses euphemisms and camouflage language such as 'a globalising world', 'exclusion', 'globalisation' and such like; it avoids the critical language which points to the real cause of Africa's problems such as 'imperialism', 'neo-colonialism' and 'capitalism'. Strong sounding words such as 'exploitation' are used neutrally and in a 'positive' manner rather than critically, for example, the document complains that Africa's resources have not been 'fully' exploited!

3.4 Nepad avoids the problem of power

The reason Africa continues to suffer is because the advanced capitalist countries have the power to dictate to us what to do. Nowhere does Nepad call for a change in the existing international power relations that compel Africa, for instance, to pay a debt whose legitimacy is highly questionable, or to succumb to an international economic system loaded against Africa.

3.5 A partnership between rider and horse

The relationship between Western Europe and Africa has been one between coloniser and colonised, exploiter and exploited. While the exact terms of this predatory relationship have evolved over time, it seems foolhardy for Mbeki and company to ask for partnership with people who still benefit from Africa's wealth at the expense of the African people. Imperialism is the problem; a partnership with it cannot be a solution.

3.6 Nepad calls for closer co-operation

He who sups with the devil must have a long spoon. Nepad calls for closer relations with the rich countries and wants Africa to be 'integrated' more into the global economic system. But economic development theorists such as Andre Gunder Frank and Samir Amin have long shown how integration leads to growing poverty and underdevelopment because the structure of insertion is designed to benefit the rich; they get richer and the poor get poorer. Third World scholars have recommended less not more integration, namely, 'de-linking'. Argentina's crisis is due to its integration which made it vulnerable to global financial and market fluctuations. The falling rand (currency) in South Africa is due to the ease with which money can move in and out of the country - an indicator of integration into the global markets.

3.7 Nepad wants market-oriented policies

Nepad wants 'market-oriented policies', that is, more capitalism, more profit-driven policies, more competition, more privatisation. Mbeki forgets that it is exactly the doctrine and practice of putting profit before people which led to slavery, colonialism, apartheid and neo-liberalism.

3.8 Nepad wants more exploitation

Like a salesperson displaying his or her wares for sale, Nepad waxes lyrical about how Africa 'is an indispensable resource base' which needs further exploitation. After years of being raped somehow Africa is casting itself as a prostitute looking for prospective customers. Nepad claims that 'the richness of Africa's culture remains under-exploited'. This mentality is the same which motivated African leaders to promote the planting of cash crops for sale overseas, in line with World Bank-inspired export-led growth strategies, while the children died back home due to starvation. In South Africa Mbeki's party, the ANC, has been complained of 'rich foreigners' buying land cheaply due to the devaluation of the rand. This shows the contradictions of neo-liberal logic.

3.9 Nepad wants more loans and aid

Implicit and explicit in Nepad is a call for money (capital) to be invested in or given to Africa. Where Nepad calls for more loans and aid it forgets the debt trap Africa is already in and the conditionalities which come with such loans. Aid has often been tied to purchasing goods produced by the 'donor' country, proving right the biblical observation that 'it is better to give than to receive'. Pakistan has recently received billions of dollars in loans and aid in order to fate the USA's imperialist project.

4. Nepad and hypocrisy

Mbeki calls for good governance and an end to corruption in Nepad, but in his own backyard his ANC comrades are busy enriching themselves through ill-gotten government contracts and kickbacks. Recently Tony Yengeni, then ANC parliamentary chief whip, received 'presents' from Daimler-Chrysler in the arms deal scandal. Social movements are beginning to question the ethics of governments who rule in the name of the people while answering to the multi-national corporations; of government leaders who receive vast amounts in salaries and perks while children die of hunger; and of international financial institutions which promote the privatisation of water, health care and education thus pricing these out of reach of the majority of the people. Nepad seems to follow the logic and values of the world's economic and political elite and as such can never take forward the cause of ordinary Africans.

5. Reject Nepad, campaign against it!

Based on these few points above it is my strong recommendation that the African Social Forum rejects Nepad and its model of economic development. Let us spend the first year of our forum studying and educating the African masses about the evils of the neo-liberalism contained in Nepad. We must suggest alternatives to this self-defeating strategy and build mass struggles in defense of African economic interests.

Phansi Nepad phansi! Down with Nepad!

• • •

MOHAU PHEKO, AFRICA TRADE NETWORK

NEW OR OLD PARTNERSHIP FOR AFRICAN WOMEN?

4 May 2002

It is not the first time that Africa's leaders are actively working on a set of new continent-wide development strategies. Kwame Nkrumah was the first. With the gap between the world's rich and poor nations growing ever wider, it is more imperative than ever to end the marginalisation of Africa and the global social exclusion of her people.

The new African initiative, in the words of African governments, 'is a pledge by African leaders, based on a common vision and a firm and shared conviction, that they have a pressing duty to eradicate poverty and to place their countries, both individually and collectively, on a path of sustainable growth and development.' They see the Programme anchored on the determination of Africans to extricate themselves and the continent from the malaise of underdevelopment, in particular the exclusion of Africa in a globalising world.

The New Partnership for Africa's Development (Nepad) gives African women the opportunity to examine whether previous partnerships around development have benefited them. It is an opportunity to analyse whether Nepad offers a framework for a new relationship and partnership with African women. A partnership that can move them away from merely surviving to advancing them as key players in the development of their countries, economically, politically, culturally, and in ways that give them the space to influence the discourse around partnership.

The word partnership is one of the most popular concepts in international development today. Partnerships vary. There is one where individuals freely and deliberately create partnership for the purposes of promoting or achieving their common objectives or interests. This emerges after a long process of consultation and arriving at the same place with the same vision.

There is another type of partnership. A partnership that promotes the interests of a certain class, gender, race, or interest groups. This is an imposed or engineered partnership by a few individuals over the collective. The question I want to pose is, which partnership does Nepad offer African women?

All women on the African continent have a sacred memory drawn from the long battle to free ourselves from colonisation, racism, bigotry, and so-called 'civilising agendas' attempting to modernise Africa through capitalism. In this regard, African women generally, and African feminists particularly, have been linking women's issues to other concerns as part of their critique of development models, especially the manner in which structural adjustment programs have impacted upon women in Africa.

A document 'Development, Crisis and Alternative Visions: Third World Women's Perspectives' - written prior to the World Conference on Women for the Nairobi forum marking the end of the UN Decade for women (1975-85) and presented by DAWN (Development Alternatives for Women in a New Era)- has influenced the debates on development policies, and has given African women a voice on issues of macro-economic policies. This paper was a significant turning point because it highlighted how women's creative strategies emerged in the struggle against the impact of various crises: debt, famine, militarisation, and fundamentalism on women's lives. It concluded that the evidence has been on the wall for a long time that African women's ability to fully enjoy human rights is integrally linked to their economic empowerment, and that the starting point must be with poor women.

It is clear that in the 21st century this conclusion continues to be vindicated. It is seen in the growing pauperisation of African women; the increasing number and rate in which women are being informalised in the economy; the feminisation of poverty; the increase of gender violence; and in the shrinking political space to debate structural adjustment programmes which have placed a great burden on African women.

Coupled with this is the emerging global order that is driven and characterised by the enormous economic growth and worldwide expansion and penetration named globalisation, facilitated and promoted by liberalisation. Women are caught in a quagmire of declining social expenditure in key sectors like education, health, electricity, water, food security and environmental sustainability.

More significantly, this contestation between economic and social policy has impacted on the social and political fabric. It has changed relations with governments in favour of the private sector and multinational corporations producing for profit. African women are paying a high price for the negative impact of these policies that are increasing the gap between rich and poor.

In this scenario, it is clear that women in African have long opted for the need for an alternative vision of the economy and development in Africa. The challenge has been to counter the notion that markets are adequate in meeting women's need. It has been necessary for African women pose this challenge with their demand for the reconstruction of the state in an effort to make it more responsive and accountable for its actions.

Having said that, Nepad poses a dilemma for African women. I cannot help feeling a tragedy is being enacted on African women. A tragedy equal to or greater than Rwanda may be in the pipeline. African women, the poorest people in the world, are being sacrificed on the altar of neo-liberalism and global capitalism through Nepad.

Nepad at the outset states that African leaders are implementing it on behalf of their people and not with the African people. This is a significant nuance that will be a deciding factor in terms of how African women participate within Nepad.

Besides being gender blind, it has experienced a very low profile among the rank and file at the national and even continental level. The idea, according to the managers of this initiative, is to hand it over to a marketing company that can begin to raise awareness about it among the African people. This brings into question the nature of this 'partnership.' A plan that is supposed to fundamentally change our lives has curiously not been a part of the discourse and the subject of debate within African communities from its conception.

How then does it become implemented? Who is it being implemented for? For African women these are old questions. In our struggle fighting for our space in political decision-making we have posed the same questions around the development discourse: what kind of partnership, what type of consultation, what kind of participation and collaboration? These questions are ones that have led us to a consensus of the need for a restructuring of relationships at the national, regional and global levels.

An in-depth analysis of the Nepad document underscores its dependency on World Bank and IMF policies in Africa. It refers for example to the Bank's Poverty Reduction Strategies as a key way of routing poverty out of Africa. African women have consistently offered a sharp critique to the failed policies of the IMF and World Bank. In essence Nepad amounts to a re-subscription by governments to these policies of structural adjustment programmes (SAPs). Given the trajectory of Africa's limited engagement in global and political partnerships and the failure of development that these unequal relations have brought to Africa, their reintroduction and reintegration through Nepad show a paucity of innovation and thinking around development, and nullifies the negative impact that these policies have had on the livelihoods of women.

Research and experience by African women show how these policies have displaced the development vision of many African countries and destroyed the industrialisation process necessary to make Africa a formidable force in world affairs. One of the objectives of Nepad is 'to promote the role of women in social and economic development by reinforcing their capacity in the domains of education and training; by the development of revenue-generating activities; by facilitating access to credit; and assuring their participation in the political and economic life of African countries.' What is new about this? There is nothing profound or life-altering about this.

When one looks at the Beijing Platform of Action, the conclusions of the United Nations Conference on Environment and Development 'Agenda 21' present a radical shift. These development summits adopted the call for the participation of women as equal partners in economic, social and political development, as well as in all sectors of economy in decision-making, and in the areas of science and technology.

Nepad is far behind, when it keeps women in areas of the economy that perpetuate exclusion from the macro-economy. Nepad's lack of reference, in terms of analysis and experience of the African women and people regarding these policies, is a glaring omission resulting in a rather peculiar conclusion about how Africa has experienced SAPs.

SAPs have not only panel beaten our fiscal and monetary policies, but they have fundamentally destroyed the social policies of many countries in Africa. It is women, the majority in Africa who have suffered through privatisation, HIV/Aids, job losses, and declining literacy and nutrition rates. It is therefore necessary for women to re-articulate an agenda that will bring back elements of the developmental state, and a strong state that can invest liberally in its people.

Nepad calls for investment in education and infrastructure. African women can hardly disagree with this. However, African women phrased this in a much better way than Nepad. When the Women call for investment, they have realigned it with the visions, needs and aspirations of the African people. This means that any education and infrastructure developments should work in the interests of the African women and people, and not export- or investor- oriented, as articulated in Nepad.

Nepad fails to build on many documents developed around African development. The Lagos Plan of Action, the African People's Consensus document and a score of other documents developed or facilitated by the OAU. The failure to select the positive aspects of these documents constructs a Nepad in a vacuum.

Globalisation is treated as a 'fact' and 'reality' without a deeper probing of our memory and experience of globalisation, which has existed for centuries in various forms in Africa. Women need to clearly define globalisation as a new word for imperialism for the manner in which it serves to consolidate the West's economic and political domination. The relationship between the spread of markets and the changing nature of poverty is not examined in Nepad. It ignores the fact that poverty in Africa is shaped by gender, class, ethnicity and religion and by unequal relations in the international economy.

Nepad fails to give a clear history of domination in Africa and the impact it has had on women economically, socially and politically. It describes globalisation as neutral, yet the proof is there to show that Africa's processed goods are closed to western markets because of the growing wall of protectionism in the industrialised countries. Because of this shallow analysis of globalisation, Nepad goes on to demand coherence of documents such as AGOA (US African Growth and Opportunity Act) Cotonou Agreement between Africa, Caribbean and Pacific countries and the European Union, as well at the WTO (World Trade Organisation). These are all instruments of neo-liberalism leading to the enslavement of African women.

Nepad reinforces these by presenting women as 'mere victims' of development, with no alternatives. The power relations in the world are never challenged in the document. This is a crucial debate and a discourse that African women have articulated for decades. Regional integration is not recognised as a significant process of strengthening Africa's economy and collaboration within Africa. It views it as a stopgap and a way to jump onto the globalisation train.

This is a complex, compromised document produced in another reality that argues that in order for Africa to 'recover' it must take responsibility for itself. This is a dangerous notion because it ignores the other reality of wars, corruption, debt that the West has and continues to contribute to in order to support its strategic economic interests.

The women of Africa are unambiguous. The problems of Africa are not only internal; they are also external to it. Africa cannot reform without the West reforming its policies' contempt and cynicism in a global environment that is actively hostile towards to Africa. In the midst of this hostility, Africa is told there is no alternative. The response and solidarity of the Northern women's movement needs to join African women by stating clearly to their government that there must be an alternative. In Nepad's place, they need to call for a reconstruction of the entire global economic system in favor of poor African women.

In challenging the key themes of Nepad such as concepts of global governance, globalisation, agriculture, technology, international aid, foreign direct investment, education, economic management, regional integration, political will and a host of other ideas put forward in the document, African women will need political and economic support to prevail against the current power structures.

• • •

Yash Tandon, Southern and Eastern African Trade, Information and Negotiations Initiative, Harare

Nepad = Sap+Gats+DSB

Seatini Bulletin, 5.4, 28 February, 2002

Introduction

The African civil society is gradually waking up to the *New Partnership for Africa's Development* - Nepad. The reaction so far, from the more radical section of it, has not been very positive. One of these is the Bamako Declaration passed by participants from some 200 social movements, organisations and institutions from 45 African countries met in Bamako, Mali, from 5 to 9 January 2001 in an African Social Forum. The relevant paragraph reads as follows: 'The Forum rejected neo-liberal globalisation and further integration of Africa into an unjust system as a basis for its growth and development. In this context, there was a strong consensus against initiatives such as Nepad (New Partnership for African Development) that are inspired by the IMF-World Bank strategies of structural adjustment programmes, trade liberalisation that continues to subject Africa to an unequal exchange between its exports and its imports, and strictures on governance borrowed from the practices of Western countries and not rooted in the culture and history of the peoples of Africa.'

By contrast, international organisations such as the World Bank and the IMF as well as representatives of global capital appear to see in Nepad a possible way out of Africa's stubborn poverty and underdevelopment. (See, for example, Mills, J. and J. Oppenheimer, 'Partnerships only way to break cycle of poverty,' Financial Times, 1 October, 2001; and Gondwe, G. and C. Madavo (2001), 'New swipe at fighting poverty,' Financial Times, 7 October, 2001). Also Nepad has been welcomed by the G7/8 countries at their meeting in Genoa in July 2001, and by the Davos Conference in New York in January 2002, as well as by the African Union at its Lusaka meeting in October 2001.

From civil society, as stated earlier, it is still an early reaction. One of their gripes is that, although Nepad talks about 'ownership' of the process by the African people, and indeed exhorts the people to mobilise themselves behind Nepad, they have not been consulted in the process. After the leading African Heads of Government (those of South Africa, Nigeria, Senegal and Algeria) had discussed Nepad among themselves, they appear to have gone first to the Western capitals and the representatives of international private capital before consulting with their own people. Presumably, the people will follow. But the mood in Africa is changing; and putting the representatives of the donor countries and international private capital ahead of the people of Africa in the consultation process was not, to say the least, a very wise strategy. It begs the famous question that Rene Dumont had raised in the 1960s about Africa's development: Is this yet another 'false start'?

We hope not. There are aspects of Nepad that must be welcomed by African civil society, even if they have not been consulted. Maturity demands patience and wisdom, even if the leaders often make mistakes, for otherwise Africa would risk perpetually dividing itself. Therefore, let us first count the positive aspects of Nepad.

Positive features of Nepad

Some of these are:

- The need to negotiate a new relationship with their development partners, which is the central idea behind Nepad;

- Also central to the spirit of Nepad is the idea that through the 'African Renaissance' project, the African continent that has been 'plundered for centuries' will 'take its rightful place in the world'
- Focus on 'African ownership and management'
- The notion of 'self-reliance'
- The importance of national and regional priorities in the formulation of development plans
- The notion that these plans must be prepared through participatory processes involving the people
- Some of the goals are the same as those set by the United Nations in several of its global conferences, such as, reducing extreme poverty by half by 2015; a sustained average gross domestic product (GDP) growth rate of above 7 per cent per annum for the next 15 years, etc.

The above principles and objectives are noble, and must be endorsed by all the people of Africa. Even if the people are not consulted in the process of formulating the above, one cannot deny that the above do summarise at least some of their most important aspirations.

As always, however, worthy aspirations often get confounded when it comes to the details. Exactly how are these aspirations going to be realised?

Nepad in practice

There can be no doubt that the path that Nepad offers is the neo-liberal path that is espoused by the IMF, the World Bank and the WTO. Neo-liberalism has become a code word for the contemporary development theory. This theory puts 'integration' into the globalised economy on the basis of the liberalisation of markets and the free movement of capital at the centre of the development paradigm. Thus, Nepad's key strategy is encapsulated by the sentence: 'The African Renaissance project, which should allow our continent, plundered for centuries to take its rightful place in the world, depends on the building of a strong and competitive economy as the world moves towards greater liberalisation and competition.' Some might see in this an ironical conjugation between 'African renaissance' and the 'the building of a strong and competitive economy as the world moves towards greater liberalisation and competition.' Can this 'renaissance' really take place in further integration of Africa into an asymmetric globalised system that is dominated by a few countries?

Nepad seems to think it can and should. The leaders of Africa do not see any other alternative to integrating into the neo-liberal globalised model of development. Nepad appears to lean towards the creation of the 'right' kind of conditions within Africa - good governance as understood by the Northern partners, open economy, and partial measures on debt relief, increased aid from the North, and greater access to their markets.

At one point (paragraph 7), Nepad does recognise that globalisation 'has increased the ability of the strong to advance their interests to the detriment of the weak', but this brilliant and incisive observation on the current asymmetrical power relationship is quickly forgotten. It is only a descriptive statement; for Nepad it has no strategic or tactical significance. Nowhere, for example, does Nepad recognise that 'liberalisation' and the 'open economy' are practically forced on Africa, of which the fourth WTO Ministerial Conference at Doha was a living testimony.

Nepad also admits, indirectly, that the structural adjustment programmes (SAPs) have failed, in that they paid 'inadequate attention to the provision of social services' [para 24], but it fails to recognise the claims of African people that SAPS have not just failed to pay attention to social services, they have been at the very root of Africa's economic and social crises.

The Nepad way and the people's way

This is where we part company with Nepad's authors. We endorse its noble aims, but we cannot endorse its chosen strategy. What, then, do we have to offer as an alternative? The following are some of the elements of an alternative strategy to achieve the same noble goals of 'self-reliance' and 'ownership' of the process of development that Nepad aspires.

The point to start is not further integration of Africa's economy into the process of globalisation that Nepad suggests. The point to begin is with human needs. This is not a pedantic, but a profoundly strategic, difference. For example, the people of Soweto in South Africa need, among other things, access to drinkable water. There are two ways of going about it - the Nepad-way, and the peoples'-way. In the Nepad-way, you open this essential service of water provision to international competition; whoever is able to bring capital from outside can have control over the distribution of water, and must be able to charge 'cost recovery' price to the water-users. If people cannot pay, then their water pipes must be closed until they are able to pay. In the process, the Government of South African must create a climate of confidence (above all, the ability of the investor to externalise his profits and eventually the capital value of his assets) so that an investor is induced to come to South Africa rather than to, say, Vietnam or Chile or Rumania (because capital is global, and must be induced with attractive terms to come to Africa, so say our leaders.) This is the Nepad way.

The people's way starts with the recognition that whether or not foreign capital comes to South Africa to provide water to the people, water is a basic human right. Its provision to all households in Soweto (our example in this case) is Government's responsibility that cannot be turned on or off on the basis of the peoples' ability to pay for the water. Access to water is a human right not a privilege. And the same is true of food, adequate housing, electricity, basic education and essential transport. Subject these to the whims of profit, and you have subverted the human rights of the people.

Nepad=Sap+Gats+DSB

Nepad admits that the Structural Adjustment Programme (Sap) had paid 'inadequate attention to the provision of social services.' African governments knew, in advance, that Saps would lead to the diminishing of social services to the people. The IMF was stringent in its demand that in return for accepting its money, it expected governments to cut down on budget deficits, which meant, in practical terms, expenses for things like health and education. In recognition of this, Governments were then advised to set aside a 'social fund' to cushion the effects of Saps.

In none of the countries in Africa that accepted Sap did the social fund prove adequate to fill the social gap that Sap created. This is what Nepad is saying. So what is its solution? Nepad's solution is to place these services in the globalisation basket, and let private capital (foreign, as it would mostly turn out) to finance the provision of these services. African countries must attract foreign direct investments (FDIs) to finance the provision of these services. Thus, from a peripheral matter (as under Saps), services now occupy a central place for investments on a competitive bid. African states must now fight amongst themselves to attract FDIs so that these can be employed to provide water, electricity and other services, to the population of Africa.

This is not only a pipe dream (such investments are not likely to materialise), but also a dangerous one. Why? Because in trying to attract foreign capital for essential services, African governments are going to be dragged into a downward spiral of offering to the owners of capital competitive terms, including tax incentives or tax holidays, free land, borrowing in local currency, and so on. Indeed, such competition may take place not only between states but also between provinces within the same state. Thus, in South Africa, Gauteng may compete with Cape Town and with other provinces.

Furthermore, services are one of the mandated issues for negotiations under the General Agreement on Trade in Services (Gats) provision of the WTO. Countries are expected to make offers on the kinds of services they would want to put up front for negotiations under the WTO. In bringing services into the centre of its 'vision' for the future of Africa, what Nepad does is to risk the lives of African people, their access to basic essentials of life, into a volatile and fluid global investment situation. Does this sound too alarmist?

No, it is not being alarmist, for this is the precise logic of Nepad. Saps were 'inadequate', says Nepad, because they neglected social services, so let us put the services, too, into the investment basket. Nepad thus is Sap+Gats. But it is more than that. Once a matter is brought under the purview of the WTO, it is subject to the provisions of the Disputes Settlement Body, with all its attendant legalism, appeal panels, and sanctions. The DSB, it is widely known, is an asymmetrical system, where the rich countries can both afford the legal costs and impose sanctions, but the poor can afford neither.

It is possible that the authors of Nepad did not have the time nor the necessary advice from those who should have known better that the route they have chosen to bring the 'renaissance' of Africa could well be Africa's final and utter submission to the rule of the IMF plus the WTO. In effect, Nepad is the sum of Sap, plus Gats, plus DSB.

Conclusion

The sentiment behind Nepad is noble. It is to put Africa on a 'self-reliant' path to development where the processes are owned by Africans themselves. But, as they say, the road to hell is often paved with good intentions. The intentions notwithstanding, the practical effect of Nepad would be to surrender the human rights of the people of Africa (their rights to food, water, energy, etc.) to the whims of a volatile and untrustworthy global capital. If the experience of Argentina does not give wisdom, then Africa sadly will learn, bitterly, from its own experiences.

It is, however, not necessary to go the Nepad-way in terms of strategy. There are alternatives. Nepad's noble intentions may be embraced, yes, but the strategy for self-reliance is .. Self-reliance. African governments must pledge to provide the basic services to the people - drinking water, basic food, essential housing and transport, and access to energy - as necessary elements of their basic human rights. They must then work upwards from there and see how the production and distribution (including savings and investments) are organised in order to meet these basic needs. Leave these matters to the whim of international capital, and Africa would find itself in a worse mess than it is in now.

• • •

Tetteh Hormeku, Third World Network-Africa, Accra, and **Gerry Barr,** Canadian Council for International Cooperation, Ottawa

Africans left out of plan for future

3 May 2002

The Prime Minister of Canada, with other G-8 leaders and some African heads of government, has been planning Africa's future. But they have left a crucial partner out of the picture - the citizens of Africa's nation states. The *New Partnership For Africa's Development* is a major, continent-wide development plan for Africa that has the full support of Prime Minister Jean Chretien. And it will be a main topic of discussion when the G-8 heads of government meet this June in Kananaskis, Alberta. But in Montreal this weekend (May 4-5), as Canadian officials gather African experts for feedback on the development plan, they are likely to run into a major speed bump on the road to Kananaskis.

Many of the Africans gathering for the conference in Montreal will be asking for the development plan to be 'sent back home' for public debate. Although the plan for social and economic development brings in many key issues like access to essential medicine, peace and security, trade and investment, food security, democracy and good governance, few Africans knew about this document until recently. As the initiative becomes better known, it is clear that many are uncomfortable with a plan that repackages old and unsuccessful strategies. Some of the development plan's 'reforms' have been tried in Africa before.

'Structural adjustment' programs, promoted by the World Bank and International Monetary Fund, have weakened and enfeebled many of Africa's national economies and governments. Sub-Saharan Africa, home to almost a quarter of the developing world's hungry, saw 28 of its countries become poorer between 1980 and 1996 during a period of the widest, most rapid trade liberalisation. The main idea of the *New Partnership For Africa's Development* is that aid dollars should be spent to effect national (legal and institutional) reforms that will open the continent to private sector foreign direct investment and that this investment will reduce poverty.

But there are problems. First, economic growth and foreign direct investment often do not mean reduced poverty. Trade and investment increased sharply in Latin America between 1990 and 1997, but poverty and economic disparity grew right along with the economies. To reduce poverty, citizens must be involved - especially the poor and powerless - in negotiating new policies and respect for rights that will improve their livelihoods. The development plan's limited vision of democracy and governance doesn't make room for that empowerment process.

Second, foreign direct investment may not come in the wake of the reforms that are being advocated. Many of these reforms have been in place for years in Africa's national economies, but foreign direct investment has become increasingly rare. Africa's share of global foreign direct investment was 1.3% in the mid-'90s; it is less than 1% today. Most global champions of increased international aid advocate a rights-based approach to meeting development needs. But the development plan barely nods at a rights-based approach. For example, access to social services is not affirmed as a fundamental right in this plan. The right to education and health is not stressed. The purpose of investment in the social sectors in Africa, the document declares, is to enable Africa 'to participate in the globalisation process.' Health, according to the document, should be promoted because it 'contributes to an increase in productivity and consequently to economic growth.'

In fact, the right approach is just the opposite. Economic growth shouldn't be valued as an end in itself. Its value should be measured against its contribution to improving the lives of the poor. Real 'partnership' to eradicate poverty, redress injustice and reform global institutions requires changes in the developed economies of the North as much as in Africa. Rules that effectively shut out Third World (and African) economies from a role in managing international institutions like the World Trade Organisation and the International Monetary Fund need to be changed.

Many African nations have called for changes to the current global trade rules, and for the full cancellation of debt owed by the poorest countries. Some countries now spend more on debt servicing than they do on education and health, even after recent moves to cancel some of their debt. Conditions placed on loans from the International Monetary Fund - 114 conditions, on average, in sub-Saharan Africa - have shut down many national public debates on how African economies will be run and have deepened poverty and inequality in the South. These same conditions have advanced the commercial and trade interests of the world's developed economies. It is a rigged game and Africa has been losing under these rules.

The development plan's arrival on the scene, and its embrace by Chretien and other G-8 leaders, has importantly put the fate of the African continent on the international public agenda. But that fate can't be improved without the involvement of citizens, and without a commitment (from African governments and donor nations) to listen to the real alternatives proposed by Africans. Only then can the social, economic, cultural, political and civil rights of the African peoples be affirmed and realised.

(originally published in the *Toronto Star*)

• • •

Margaret Legum, SA New Economics Society

How new is this partnership?

March 2002

Preparations for the June G8 Summit this year include some high-level visits to South Africa, including Canada's PM Jean Chretien. This is because President Mbeki is seen as African author and holder of the vision of the New Economic Partnership for Africa (Nepad), of which the G8 is the other partner.

Very, very cool heads, and a lot more consultation, will be needed if Nepad is not to overwhelm Africa by making it more, and not less, dependent on world economic forces over which it has no control, and within which it is inevitably the weaker partner. The current ideology is that Africa is poor because it is not integrated in the global economic system, and Nepad will bring it in. The sub-text is that this marginalisation is due to 'poor governance' - authoritarian and corrupt leaders, tribal wars and inefficient centralised economies.

All of these discourage foreign direct investment, assumed to be the engine of economic growth. How true is all this?

First, a quote from Tanzania's former President, Julius Nyerere in 1998. 'At the World Bank they asked me *Why did you fail?* I replied. The British Empire left us with 85% illiterates, 2 engineers and 12 doctors. I retired thirteen years ago. Then our per capita income was $280, twice what it is today. Now we have a third less children in our schools, and public health and social services are in ruins. During those years Tanzania has done everything the World Bank and the IMF have demanded. So I ask *Why did they fail?*'

It is generally forgotten that the decade or so that followed Africa's independence saw steady economic, social and infrastructural growth in most countries. Then three things happened. Africa was given huge loans at low interest, partly as a solution to Europe's problems with bank liquidity, and these rates escalated over time. World prices for commodities, on which Africa's colonial economies were based, dropped like a stone. And the deregulation of world markets in capital and trade - globalisation - required Africa to compete on an equal footing with the developed world.

All of this resulted in foreign exchange crises. That brought in the IMF/World Bank with 'rescue' packages on the condition of 'structural adjustment.' It is those policies that impoverished Africa, whose share of world trade fell by over half to 0.3% in those twenty years. It is said that 'by their fruits shall ye know them.' Nyerere was quite right.

Of course, good government did not spring immaculate from the colonial experience; and of course some African leaders became corrupt and authoritarian. But, good or bad, their economies all suffered the same fate when the IMF got hold of them. There is also a deep connection between economic growth and political stability. When resources are shrinking - even in rich places - societies degenerate. The story of Eastern Europe since the fall of communism is one of barbarism, tragedy and horror - giving the lie to the idea that there is something about skin pigment that fails when it comes to governance, peace and stability.

Back to Nepad. Here, it seems, is the deal. Africa will create 'good governance' via a 'peer review mechanism.' All African states will be induced to stop corruption, wars, inefficient economies etc., by peer pressure from the others. In exchange the rich nations' private sectors will invest in Africa, and governments will begin to allow more African trade into their countries.

Note the wishful thinking in all this. First, how are African states to police each other? The current political joke is that 'Mbeki shot himself in the kneepad' (Nepad. geddit?) over Zimbabwe. So goodbye Nepad if South Africa can't even control its neighbour - let alone Rwanda or Somalia or Sierra Leone.

Second, governments cannot tell private investors where to put their money. Investors are interested in expanding markets - not in theoretical partnerships. South Africa's failure to attract investment is about its poor growth rate, not about what rich governments think of it.

As for trade, rich countries can open their markets to African trade regardless of Nepad. But they do not, because they have their own fish to fry politically at home. Mike Moore, World Trade Organisation's DG, calls the present system 'an obscenity.' He said, before the Doha round of talks: 'There is no moral consistency to talk of free trade, and then to block trade in some areas - African exporters.'

Finally, what exactly is in it for the G8? Is it really about their consciences? Or is about seeing Africa as a wasted resource as far as investment and trade is concerned? If the latter, we need to be careful. Nobel Laureate, Joseph Stiglitz, warned us in Cape Town last week that our own development needs are not best served by foreign investment or opening our trade, but by developing our own savings through local market activity. In other words we need to become less dependent on outsiders. If Nepad became *Gear* writ large, we would be ignoring the Stiglitz view, as well as Africa's history over the past twenty years.

If the G8 really wants to help, it will focus on massive Marshall Aid type programmes of grants (not loans) for public health, education and transport throughout the continent. They can do that by simply fulfilling their own previous commitments to aid levels. And no conditions please, except normal accounting. And then let us get on with developing our own local economies. Good governance should follow, and so also market opportunities for the G8 countries.

(Originally published in the *Mail & Guardian*)

• • •

ZWELINZIMA VAVI, CONGRESS OF SA TRADE UNIONS, JOHANNESBURG

NEPAD KEEPS OUT LABOUR, SAYS COSATU

29 April 2002 (from *Business Report*)

'Cosatu will not accept any programme aimed at giving capital a free rein. What Nepad amounts to is the Africanisation of the *Gear* strategy. How can Nepad hope to take us out of our ugly past if it's happening above our heads?'

• • •

IAN TAYLOR, DEPT OF POLITICAL & ADMINISTRATIVE STUDIES, UNIVERSITY OF BOTSWANA, GABARONE

ZIMBABWE AND THE DEATH OF NEPAD

March 2002

Few events in Africa in recent years have so excited world opinion as has the downward spiral of Zimbabwe under President Robert Mugabe and the years of chaos and terror under his rule. The slide into lawlessness, the wholesale illegal confiscation of land, the general free-fall of the Zimbabwean economy and the presidential competition between Mugabe of the Zimbabwe African National Union-Popular Front (ZANU-PF) and Morgan Tsvangirai of the Movement for Democratic Change, have been the stuff of many editorials and commentaries in all the main newspaper, both in the West and in Africa. At the same time however, the Zimbabwe case has highlighted the perpetual reluctance of African elites to criticise one of their own, particularly in the light of African leaders' reactions to what most people saw as fundamentally rigged elections. This point raises profound questions as to the seriousness and credibility of the New Economic Partnership for Africa's Development (Nepad).

Nepad was launched in October 2001 and was a supposed blueprint for Africa's regeneration. The document asserts that

'African peoples have begun to demonstrate their refusal to accept poor economic and political leadership. These developments are, however, uneven and inadequate and need to be further expedited.' There is, so Nepad claims, 'a new resolve to deal with conflicts and censure deviation from the [democratic] norm.' This springs from the view that 'development is impossible in the absence of true democracy, respect for human rights, peace and good governance.' Nepad shows, the document claims, that 'Africa undertakes to respect the global standards of democracy, which core components include political pluralism, allowing for the existence of several political parties and workers' unions, fair, open, free and democratic elections periodically organised to enable the populace choose their leaders freely.' In short, 'a democratic Africa will become one of the pillars of world democracy, human rights and tolerance.' in partnership with the developed world who have certain 'responsibilities and obligations' to support Nepad.

Tragically, that Nepad only lasted less than six months before its credibility was fatally undermined demonstrates the fickle nature of African elite politics. The much-vaunted desire to alter the 'rules of the game' on how the continent interacts with the West, without any real reciprocal change in the behaviour of African elites-an absolute precondition if such 'Partnerships' are ever to be taken seriously-now seems to be a one-way street of demands but no duties on the part of Africa's presidents. To put it bluntly, that will never wash in the global corridors of power and it is naïve of African leaders to think otherwise. Fatigue with Africa's incessant problems is already high and, even though not all of Africa's malaise is its own making, the refusal of African leaders to at least try and get their own houses in order further exacerbates such negative attitudes in London, Washington, Paris etc.

In the case of Zimbabwe, although there were repeated attempts to muddy the water over the real issues in Zimbabwe, particularly with incessant appeals to 'the land issue' and a desperate playing of the race card, the real issue was the concerted effort by Mugabe and his ZANU-PF party to retain their hold on political power. That African leaders chose to ignore this and rather seek to cast it as some sort of 'neo-imperialist' issue shows, it seems, that even now in 2002, bad governance, corruption, violence and vote-rigging will, at the final analysis, be defended to the hilt by many African presidents. Mugabe's record on the economy, setting aside the land issue, the Matabeleland massacres, the one-party state and myriad other markers of his rule, has been lamentable. After twenty years of

ZANU-PF control, not only are Zimbabwe's citizens one-third poorer than they were at independence, but, according to IMF figures, Zimbabwe has gained the dubious distinction of being the world's fastest-shrinking economy.

Sadly, rather than seeking to contribute positively to change this situation, many African leaders fell into line behind Mugabe-in effect positioning themselves in agreement with the view that there is a malevolent white racist conspiracy to recolonise Zimbabwe and make it back into Rhodesia, led by Britain's Tony Blair and his 'gay gangsters'. Thabo Mbeki, a man who likes to think of himself as some of sort of 'philosopher king', went so far as to assert at the Commonwealth meeting in Australia in March 2002 that talk of ostracising Mugabe was 'inspired by notions of white supremacy' and that such moves were pursued because white political leaders apparently felt uneasy at their 'repugnant position imposed by inferior blacks.' This type of extreme language is not the unique preserve of Mbeki. But, what is significant is that it is precisely Mbeki who has been notably active in promoting Nepad and the 'African Renaissance'. Ironically, it was Mbeki who loudly proclaimed at a conference on the African Renaissance in September 1998 that:

> We want to see an African Continent in which the people participate in systems of governance in which they are truly able to determine their destiny and put behind us the notions of democracy and human rights as peculiarly 'Western' concepts. Thus would we assume a stance of opposition to dictatorship, whatever form it may assume. Thus...we say that we must ensure that when elections are held, these must be truly democratic, resulting in governments which the people would accept as being genuinely representative of the will of the people.

Zimbabwe provided a clear test case for such noble sentiments to be measured against and for leaders such as Mbeki to translate rhetoric into action. This is particularly so in the context where the notion that ZANU-PF might be peaceably removed from power through the democratic wishes of the population was rejected out of hand by Mugabe. The government consistently targeted the judiciary, the independent media and opposition activists for repression and Mugabe himself repeatedly flouted a series of court orders barring the seizure of white-owned farmland by state-backed thugs. In January 2001 the presses of the opposition-inclined Daily News were bombed and several foreign journalists were expelled from the country. Clearly, 'a stance of opposition to dictatorship' was called for. Even more so with the murder of opposition activists openly and repeatedly encouraged from the very top and with vicious racism being deployed by Harare.

All of the above clearly goes against the supposed fundamentals of Nepad, which claims to push for Africa's development and to protect basic human rights and democracy. Africa's leaders did, momentarily, demonstrate a willingness to act with the September 2001 Abuja Agreement, brokered in Nigeria, which set out the conditions for a peaceful resolution of Zimbabwe's crisis and a programme of land reform that would take place within the rule of law. But, Morgan Tsvangirai recognised the problems with such agreements well before the Abuja document was signed, remarking that 'you know this is the saddest thing about Africa, all these flowery declarations and all without commitment. There's no commitment because there is no holding to account...The declarations are not worth the paper they're written on. Releasing such paper creates a feel-good atmosphere and, when leaders are reminded of what they have signed, they retreat into the defense of the sovereignty of nations.'

This is the fundamental issue: African leaders will rarely criticise their own. The self-interest of African elites under threat from democracy (linked surreptitiously in their eyes to notion of good governance) should not be played down. Nor should notions of solidarity and resentment at perceived 'neo-imperialist' interference in the affairs of fellow African countries. Many African leaders have highly dubious credentials themselves. Zambia's Levy Mwanawasa came to power through seriously flawed elections; aid donors have virtually given up on Malawi's Bakili Muluzi and his corrupt regime; Tanzania's Benjamin Mkapa ordered a crack-down on opposition activists in Zanzibar, resulting in many deaths etc., ad nauseam. Focusing on the fact that critics of one of their colleagues is the former colonial master neatly allows such leaders to side-step thorny issues such as democracy and accountability. After all, if they allow someone like Mugabe to be ostracised for his behaviour, who's next on the list? Better to show a united front and protect all members of the elite club. In addition, many African leaders seem to believe that they are predestined to rule, particularly if they are the head or inheritors of victorious liberation movements. Such thinking regards the country and its people as the rightful 'property' of the leader, who can and must never lose power. If Mugabe were to be ousted, this legend would be shattered, setting a precedent for the likes of Dos Santos, Moi, Mbeki etc.

Ironically, the country that world opinion looked to for solid African leadership over Zimbabwe has fallen short, to put it mildly. South African support for Mugabe undermined any speedy resolution of the problem as Pretoria's diplomacy was effectively based on a public excusing of Mugabe's human rights record and the playing down or ignoring of any reports to the contrary. Note that a South African observer delegation was amongst the first to proclaim solemnly that the elections were 'free and fair', even whilst other observers were saying the exact opposite. Note too that the ANC openly welcomed Mugabe's victory in the 2000 parliamentary elections as evidence of Zimbabwe's increasing democratic credentials. In a statement, the ANC said, 'we congratulate ZANU-PF on their victory as we realise that the election process has underscored the fact that democracy is taking root not only in Zimbabwe but in the sub-region and, indeed, in the whole of Africa.'

In a joint statement following a meeting between senior members of the ANC and ZANU-PF in 2000, the two parties announced that they had 'reached common ground' on resolving Zimbabwe's land crisis, namely that that Britain should 'unconditionally' give the Mugabe government funds for land redistribution. The ANC secretary-general Kgalema Motlanthe, ignoring the £44 million that Britain had contributed to the process of land reform but which had been stopped due to gross mismanagement and corruption, criticised London for 'refusing' to fund land redistribution. Motlanthe went on to say that 'the ANC does not accept any conditions put on funds by the British government.'

Prior to the 2002 elections, Mugabe's position was also considerably strengthened by leaders of the Southern African Development Community (SADC) who gave him their unflinching support at the organisation's 20th summit in Windhoek, Namibia in August 2000. President Joaquim Chissano of Mozambique led a chorus of statements widely viewed as clear-cut support for Mugabe, saying there had been a tendency on the part of some 'big powers' to put a 'blanket' over the history of the freedom struggle by 'portraying heroes of the freedom struggle as anti-democratic and even dictators.' 'We cannot in SADC condone these views. We are the democrats and we want democracy to work according to the will of our people in each one of our countries.' SADC leaders went further and 'congratulated' Mugabe and the 'people of Zimbabwe on the manner in which they conducted their parliamentary elections' in June 2000.

If Zimbabwe had a problem, they argued, it was that the foreign press had misrepresented Mugabe's policies. 'We are disappointed,' the leaders continued, 'by the partisan and biased manner in which a sector of the international media has misrepresented the land policy of the government of Zimbabwe which seeks to effect a just and equitable redistribution of land in a situation where one per cent of the population owns over seventy per cent of the best arable land.'

Part of the problem appears to be the inability of many African leaders to differentiate between colonial legacies in the region and the survival strategies of corrupt and undemocratic autocrats. When African leaders have shown any concern, it is over the fear that the spill-over effect from the Zimbabwe crisis would affect the entire region. In essence, whether a colleague was suppressing democracy, encouraging lawlessness and openly stimulating racism against southern African citizens was not an issue per se. It only became an issue when such activities impacted negatively on the region's economies. Yet, what African leaders do is crucial. Only strong, clear-headed African leadership can create the right conditions for a constructive process contributing to the rebuilding of Africa and an escape from the developmental impasse it has fallen into. In the case of Zimbabwe, Mugabe has delighted in snubbing extra-African initiatives (thus playing up his Africanist credentials as an African 'standing up' to the colonials), but has tended to be more receptive to African input. If African leaders had used their leverage more constructively it is possible that the situation in Zimbabwe might not have deteriorated so badly.

Unfortunately, Zimbabwe was in many ways the test case for evaluating the credibility of Nepad and a clear opportunity for African leaders to signal that they had changed their ways. It is quite clear that this has not happened and Nepad's trustworthiness lies in tatters. In fact, incredibly but not surprisingly, Africa fell over itself in talking up the legitimacy of the elections. An observer team from the AU said the elections were 'transparent, credible, free and fair', whilst Nigerian observers in Zimbabwe endorsed Mugabe's victory, saying it had 'recorded no incidence that was sufficient to threaten the integrity and outcome of the election.' The leaders of Kenya and Tanzania praised ZANU-PF's 'deserved victory', and Namibian observers proclaimed that the election was 'water tight, without room for rigging.' Putting in their worth, the South African observer team blamed the long lines of voters unable to vote despite waiting many hours on 'administrative oversights', drawing audible laughter from journalists and diplomats attending their press conference in Harare.

This should not be overly surprising, bearing in mind that one of the South African observers had previously told the Washington Post that 'I don't want to see Mugabe lose this election. He is still a hero to many of us.' For his part, Mbeki stated that South Africa would help Zimbabwe, regardless of the outcome of the presidential election.

If Mbeki and the other proponents of Nepad had been serious about encouraging an African Renaissance then surely their response to Mugabe's behaviour would have been different and signaled a brave commitment to Nepad's principles. But as Tendai Biti, an MDC MP commented on elite-produced initiatives such as Nepad, 'at the end of the day [they] became nothing but a boy's club of little tin-pot dictators justifying the negative views of the traditional Afro-pessimist... For as long as Africans do not insist on uniform international standards of respect for human rights, respect for national coffers, the sacrosanct nature of elections and a commitment towards the eradication of poverty, then the noble ideas and concepts of African unity will become a pipe dream.' The Zimbabwe debacle and the response of African leaders to this simply feeds such pessimism In a speech to a 'Review Workshop' on Nepad in January 2002, Mbeki boldly stated that 'if we cannot unite through an initiative that can permanently reshape this continent and bring about sustained improvement in the lives of our people, then we would have lost an opportunity that will not arise for some time.' The fatal undermining of Nepad's credibility by inaction over Zimbabwe has, I think, produced this 'lost opportunity.' It is most disappointing to anyone who holds out hope for Africa's future.

• • •

GEORGE SOROS, INTERNATIONAL FINANCIER, NEW YORK

A 'VERY SKEWED DOCUMENT'

12 April 2002 (SA Broadcasting Corporation interview)

'Nepad is worth the paper that it is written on. It is very much designed to meet the standards of the Washington Consensus. And therefore it's a very skewed document which I think could be improved on.'

• • •

Greg Mills and **Jonathan Oppenheimer,** SA Institute of International Affairs and Anglo American Corporation, Johannesburg

Partnerships only way to break cycle of poverty

1 October 2001

Africa is a continent eager to take responsibility for its destiny. But that will only be realised by close partnerships between governments and businesses.

The New Africa Initiative, a plan spearheaded by President Thabo Mbeki, aims to revitalise African economies through the promotion of intra-African trade and infrastructure links; the establishment of conditions for good economic and political governance; the combating of regional threats, including conflict and disease; and the promotion of resource inflows. It is, however, important to appreciate that Africa's states have different strengths, weaknesses and divergent ambitions.

Thus, the *New Africa Initiative* must be seen as a framework within which countries can pursue different policies to advance common goals.

Increased capital flows and improved technology offer Africa the opportunity to leapfrog ahead in its development.

More than half of Africa's estimated 800-million people live on less than $1 a day.

But for the continent to reach a goal of reducing poverty by half by 2015, the United Nations Conference on Trade and Development estimates that economies will have to grow by 7% to 8% a year in real terms, well above their average performance of 2,2% in 1991-97.

The requisite capital is unlikely to come from donors as total global aid flows are declining. Moreover, foreign direct investment to Africa dropped by 13% last year. Financing is unlikely to come from Africans themselves, given their low savings rates. Africa's governments must, therefore, create an environment that will encourage the needed capital from domestic and global sources. Some possibilities include the establishment of preferential tax regimes, guarantees for investors, region-wide marketing initiatives and faster privatisation. These conditions will increase the prospect of infrastructure investments and reduce business transaction costs.

A great example of this type of programme is Botswana. Its success has been founded on a sound and sensible leadership and good policies involving a close relationship with business notably through the Debswana diamond-mining entity.

The annual per capita income of $3300 is more than six times the sub- Saharan African average. Yet diamonds were discovered there only in 1969.

But a similar continental approach will require dealing first with those African states willing and able to adhere to such higher standards and integration.

In the 40 years of independence, Africa has been plagued by widespread instability and conflict. Part of the cause of its failure lies in the weak foundations and limited assets possessed by post-colonial regimes. In this way, close partnerships with business offer a path out.

(originally published in the *Financial Times* and *Business Day*)

• • •

GONDAL GONDWE AND **CALLISTUS MADAVO,** INTERNATIONAL MONETARY FUND AND WORLD BANK, WASHINGTON

NEW SWIPE AT FIGHTING POVERTY

7 October 2001

Half a century of global economic integration has helped to bring unprecedented gains in living standards to much of the world. But the rising tide of prosperity has left far too many behind in particular, most of subSaharan Africa.

In recent months, an African vision has emerged that represents a true window of opportunity. It deserves strong support from the international community.

At the Organisation of African Unity (OAU) meeting in Lusaka in July, African leaders launched the *New African Initiative*. The strategy is firmly anchored in the fundamental principles of African ownership, leadership and accountability.

This new initiative focuses on four core elements: peace, democracy and good governance; health care and educational systems, infrastructure and agriculture; the private sector and economic integration at the regional and global levels; and productive partnerships between Africa and its development partners. Together with a commitment 'to restore and maintain macroeconomic stability', this initiative is a comprehensive approach to fighting poverty in Africa. A strong, supportive international response is needed.

The International Monetary Fund (IMF) and the World Bank are doing everything possible to play a part.

The initiative expects the IMF and World Bank to make a contribution on the basis of the poverty reduction strategy adopted in 1999. Central to this approach are poverty reduction strategy papers (PRSPs). The approach emphasises country ownership, broad participation and dealing with the economic, social and structural fundamentals. It also provides a vehicle for co-ordinating international support, to ensure that aid flows truly serve African interests. These strategies, supported by the policy advice and the financial and technical assistance of the two institutions, have the potential to become highly effective tools for self-help in Africa.

In short, this approach offers a framework for partnership with the countries of Africa.

The PRSP process is still in its early stages, but there are signs that it is bearing fruit. Growth performance is holding up and even improving in a number of countries, despite today's difficult global environment. The share of gross domestic product devoted to health and education is rising in the countries participating in the strategy.

Our institutions are determined to make the most of the PRSP process. In that connection we are undertaking a review of the process, and the IMF is reviewing its poverty reduction and growth facility (PRGF), which provides loans at interest rates close to zero to countries pursuing a poverty-reduction strategy. The reviews, which will be conducted later this year, will be much more than a mere formality. We will identify potential improvements, including by actively seeking the views of member countries, civil society, other international institutions and donors.

For its part, the World Bank is moving towards more programmatic assistance to support the implementation of PRSPs, through sector-wide programmes and now Poverty Reduction Support Credits (PRSCs).

Key to accelerating economic progress in Africa is an expansion of private sector activity, and throughout the continent, countries are seeking to create the necessary conditions for this: sound institutions, a predictable legal and economic environment, and a level playing field. This is an important way to bolster the confidence of potential investors. In support of these efforts, the IMF and World Bank will help to establish Investors' Councils as means of constructive dialogue between African leaders and local and international companies. African leaders have chosen to make good governance a central element of the *New African Initiative*. This is essential for attracting private investment and making efficient use of scarce public resources. We are also ready to work with national authorities to identify ways to attack mismanagement and corruption.

Development and reform in Africa call for policies that reflect national priorities and that are fully 'owned' by countries. That is why the Bretton Woods institutions are refocusing and streamlining the conditions attached to their lending. We will focus them on the measures that are really critical to the macroeconomic, structural and social objectives of country programmes. And conditionality must leave real scope for countries to make choices consistent with their political and cultural traditions.

We also recognise that the complexity of development and poverty reduction places severe demands on countries' limited administrative capacities. The IMF, World Bank and other donors will need to provide increased and better co-ordinated technical assistance to support poverty reduction in Africa.

The IMF is planning to make an well-targeted extra effort to support capacity building. This will complement the continuing efforts of other organisations such as the World Bank, United Nations Development Programme (UNDP) and the African Development Bank.

How can the broader international community help? Much attention has been focused on debt relief. The IMF and World Bank have spearheaded the enhanced highly indebted poor countries initiative, which has brought $25bn of debt relief to 19 countries in Africa. Their debt service-to-exports ratio has been cut in half. And the annual budgetary saving of between 1% and 2,5% of GDP allows significant increases in pro-poor spending.

Now we are doing our utmost to extend the benefits of this initiative to the remaining eligible countries, especially those emerging from conflict.

But debt relief is just one element of a comprehensive approach to getting countries back on their feet. Credit is crucial for economic development.

That is why, in the longer run, African countries need to retain the trust of investors in their ability and willingness to repay what they borrow.

Therefore the IMF, the World Bank, and other development partners are working to help African countries create sound domestic financial sectors and, eventually, integrate into international financial markets.

But the most effective help for self-help will come from trade. Africa needs better opportunities for trade. It is time, finally, for the industrial countries to provide African nations with free access to their markets, especially in areas such as agricultural products, textiles and clothing.

Equally important, developing countries need to remove their own impediments to trade. Regional economic co-operation and integration are vehicles for improving competitiveness and attracting investors. We support regional trade and financial integration, but we also encourage the region to harmonise and simplify the often complex and overlapping sub-regional trade arrangements that have evolved over the years.

Financial aid is still essential. The people and governments of the industrial countries need to view aid as an investment in peace and prosperity for the whole world. Industrial countries 30 years ago promised to provide 0.7% of GNP in official development assistance (ODA). If they commit themselves to meeting this target by 2010, starting from today's average level of 0.24% of GNP, then the increase in the first year alone would amount to over $10billion. That is the amount that UN Secretary General Kofi Annan has said is needed for a comprehensive program of HIV/Aids prevention and treatment.

The international community is committed to the achievement of international development goals which aim to halve absolute poverty by 2015. But time is passing, and we need to make faster progress in converting these basic goals into tangible gains in wellbeing. The PRSP process offers a potentially powerful vehicle for promoting country-owned development programmes and for monitoring poverty-reduction efforts by individual poor countries, and the IMF and World Bank are discussing with other partners, including the United Nations, and with African countries, how to use it most effectively.

Success in the fight against poverty is key to stability and peace in the 21st Century. Nowhere are the battle lines clearer than in

Africa. The rest of the world must not let the continent down. The way forward has to be one of strong support for Africa's efforts, on the basis of a true partnership and a recognition of the global benefits that will flow from a more prosperous Africa.

(originally published in the *Financial Times* and *Business Day*)

4

The New Partnership for Africa's Development: An Annotated Critique

The following pages include the original October 2001 text of the *New Partnership for Africa's Development,* accompanied by detailed footnotes analysing the document.

The final draft of the footnotes was compiled in May 2002 by critical intellectuals associated with the Alternative Information and Development Centre. The critique is heavily focused on South Africa in part because of the experiences and research backgrounds of the contributors. This is not an unnecessary intervention, for we *mainly* seek to inform other progressives in the rest of Africa, and across the world, about contradictions, controversies and hypocrisies associated with South Africa, Nepad's host (secretariat) country and catalyst. Because Pretoria politicians and Johannesburg capitalists will be the main African beneficiaries of Nepad, the phrase 'subimperialism' is being increasingly applied to South African initiatives on the continent.[1]

Nevertheless, what must be acknowledged immediately is that the freedom to write far-reaching commentaries of this sort reflects the strength of South Africa's democratic constitutional form, the still-fluid power relations in the society and the openness to democratic debate within the ANC-Cosatu-SACP 'Alliance.' This freedom we do not take for granted, and hence our exercise of robust criticism is a celebration of the space that exists to - in our view - continue speaking truth to power.

1. For example, an article in the business section of South Africa's (pro-Nepad) Sunday Independent (5 May 2002) even openly asked 'Should South Africa be stopped or cooperated with? This is the debate raging in Kenya and other African countries as fears mount that South Africa may take control of the continent's business.'

Three minor methodological points must be made at the outset. Firstly, Nepad is repetitive, and hence necessarily so must this annotated critique repeatedly dwell on core problems. Secondly, there were very minor editing changes made between October 2001 and the present version of Nepad (http://www.Nepad.org), which mean that there are slight inconsistencies in numbering following paragraph 87. Thirdly, while Nepad is a relatively short document that does not seek to provide details in all its areas, we believe that it is already time to assess the *logic* of the document and extrapolate the likely detailed strategies from South Africa's own experience. In some ways, this is a best-case experience, given the relative wealth, resources, social mobilisation and international support the government has enjoyed since 1994.

Finally and most importantly, although the authors agree that top-down improvements in Africa's dire situation are welcome, this critique takes the viewpoint that *genuine solutions to the major problems affecting Africa will really only come from the bottom up.* It is for that reason that aside from citing a variety of popular statements of African developmental aspirations - including South Africa's own 1955 *Freedom Charter* and 1994 *Reconstruction and Development Programme* - we have not made any presumptuous attempt to lay out 'the alternative' to Nepad.

The progressive alternative will come, as did the *Charter* and *RDP*, from the concrete social struggles of the organised popular forces, and from their eventual collection of campaigns and demands into a robust 'African People's Consensus' (as the process has been termed in various continental meetings), followed by a . formal development strategy and programmes. That process is still unfolding, unless it is to be distracted by Nepad.

The New Partnership for Africa's Development

I. INTRODUCTION

1. This *New Partnership for Africa's Development* is a pledge by African leaders,[1] based on a common vision and a firm and shared conviction, that they have a pressing duty to eradicate poverty and to place their countries, both individually and collectively, on a path of sustainable growth and development, and at the same time to participate actively in the world economy and body politic. The Programme is anchored on the determination of Africans to extricate themselves and the

---

Nepad: An Annotated Critique

1. In the formulation of Nepad, the word 'leaders' refers exclusively to heads of state. Three men were most responsible for the document during 2000-01: Thabo Mbeki of South Africa (the catalyst), Abdelaziz Bouteflika of Algeria and Olusegun Obasanjo of Nigeria. The three leaders' governments have faced intense criticism for violating the human rights of their citizenries on a large scale, on the basis of what was sometimes described as a 'genocidal' HIV/Aids policy (South Africa) and of rampant civil/military/religious oppression (Algeria and Nigeria).

To illustrate, in January 2002, Nigerian police teargassed a non-violent demonstration of workers protesting fuel price increases, and then arrested the president, two vice presidents and national auditor of the Nigeria Labour Congress (NLC), the presidents of the bank and public service unions and of the academic staff union of the universities, the chair and treasurer of the NLC's capital territory council and secretary of the NLC's state councils of Ogun, and the acting general secretary of the textile union.

During the formulation of Nepad, no civil society, church, political-party, parliamentary, or other potentially democratic or progressive forces were consulted by Pretoria. In contrast, extensive consultations occurred with the World Bank and IMF (November 2000 and February 2001), transnational corporations and associated government leaders (at Davos in January 2001), the G-8 (in Tokyo in July 2000 and Genoa in July 2001), the European Union (November 2001) and individual Northern heads of state. Only in April 2002 was the first major civil society consultation held, with the Congress of South African Trade Unions (Cosatu).

continent from the malaise of underdevelopment and exclusion in a globalising world.[2]

2. The poverty and backwardness of Africa stand in stark contrast to the prosperity of the developed world. The continued marginalisation of Africa from the globalisation process and the social exclusion of the vast majority of its peoples constitute a serious threat to global stability.[3]

3. Historically accession to the institutions of the international community, the credit and aid binomial has underlined the logic of African development. Credit has led to the debt deadlock, which, from installments to rescheduling, still exists and hinders the growth of African countries. The limits of this option have been reached. Concerning the other element of the binomial – aid – we can also note the reduction of private aid and the upper limit of public aid, which is below the target set in the 1970s.[4]

4. In Africa, 340 million people, or half the population, live on less than US $1 per day. The mortality rate of children under 5 years of age is 140 per 1000, and life expectancy at birth is only 54 years. Only 58 per cent of the population have access

---

2. The aspirations expressed are necessary, but the onus is placed immediately on Africa, even though it appears virtually impossible to fulfill conditions of 'sustainable development' and good governance under the conditions of the current global regime. Nepad begins by framing the problems using phrases such as 'exclusion' and 'a globalising world' - instead of the critical language traditionally used by progressive African analysts, e.g., 'neocolonialism' and 'imperialism.' And where at the outset a tough phrase does emerge - 'eradicate poverty' - it is often supplanted later in Nepad with the mandate to merely 'reduce' poverty.

3. The automatic presumption is that the 'poverty' and 'backwardness' of Africa are as a result of 'exclusion' and 'marginalisation' from 'globalisation.' A different presumption, not even considered, is that mass poverty is an intrinsic feature of globalisation, generated within the logic of the system, much as it was a corollary of apartheid in South Africa. Indeed, the presumption that globalisation correlates to growing poverty and inequality is now widely acknowledged as an entirely valid argument, given that the most profound, rapid cases of impoverishment (e.g. Argentina at present) occur because of excessive vulnerability and dependency upon global financial, trade and direct-investment markets.

4. Although convoluted, the argument is correct. The ambivalence of the Nepad critique of imperialist economic relations is here evident. But the implication of 'the limits of this option' is, amongst progressives, to

to safe water. The rate of illiteracy for people over 15 is 41 per cent. There are only 18 mainline telephones per 1000 people in Africa, compared with 146 for the world as a whole and 567 for high-income countries.

5. The *New Partnership for Africa's Development* calls for the reversal of this abnormal situation by changing the relationship that underpins it. Africans are appealing neither for the further entrenchment of dependency through aid, nor for marginal concessions.[5]

6. We are convinced that an historic opportunity presents itself to end the scourge of underdevelopment that afflicts Africa. The resources, including capital, technology and human skills, that are required to launch a global war on poverty and underdevelopment exist in abundance, and are within our reach.[6] What is required to mobilise these resources and to use them properly, is bold and imaginative leadership that is genuinely committed to a sustained human development effort and poverty eradication, as well as a new global partnership based on shared responsibility and mutual interest.[7]

---

call for debt cancellation, repudiation, a debtor's cartel, and reparations. The problem, in short, is not (as Nepad has it) the *lack* of credit and aid. Official aid comes with neo-liberal strings attached, often has a corrupting and wasteful impact, and mainly trickles back up to the country of origin, in the form of tied purchases of goods and services by home-country multinational corporations. As a result, progressive African civil society groups within the Harare-based African Debt and Development Network have been calling for aid to be canceled, along with the debt.

5. This is a radical statement. Its logic, however, is immediately forgotten.

6. This has been true, objectively, for around a century. There is no analysis in Nepad of why the contemporary period offers the best opportunity. On the contrary, given the prevailing power relations and the West's lack of interest in what *The Economist* recently labelled 'the hopeless continent,' the opposite is true. Until prevailing international power relations are changed, this may be the least hopeful conjuncture in which to propose partnership. However, were genuine African leadership in greater supply, it would be the most hopeful conjuncture to break the most exploitative international debt, trade and investment relationships that actively underdevelop Africa.

7. If 'leadership' is the missing ingredient, Nepad should have a great deal to say about what caused the demise of strong African leaders during the era of independence struggles (1950s-80s). The topic is immediately

7. Across the continent, Africans declare that we will no longer allow ourselves to be conditioned by circumstance. We will determine our own destiny and call on the rest of the world to complement our efforts. There are already signs of progress and hope. Democratic regimes that are committed to the protection of human rights, people-centred development and market-oriented economies are on the increase.[8] African peoples have begun to demonstrate their refusal to accept poor economic and political leadership.[9] These developments are, however, uneven and inadequate and need to be further expedited.

8. The *New Partnership for Africa's Development* is about consolidating and accelerating these gains.[10] It is a call for

---

dropped, unfortunately. But suffice to say, had the early stages of mid/late-20th century globalisation not been so effective – i.e., if colonial and apartheid prisons had not been so full of great men and women, coups not so easily arranged by Cold Warriors, and US government assassination lists not so ambitious – genuine African leaders would have been in greater supply.

8. It is sophistry – characteristic of Nepad – to imply, presumptively, that 'protection of human rights, people-centred development and market-oriented economies' are mutually compatible, when evidence suggests that the latter venture typically trumps and eradicates the two former.

Interestingly, even the Nigerian government recognised this when Obasanjo's office issued a statement in March 2002 breaking with the market-oriented economics of the International Monetary Fund. The rationale was that Nigeria 'values the benefits of political stability, democratic consolidation, credibility and accountability. It does not wish, therefore, to continue with arrangements where only narrowly defined macroeconomic targets come into play' (Agence France Press, 5 March 2002).

9. The period of 'IMF Riots' against literally dozens of corrupt, *comprador* African regimes began, in fact, in the early 1980s. In many cases, these immediately led to a change in regime, or catalysed a process by which democratic civil society and opposition parties took centre stage in African politics for the first time. In most cases, the IMF Riots were caused by the old regimes' implementation of IMF and World Bank policies. Later, we will see, Nepad calls for the present generation of African leaders to implement virtually identical IMF and World Bank policies. A new generation of IMF Riots can be safely predicted.

10. In fact, the rise of democratic regimes in Africa was at its most rapid during the early 1990s. But then dramatic slippage occurred as more sophisticated modes of ruling-party endurance, repression and divide/rule strategies emerged in key 1990s sites of struggle such as Kenya, Namibia, Zambia and Zimbabwe.

a new relationship of partnership between Africa and the international community, especially the highly industrialised countries, to overcome the development chasm that has widened over centuries of unequal relations.

II. AFRICA IN TODAY'S WORLD: BETWEEN POVERTY AND PROSPERITY

9. Africa's place in the global community is defined by the fact that the continent is an indispensable resource base that has served all humanity for so many centuries.[11]

10. These resources can be broken down into the following components:

    - The rich complex of mineral, oil and gas deposits, its flora and fauna, and its wide unspoiled natural habitat, which provide the basis for mining, agriculture, tourism and industrial development (Component I);

    - The ecological lung provided by the continent's rain forests, and the minimal presence of emissions and effluents that are harmful to the environment – a global public good that benefits all humankind (Component II);

    - The paleontological and archaeological sites containing evidence of the evolution of the earth, life and the human species. The natural habitats containing a wide variety of flora and fauna, unique animal species and the open uninhabited spaces that are a feature of the continent (Component III);

    - The richness of Africa's culture and its contribution to the variety of the cultures of the global community (Component IV).[12]

11. The first of these, *Component I*, is the one with which the world is most familiar. The second, *Component II*, has only

---

11. This is a depressingly narrow perspective on how Africa serves humanity: merely as 'resource base.' Is Africa 'indispensable'? Most of Nepad is devoted to explaining that Africa is 'marginalised,' not indispensable.

12. This is a poetic list, but the phraseology appears as a cry for Africa to be increasingly *exploited* by the rest of the world. Moreover, the main experiences of Africa's resistance to exploitation are ignored: the anti-slavery, nationalist, revolutionary, anti-apartheid and anti-neoliberal movements over the past two centuries.

come to the fore recently, as humanity came to understand the critical importance of the issue of the environment. The third, *Component III*, is also now coming into its own, emerging as a matter of concern not only to a narrow field of science or of interest only to museums and their curators. The fourth of these, *Component IV*, represents the creativity of African people, which in many important ways remains under-exploited and under-developed.

12. Africa has a very important role to play with regard to the critical issue of the protection of the environment. African resources include rain forests, the virtually carbon dioxide-free atmosphere above the continent and the minimal presence of toxic effluents in the rivers and soils that interact with the Atlantic and Indian Oceans and the Mediterranean and Red Seas. The *New Partnership for Africa's Development* will contain a strategy for nurturing these resources and using them for the development of the African continent, while at the same time preserving them for all humanity.[13]

13. It is obvious that, unless the communities in the vicinity of the tropical forests are given alternative means of earning a living, they will co-operate in the destruction of the forests.[14] As the preservation of these environmental assets is in the interests of humanity, it is imperative that Africa be placed on a development path that does not put them in danger.

14. Modern science recognises Africa as the cradle of humankind. As part of the process of reconstructing the identity and self-confidence of the peoples of Africa, it is necessary that this contribution to human existence be understood and valued by Africans themselves.[15] Africa's status as the birthplace of humanity should be cherished by the whole world as the

13. At this point in the document, it would show integrity to concede that the country with the worst levels of greenhouse gas emissions per person, corrected for income levels, is South Africa. As discussed below, under the neo-liberal macroeconomic policy that promotes foreign investment in minerals beneficiation, this problem has become worse since the demise of apartheid.

14. Here would be an opportunity to target the transnational corporations and banks involved in rainforest destruction (http://www.ran.org) but Nepad fails to do so.

15. Nepad here establishes a psychological auto-critique of the deconstruction of the organic 'identity and self-confidence' of many

origin of all its peoples. Accordingly, the *New Partnership for Africa's Development* must preserve this common heritage and use it to build a universal understanding of the historic need to end the underdevelopment and marginalisation of the continent.

15. Africa also has a major role to play in maintaining the strong link between human beings and the natural world. Technological developments tend to emphasise the role of human beings as a factor of production, competing for their place in the production process with their contemporary or future tools. The open uninhabited spaces, the flora and fauna, and the diverse animal species that are unique to Africa offer an opportunity for humanity to maintain its link with nature.[16]

16. Africa has already made a significant contribution to world culture through literature, music, visual arts and other cultural forms, but her real potential remains untapped because of her limited integration into the global economy.[17] The *New Partnership for Africa's Development* will enable Africa to increase her contribution to science, culture and technology.

Africans – a problem which can be traced in large part to the penetration of cheap, tacky Western culture associated with globalisation.

Tragically, important paleontological sites in Ethiopia, Kenya and even South Africa are not given sufficient resources and protection, nor is pre-colonial history sufficiently researched and promoted across Africa. Aside from structural adjustment programmes which have cut research, teaching and scientific budgets, the ideology of modernisation – which pervades Nepad – is also to blame.

16. What should also be admitted here, were Nepad to do an honest inventory of Africa's problems, is that the manner in which this occurs under present circumstances of globalisation is via: the commodification of nature, 'biopiracy,' eco-tourism generally limited to the very wealthy, big-game hunting, and the displacement of people and farmworkers (as capital-intensive commercial agricultural is intensified and as agricultural areas are converted to game-farming).

South Africa has been the most notorious site of these problems in recent years. To make matters worse, during the 1990s, both apartheid-era and post-apartheid authorities together lobbied against the CITES convention provisions that protected the elephant herds of Kenya, Tanzania and other African countries from ivory-seeking poachers.

17. A frank assessment of why Africa's cultural heritage is undeveloped would stress the opposite: the swamping of African culture by cheap

17. In this new millennium, when humanity is searching for a new way to build a better world, it is critical that we bring to bear the combination of these attributes and the forces of human will to place the continent on a pedestal of equal partnership in advancing human civilisation.[18]

• The historical impoverishment of a continent

18. The impoverishment of the African continent was accentuated primarily by the legacy of colonialism, the Cold War, the workings of the international economic system and the inadequacies of and shortcomings in the policies pursued by many countries in the post-independence era.[19]

---

imports associated with globalisation, along with the Bretton Woods institutions' single-minded focus on African export-led growth through structural adjustment over the past two decades. Structural adjustment entailed debilitating state subsidy budgets for arts and culture, with the exception of very minor programmes to promote a few commodifiable cultural industries for tourists and international curio shops.

The South African government's own budget cuts in these areas, and failure to undo the damage that apartheid did to the historical record of indigenous culture, are exemplars of the problem.

18. To strive for an 'equal' international partnership requires, first and foremost, an analysis of power relations and how to change them, which is what Nepad most studiously avoids.

For the sake of appeasing a post-war British public which was growing queasy about colonialism, 'Partnership' was also the name of the idea for slightly-adjusted race-relations promoted by the leader of settler-colonial Zimbabwe during most of the 20th century, Lord Godfrey Huggins. Huggins explained to his white Rhodesian constituents that he meant the 'partnership between the rider and the horse.'

Likewise, the idea of partnership is unveiled in South Africa where the ANC government regularly comments on its good relations with its 'social partners,' big business and labour. In reality, labour is up in arms about neo-liberal policies, while the biggest businesses have deserted South Africa. in order to establish their financial headquarters in London, where they drain profits and dividends, which in turn was the main cause of the rand crashing at an unprecedented rate during 2000-01.

19. Because this list says everything, it says nothing. Because blame is not explicitly attributed, the opportunity to make a case for reparations – as was done by many African government delegates and civil society activists at the UN World Conference Against Racism hosted by South Africa in September 2001 – is missed.

19. For centuries, Africa has been integrated into the world economy mainly as a supplier of cheap labour and raw materials. Of necessity, this has meant the draining of Africa's resources rather than their use for the continent's development. The drive in that period to use the minerals and raw materials to develop manufacturing industries and a highly skilled labour force to sustain growth and development was lost.[20] Thus, Africa remains the poorest continent despite being one of the most richly endowed regions of the world.

20. In other countries and on other continents, the reverse was the case. There was an infusion of wealth in the form of investments, which created larger volumes of wealth through the export of value-added products. It is time that African resources are harnessed to create wealth for the well-being of her peoples.

Notably, Pretoria actively opposed Africa's attempts in these regards, and tried to suppress discussion of reparations. There were both ideological (comprador) and pragmatic reasons, as the South African government attempted unsuccessfully to prevent the low-level US delegation's walk-out, and succeeded in appeasing the European Union, in search of a much more moderate official statement against colonialism.

20. 'This period' extends to the present time. Africa's industrialisation had increased dramatically in several parts of the continent during the deglobalisation period of the 1930s and elsewhere during the inward-oriented post-Independence years of the 1960s-70s. The structural adjustment era rolled back this progress.

Virtually all World Bank and IMF dictates during this era have included demands that African countries cut budgets; increase users fees for state services; privatise state enterprises (including even municipal services); lift price controls, subsidies and any other distortions of market forces; remove currency controls; devalue the currency; impose higher interest rates; deregulate local finance; remove import barriers such as trade tariffs and quotas; lower the social wage and funding for education/ skills-training programmes; and promote the export of raw materials to increasingly-glutted world markets.

Perhaps the most notorious recent example was in Mozambique during the late 1990s, when the country's single largest industry, cashew nut processing, was destroyed by World Bank dictates, via debt-relief conditionality (privatisation plus liberalisation plus retraction of a 10% export tax on raw cashews). Nepad endorses more of the same, via HIPC and the Paris Club debt workout process.

21. Colonialism subverted hitherto traditional structures, institutions and values or made them subservient to the economic and political needs of the imperial powers. It also retarded the development of an entrepreneurial class, as well as a middle class with skills and managerial capacity.[21]

22. At independence, virtually all the new states were characterised by a shortage of skilled professionals and a weak capitalist class, resulting in a weakening of the accumulation process.[22]

---

21. Colonialism also destroyed social structures and settler-colonialism deliberately drove Africans from their land so as to set up migrant labour-sourcing systems that particularly required the superexploitation of women. (Women had the roles, during male migrancy, of child-rearing, nursing sick workers and looking after pensioners, which in normal capitalist societies the state and employers would have subsidised - but African women were forced to provide these services on their own, so that once the usefulness of male workers ended, they were tossed back to 'native reserves.')

Again, were it not for the Nepad authors' ideological opposition, a demand for reparations would be logical here. The 'middle-class' that colonialism promoted, it should be mentioned, was characterised by *compradorism* (as Frantz Fanon brilliantly analysed): a subservient group of local Africans who served the interests of colonial *and* neocolonial exploitation, in part by refusing to speak truth to Western power - as also characterises Nepad.

22. The use of phrases such as 'capitalist class' should not disguise Nepad's profound conservatism. Contributing to the lack of skilled labour and an organic capitalist class was the inherited structure of the capitalist component of African economies, which was towards raw materials extraction whose marketing on international markets was mediated by international oligopolistic cartels of large transnational corporations. They, in turn, extracted far greater profits from the insertion of African economies into the world economy in this manner, than did Africans. It was in the interests of these firms and Western consumers that this system continue, and that it be labeled 'globalisation' and made to seem inevitable. The destruction of skilled workforces, deindustrialisation of protected industries, denuding of national industrial policy, privatisation of major state-owned industry (often leading to their total demise), and defunding of the social wage were all universal characteristics of structural adjustment programmes imposed by the World Bank and IMF. The logical implication is to resist these programmes and demand the end of interference by the Bretton Woods institutions.

The key economic problem at the point apartheid was defeated in South Africa, incidentally, is not 'a weak capitalist class, resulting in a weakening of the accumulation process' but the opposite: a strong capitalist class

Post-colonial Africa inherited weak states and dysfunctional economies that were further aggravated by poor leadership, corruption and bad governance in many countries.[23] These two factors, together with the divisions caused by the Cold War, hampered the development of accountable governments across the continent.

23. Many African governments did not empower their peoples to embark on development initiatives to realise their creative potential.[24] Today, the weak state remains a major constraint

---

which demanded austerity policies and liberalisation, so that its own narrow process of capital accumulation could be enhanced. (A weaker capitalist class during South Africa's transition to democracy would have been most welcome, from the standpoint of social change and the redistribution of apartheid wealth.) This accumulation process has been most notable in two areas that have caused profound harm to the South African economy: financial profiteering/speculation, and the flight of funds to London and offshore banking centres. The post-apartheid government acquiesced to virtually all the wishes of that capitalist class: dramatically lower corporate taxes (from 48% in 1994 to 30% by 1999); much less onerous exchange controls; lower import tariffs; the demutualisation of the major insurers; permission to relist the largest companies in London; and no state resistance to the loss of more than a million formal-sector jobs.

23. The phenomenon of neocolonialism, as critiqued by many great African intellectuals and leaders, deserves more comment. The near-universality of the experience in Africa, and in many other Third World settings, was functional to an earlier epoch of globalisation, as well as to geopolitical arrangements associated with formal decolonisation and the Cold War.

But the problems continue today, as witnessed in South Africa. The functionality of African corruption and malgovernance to the international capitalist system, was shown when Daimler-Chrysler arms-dealers allegedly bribed the second-ranking ANC official in parliament, Tony Yengeni, and when the then defense minister, Joe Modise, directly promoted an inexplicable $6 billion arms acquisition deal which benefited a company in which he was involved.

As discussed below, there are rare efforts to address these problems - such as that by Lesotho to prosecute the beneficiary of bribes extended by some of the largest companies in South Africa (e.g., Anglo American Corporation) and Sweden (ABB) - which Nepad should celebrate, were the ongoing character of bribery and corruption in Africa not so embarrassing.

24. The coy phrases 'bad governance' and 'failure to empower their peoples' cannot substitute for the harsh reality of African state repression under conditions of worsening economic stress since Independence. Were

to sustainable development in a number of countries. Indeed, one of Africa's major challenges is to strengthen the capacity to govern and to develop long-term policies. At the same time, there is also the urgent need to implement far-reaching reforms and programmes in many African states.

Nepad honest, it would expose the propensity of African nationalist regimes - often propped up by the West, including during the 1990s - to murder, torture or otherwise oppress their political opponents, especially those promoting human rights and social justice.

The Zimbabwe African National Union is only the latest case of tyrannical repression of a labour-based opposition. Once Harare began implementing a standard structural adjustment programme in 1991, which failed immediately leading to protests by trade unions, students and social movements, the West contributed to the repressive regime. The British and US governments engaged in extensive military cooperation with the Zimbabwe Defense Force. The World Bank labeled the structural adjustment programme 'highly successful' (the highest possible mark) in its first (1995) evaluation, in spite of the plummeting living standards and deindustrialisation. More recently, after falling out of favour with the West when he redistributed land and defaulted on Zimbabwe's debt during the late 1990s, Robert Mugabe benefitted enormously from Pretoria's ideological and material support since the upsurge in violence began in February 2000.

Some South African labour and social-justice movements have succumbed to intimidation by the ANC government, in part because of recent ruling-party propaganda attacks on: the leaders of millions of anti-privatisation strikers (August-September 2001); thousands of community residents in Soweto suffering from unaffordable services (who were labeled 'thugs and criminals' in December 2001); three top ANC leaders (based in business) who were alleged to have plans to overthrow Mbeki (May 2001); and leading opponents of government HIV/Aids policies, who during 2000 were labeled by Pretoria (according to newspaper reports) as agents of pharmaceutical corporations and even of the CIA. Those Aids policies, which follow logically from the 'dissident' (or 'denialist') philosophy that disputes a link between HIV and Aids, were described in March 2002 by the head of the Medical Research Council as 'genocidal.'

Although in April, a U-turn apparently occurred on the use of anti-retroviral drugs for prevention/treatment in cases of mother-to-child-transmission and rape, this was widely seen as a manifestation of western pressure, not a sincere change of opinion by Pretoria. Immediately beforehand, a bizarre 114-page Aids-denialist document (allegedly written by Mbeki himself though credited to his close ally Peter Mokaba) was officially circulated throughout the ANC, suggesting that South Africa's ruling party retains an ongoing, debilitating division on the issue that most profoundly affects the society.

24. The structural adjustment programmes of the 1980s provided only a partial solution. They promoted reforms that tended to remove serious price distortions, but gave inadequate attention to the provision of social services.[25] As a consequence, only a

---

25. One test of robust analysis is to pose the opposite premise, to determine whether the subsequent hypotheses are worth exploring:

- What if structural adjustment represented not 'a partial solution' but instead, reflecting local and global power shifts, a profound defeat for genuine African nationalists, workers, peasants, women, children and the environment?
- What if the structural adjustment programmes of the 1980s-90s were the result not of independent Africans searching honestly for 'solutions,' but instead mainly reflected the dramatic shift in power relations at both global scale (where financial and commercial circuits of capital were in ascendance) and within individual African states, away from lobbies favouring somewhat pro-poor social policies and (at least half-hearted) industrial development, towards cliques whose strategies served the interests of acquisitive, overconsumptive local elites, Washington financiers, and transnational corporations?
- What if 'promoting reforms' really amounted to the IMF and World Bank imposing their one-size-fits-all neo-liberal policies on desperately disempowered African societies, without any reference to democratic processes, resistance or diverse local conditions?
- What if the removal of 'serious price distortions' really meant the repeal of exchange controls (hence allowing massive capital flight), subsidy cuts (hence pushing masses of people below the poverty line), and lowered import tariffs (hence generating massive deindustrialisation)?
- What if 'inadequate attention to the provision of social services' in reality meant the opposite: excessive attention to applying neo-liberalism not just to the macroeconomy, but also to health, education, water and other crucial state services? And what if the form of IMF/Bank attention included insistence upon greater cost recovery, higher user-fees, lower budgetary allocations, privatisation, and even the disconnection of supplies to those too poor to afford them, hence leading to the unnecessary deaths of millions of people?
- What if 'inadequate attention to the provision of social services' is not anywhere correlated to the inability of countries to 'achieve sustainable higher growth,' but rather serves as a nice-sounding justification for 'adjustment with a human face,' as UNICEF coined the compromise that Nepad apparently seeks?

few countries managed to achieve sustainable higher growth under these programmes.[26]

25. Indeed, Africa's experience shows that the rate of accumulation in the postcolonial period has not been sufficient to rebuild societies in the wake of colonial underdevelopment, or to sustain improvement in the standard of living. This has had deleterious consequences on the political process and led to sustained patronage and corruption.[27]

26. The net effect of these processes has been the entrenchment of a vicious cycle, in which economic decline, reduced capacity and poor governance reinforce each other, thus confirming Africa's peripheral and diminishing role in the world economy. Thus, over the centuries, Africa has become the marginalised continent.[28]

27. The *New Partnership for Africa's Development* seeks to build on and celebrate the achievements of the past,[29] as well as

---

26. Which countries? Botswana didn't undergo formal structural adjustment. The three main World Bank success stories of the 1980s-90s were Uganda, Ghana and Zimbabwe. All subsequently suffered major setbacks, especially the latter two, directly attributable to the distortions caused by reorientation of the economy away from people's needs, towards export-led growth which ultimately proved illusory.

South Africa adopted a home-grown structural adjustment programme in 1996, whose results were devastating to employment and the value of the currency, amongst other variables, as discussed below.

27. The causality can be debated. In most African countries, the rate of profit for transnational corporate investment has been extremely high (in the 30% of equity range). It can be shown in case after case (perhaps most notably in the case of the Democratic Republic of the Congo) that a high rate of accumulation - not for the country, but for transnational corporations - required corruption and tyranny, so the looting would continue undisturbed by popular opposition.

28. The use of 'marginalised' in this context is pernicious, for it makes it appear that the solution to Africa's problem is necessarily a more active embrace of globalisation - which in reality is the euphemism for the historical process (slavery-imperialism-colonialism-neocolonialism-neo-liberalism) that is most responsible for the development of Africa's underdevelopment.

29. But none of these achievements - especially mass civil-society protests that threw off the yokes of slavery, colonialism and apartheid - are specifically mentioned in Nepad. Nor are the constructive, suggestions made by an earlier generation of African nationalists in the Lagos Plan

reflect on the lessons learned through painful experience, so as to establish a partnership that is both credible and capable of implementation. In doing so, the challenge is for the peoples and governments of Africa to understand that development is a process of empowerment and self-reliance. Accordingly, Africans must not be wards of benevolent guardians; rather they must be the architects of their own sustained upliftment.[30]

- **Africa and the global revolution**

28. The world has entered the new millennium in the midst of an economic revolution.[31] This revolution could provide both the context and the means for Africa's rejuvenation. While globalisation has increased the cost of Africa's ability to compete, we hold that the advantages of an effectively managed integration present the best prospects for future economic prosperity and poverty reduction.

29. The current economic revolution has, in part, been made possible by advances in information and communications technology (ICT), which have reduced the cost of and increased the speed of communications across the globe,

---

of Action mentioned, much less taken forward - on the contrary, Nepad celebrates the WTO, IMF, World Bank and transnational corporations.

30. This is, again, inspiring rhetoric. But Nepad, in reality, shuns 'self-reliance' and the self-upliftment of the mass of Africans, as witnessed by the total lack of civil society consultation in the drafting of the document.

31. Pretoria perpetually endorses technicist interpretations of international economics, including rhetoric about the info-communications 'revolution.' In reality, however, there are enormous problems of both sustainability and relevance associated with the alleged 'New Economy' (a phrase that immediately went out of fashion with the massive dot.com crash of 2000). These include severe cutbacks in the sectors of the ICT industry most relevant to mass expansion of services to low-income people. Moreover, the worsening digital divide in Africa allows elites and the middle classes to gain expensive access to cellphones and computers, distancing themselves further from the masses of the citizenry.

South Africa's own efforts to come to grips with ICT challenges are analysed below. They include the failure of the Universal Service Agency 'telecentres,' due to financial unaffordability, and the unsustainable expansion of unaffordable telephone lines (known as 'churning') through the majority state-owned telecommunications monopoly, which has been dramatically reducing cross-subsidies.

abolishing pre-existing barriers of time and space, and affecting all areas of social and economic life.[32] It has made possible the integration of national systems of production and finance, and is reflected in an exponential growth in the scale of cross-border flows of goods, services and capital.[33]

30. The integration of national systems of production has made it possible to 'slice up the value chain' in many manufacturing and service-sector production processes.[34] At the same time, the enhanced mobility of capital means that borrowers, whether governments or private entities, must compete with each other for capital in global rather than national markets.[35]

---

32. The effect of ICT on most Africans has been marginal on a day-to-day basis. However, the rapid rise of the sector over the past two decades has been central to the overall growth of international income inequality and distorted power relations associated with globalisation. These have had their mirror in Africa during the 1980s-90s in lowered standards of living for hundreds of millions of people, and more rapid environmental destruction.

33. In reality, while there has been fairly rapid growth in world trade since the world recession of the early 1980s, the level of globalisation (measured by trade as a percentage of national output) is still in the range it was in 1913, long before the ICT revolution. More importantly, even prior to the dot.com crash and downturn in the world economy, global economic growth had already slowed dramatically during the two-decade period of the alleged economic revolution, compared to the prior two decades, and the lowest-income countries' economies were worst affected (http://www.cepr.net).

34. This is precisely the problem that Africa suffered during the era of colonial exploitation: being just a slice (raw materials) of a production process. The immediate post-colonial era at least included a few attempts at more balanced, self-reliant economic development, prior to their destruction due to structural adjustment policies imposed by the Bretton Woods institutions.

35. It is incorrect to argue that borrowers 'must' search for capital in international markets. This is only true insofar as hard-currency resources are required. For most of the investment that is urgently needed in Africa, in basic water systems, roads, food security and the like, the hard-currency input is negligible and foreign capital is not required. Indeed, because of declining currencies, it is usually far more expensive to pay for African development projects using foreign loans, which must be repaid with increasingly-expensive foreign currency, hence requiring economies to shift increasingly to export-led growth rather than internally-balanced

Both these processes have increased the costs to those countries that are unable to compete effectively.[36] To a large extent, these costs have been borne disproportionately by Africa.[37]

---

development. (The hard currency is then often squandered on wasteful luxury goods or used to repay illegitimate foreign debt.)

In the same vein, an enormous mistake was made by the South African government towards the end of the apartheid era, and amplified in the period 1998-2001, when Pretoria allowed the country's largest companies - Gencor/Billiton, Anglo American Corporation, Old Mutual, South African Breweries, Didata, DeBeers and others - to effectively change their location of ownership, from Johannesburg to London. The excuse used was, as in this Nepad paragraph, the alleged need to access capital more inexpensively in international markets. But this gift to the main beneficiaries of apartheid - white businesses who set up the migrant labour system - was repaid by the largest-ever drain on the current-account balance in South African history, as profit/dividend repatriation became extreme especially during 2000-01, leading directly to a crash in the value of the South African currency.

36. The extremely high real cost of capital that prevailed during most of the 1980s-90s was *not* caused by lack of competitiveness - as witnessed by the desperation with which Western financial centres offloaded credits to Third World borrowers (until the early 1980s) and then portfolio investments in emerging markets (during the 1990s). Instead, the cost of capital reflected, firstly, international monetarism catalysed by Paul Volcker's increase in interest rates at the US Federal Reserve in 1979; secondly, the transmission of the monetarist ideology through structural adjustment programmes across the world, simultaneous with financial liberalisation which gave financiers more outlets for their investible funds; and thirdly, higher risk ratings in Third World countries, which were generally unjustified, since only a very few (e.g., South Africa in 1985, Brazil in 1987, Russia in 1998, Zimbabwe in 1999, Ecuador in 2000, Argentina in 2001) failed to immediately service or reschedule their debts, accept IMF bailout loans to allow investor exit, or permit profit/dividend repatriation.

37. At last, this sentence is based upon valid analysis. However, Africa's suffering mainly occurred because state elites - egged on by the Bretton Woods institutions, like-minded conservative advisors, arms merchants and other transnational corporate sales agents - fell head over heels into the Third World debt trap. They then failed to organise collectively to demand better terms, or to establish a debtors' cartel - as Fidel Castro and Julius Nyerere had called for in 1983. Nepad continues the tradition of subservient African leaders by refusing to question the moral legitimacy of debt repayment, even though the Jubilee campaign has raised this issue to an unprecedented level of consciousness at the world scale. Post-apartheid

31. While no corner of the world has escaped the effects of globalisation, the contributions of the various regions and nations have differed markedly. The locomotive for these major advances is the highly industrialised nations.[38] Outside this domain, only a few countries in the developing world play a substantial role in the global economy.[39] Many developing countries, especially in Africa, contribute passively, and mainly on the basis of their environmental and resource endowments.

32. It is in the distribution of benefits that the global imbalance is most glaring. On the one hand, opportunities have increased to create or expand wealth, acquire knowledge and skills, and improve access to goods and services – in brief, to improve the quality of life. In some parts of the world, the pursuit of greater openness of the global economy has created opportunities for lifting millions of people out of poverty.[40]

South Africa is the most notorious of African countries for denial of its Third World debt crisis.

38. Actually, the fastest-growing economies during the 1980s-90s were not those of the highly industrialised West or Japan, but the Newly Industrialising Countries of East Asia. As for the trajectory of the West's alleged economic 'locomotive,' it was certainly possible by October 2001 to remark upon the New Economy's train smash - but to do so would spoil Nepad's techno-driven story.

39. South African elites like to consider themselves amongst this group. Indeed, since 1994, they have presided over the board of governors of the IMF and World Bank, the Non-Aligned Movement, the United Nations Conference on Trade and Development, the Commonwealth, the Organisation of African Unity, the Southern African Development Community (SADC), the World Commission on Dams, and a host of other important international and continental bodies. But the question that typically goes unasked in Pretoria, is what good has it done the people of South Africa, and the Third World, to have had the South African government playing this 'substantial role in the global economy' - given that they have worked in the *comprador* spirit of Nepad rather than as strong advocates for poor people's interests?

40. This argument has been frequently debated. There is increasing evidence to show the opposite. Even in countries like China and India where proletariat, middle-class and elite populations have grown, so too have the ranks of the unemployed and deeply impoverished. Those countries celebrated as globalisation poster-children, like Southeast Asia, experienced horrendous crises during the late 1990s, whereas prior to liberalising investment and finance they boasted higher growth rates.

33. On the other hand, greater integration has also led to the further marginalisation of those countries that are unable to compete effectively. In the absence of fair and just global rules, globalisation has increased the ability of the strong to advance their interests to the detriment of the weak, especially in the areas of trade, finance and technology.[41]

---

41. This is a fine statement, but it bears asking, *if 'fair and just global rules' are impossible to establish, as appears to be the case under prevailing power relations and rising US belligerence, then is it not time to question the imperatives of globalisation?*

Moreover, it also bears asking, *if the rules were not fair and just - e.g., in the Uruguay Round of the General Agreement on Tariffs and Trade (1993) and subsequent trade agreements, and in relation to international flows of financial capital - then why did South Africa's post-apartheid rulers join Gatt in 1994, sign on to various subsequent free-trade agreements with the European Union and United States in 1998-2000, and lift the country's main defense against financial capital (the financial rand) in March 1995?*

In 1999, Mbeki agonised over the rules of the game, in particular, just as the EU-South African trade deal was to be signed:

> ...the problem we are facing even as we stand here, of arriving at the point when we can conclude the bilateral agreement between our country and the European Union. Stripped of all pretence, what has raised the question whether the agreement can be signed today or not, is the reality that many among the developed countries of the North have lost all sense of the noble idea of human solidarity. What seems to predominate is the question, in its narrowest and most naked meaning - what is in it for me! What is in it for me! - and all this with absolutely no apology and no sense of shame. (Mbeki, T. (1999), 'Speech at the Launch of the African Renaissance Institute,' Pretoria, 11 October.)

Yet he and trade minister Alec Erwin subsequently accepted those rules (including silly provisions concerning use of the terms grappo, ouzo, port and sherry, at the insistence of Southern Europeans). This they did not only on behalf of South Africa, but on behalf of the entire Southern African region (because of impending SADC free trade), whose leaders *had not been consulted by Erwin.* The devastating consequences of trade liberalisation in SADC include South Africa's neighbours - Botswana, Swaziland, Namibia and Lesotho - in the regional customs union, whose tariff revenues have been slashed. In turn, this is forcing huge cuts in government budgets, which typically affect social spending, women and children.

It has limited the space for developing countries to control their own development, as the system has no provision for compensating the weak.[42] The conditions of those marginalised in this process have worsened in real terms. A fissure between inclusion and exclusion has emerged within and among nations.

34. In part, Africa's inability to harness the process of globalisation is a result of structural impediments to growth and development in the form of resource outflows and unfavourable terms of trade.[43] At the same time, we recognise that failures of political and economic leadership in many African countries impede the effective mobilisation and utilisation of scarce resources into productive areas of activity in order to attract and facilitate domestic and foreign investment.[44]

---

42. The main reason for this, which Nepad dares not say, is that the weak have very few threats to make against the powerful. Fake threats such as counterproductive radical-Islamic terrorism, which strengthened not weakened the forces of reaction in the United States, are no substitute for the potential threat of a united Africa which acts in its self-interest. The best example was the denial of consensus by the Organisation of African Unity at the December 1999 World Trade Organisation summit in Seattle.

In contrast, South African trade minister Erwin was notably peeved at the failure of Seattle to establish a new WTO round, and only joined the OAU caucus statement at the last moment, grudgingly, and demanding edits. He then actively pursued a new round during 2000-01 in meetings with both intransigent and weak African trade ministers, and according to press reports which went unrefuted, he worked very hard to split the African delegation in November 2001 at Doha to prevent another Seattle debacle.

43. This is indeed the fundamental problem, added to which is that once Africa fell into debt-dependency, the Bretton Woods institutions imposed inappropriate austerity policies which ruined the capacity of states to lead industrialisation, and which lowered effective demand in the economy, in part through lowering the social wage of the masses. For Nepad to criticise the structural constraints without mentioning the neo-liberal policies associated with systematic economic disempowerment is cunning, but fraudulent.

44. The phrase 'in order to' implies that the objective is investment, rather than meeting needs. Often, the two are compatible, but often they are not. If private-sector investment in Africa's productive sectors has been weak, one problem may be inappropriate state policies. But another might be the intrinsic lack of profit in these areas, given the low level of

35. The low level of economic activity means that the instruments necessary for the real injection of private funds and risk-taking are not available, and the result is a further decline.[45] In this self-perpetuating cycle, Africa's capacity to participate in the globalisation process is severely weakened, leading to further marginalisation.[46] The increasing polarisation of wealth and poverty is one of a number of processes that have accompanied globalisation, and which threaten its sustainability.[47]

African consumers' buying power, a problem which can only be solved by replacing the profit motive with state production on a subsidised basis. This is certainly recognised in crucial areas in South Africa, such as water provision, where the government came under pressure (in part due to a cholera epidemic in 2000-01) to promise a lifeline supply of water to residents, which in turn has subsequently proven to be a major disincentive to private investors. This universal dilemma - the need for African state-led development due to the private sector simply opting out, or due to its own crises - goes unmentioned in Nepad.

45. 'Instruments' is a confusing term, because it might refer to financial institutions which mobilise savings for onlending to investors, or it might mean investors themselves. Yet where such instruments are 'not available,' the standard historical solution has been to introduce a state enterprise (a development-finance corporation, or a state-owned investment initiative) which mobilises private-sector funds, engages in joint ventures with the private sector, taxes the private sector for specific project-related reasons, or otherwise controls the contours of investment. Yet since the 1980s, Bretton Woods dictates have specifically prohibited such state interventions and indeed have decapacitated states from establishing instruments that the private sector neglected to provide - a fact that Nepad is once again too diplomatic (and short-sighted) to mention.

46. Again, Nepad reinforces the deceitful linkage between marginalisation and the alleged lack of globalisation - and in doing so, completely ignores the possibility of the contrary case, i.e., in favour of *de*globalisation so as to end the debt dependency, declining terms of trade and *comprador* relationships with the most exploitative international economic processes, that continue to destroy African economies, societies and environments.

47. This last phrase is possibly the most important in the document, but also the most empty. Nepad fails to elaborate: How is globalisation's 'sustainability' threatened? What can Africans do to ensure the West comprehends this threat, and that consequently a massive transfer of resources must occur? Nepad owes it to Africans and their supporters across the world to outline a non-terrorist means of translating globalisation's non-sustainability into a meaningful change in power relations. Because it does not, and probably cannot do so because of the authors' subservience,

36. The closing years of the last century saw a major financial collapse in much of the developing world, which not only threatened the stability of the global financial system, but also the global economy as a whole.[48] One of the immediate effects of the financial crisis was the exacerbation of existing levels of deep, structural poverty in which about half of the world's population lives on less than US $2 per day, and a fifth on less than US $1 per day.

37. There also exist other factors that pose serious longer-term risks. These include the rapid increase in the numbers of the socially excluded in different parts of the world, contributing to political instability, civil war and military conflict on the one hand, and a new pattern of mass migration on the other.[49] The

---

Nepad's case for further participation in globalisation is weakened by such vague references to unsustainability.

As a footnote, the World Summit on Sustainable Development – the world's largest-ever official conference – is to be hosted by South Africa in September 2002, ironically in a globalisation-showcase setting (the opulent Johannesburg suburb of Sandton) that is probably the most unsustainable in Africa, for numerous environmental, social and economic reasons.

48. This is the kind of 'threat' that might, as argued above, make sense in order to show that globalisation is 'not sustainable.' But to do so would require Nepad to more forcefully hint that there will be more crises like those suffered by East Asia, Russia, Latin America and South Africa during 1997-99 – where currency values fell by a third in most cases and repayment of foreign debt (or in South Africa's case forward-cover book liabilities) became onerous. The 2000-01 Turkish and Argentine crises suggest that the problem was not limited to 'the closing years of the last century' and might be far more permanent.

However, to do so would in turn require Nepad to promote two other corollaries: collective default on African and Third World debt so as to again 'threaten the stability of the global financial system'; and prohibition of developing country funds invested in the IMF/World Bank (e.g., South Africa's 1% share) to bale out Western investors, as would normally happen. In the next sentence, Nepad does not mention that while poverty increased dramatically in the wake of the 1997-99 emerging markets crisis, foreign investors (especially New York and London financiers) generally recovered their funds, and new US investors in debt-ravaged Asian firms were able to pick up assets at fire-sale prices.

49. There is not, at this stage, a bona fide case to be made that the threat from the masses of excluded people needs taking seriously by the world's economic managers. The terrorist incidents of 2001 were not organised by the 'socially excluded' but by wealthy, alienated Muslims. The 'political

> expansion of industrial production and the growth in poverty contribute to environmental degradation of our oceans, atmosphere and natural vegetation.[50] If not addressed, these will set in motion processes that will increasingly slip beyond the control of governments, both in developed and developing countries.

---

instability, civil war and military conflict' that ordinarily and directly follow failed structural adjustment programmes - from Argentina to Zimbabwe, including most of Africa's basket cases - are sometimes slightly disruptive and embarrassing to the West. But they are just as often seen as excellent opportunities to sell expensive high-tech weapons.

South Africa itself demonstrates the point, with its unaffordable $6 billion purchase of mainly offensive armaments from European producers. And mass migration is either welcomed by citizens of the West who are too lazy to engage in unpleasant manual labour, or repelled by xenophobes, depending upon the level of migration, balance of forces and ideological circumstances in particular countries.

There is little, in reality, to suggest that any of these problems represent threats to the 'sustainability' of globalisation, as implied above. International neo-liberal agents have found numerous ways to marginalise such threats, or insulate themselves. The Clinton Administration's model of malign neglect in the case of the 1994 Rwandan civil war, which was subsequently repeated with triple the number of unnecessary deaths in the Democratic Republic of the Congo during the late 1990s-present, should be ample illustration of the West's lack of compassion when it comes to African geopolitics. The rare exceptions (e.g., the success of British peacekeepers in Sierra Leone) prove the rule (e.g., the US debacle in Somalia).

50. Several contradictory processes are conflated in this pop-environmental reading of the relationship between poverty and ecological degradation. As noted above, Africa's main economic problem is not excessive pollution-intensive industrialisation, but insufficient industrialisation, which in turn leads to greater reliance for export earnings upon ecologically-destructive raw material extraction (e.g., the rain-forests and strip-mines, or the substitution of cash crops for food crops). Globalisation has exacerbated these processes, because the 'environmental degradation of our oceans, atmosphere and natural vegetation' is mainly a function of transnational and local corporate irresponsibility: e.g., overexploitative EU and East Asian fishing trawlers, pollution-intensive South African mines and metal companies which defile the air and water without paying the externality costs, and forestry companies whose alien-timber plantations destroy the integrity of African soils.

In some cases, obviously, the colonial/apartheid displacement of large populations from good farms to infertile areas led to worsening

38. The means to reverse this gloomy scenario are not yet beyond our reach. Improvements in the living standards of the marginalised offer massive potential for growth in the entire international economy, through the creation of new markets and by harnessing increased economic capacity. This will bring with it greater stability on a global scale, accompanied by a sense of economic and social well-being.[51]

39. The imperative of development, therefore, not only poses a challenge to moral conscience; it is in fact fundamental to the sustainability of the globalisation process.[52] We readily admit that globalisation is a product of scientific and technological advances, many of which have been market-driven.[53] Yet, governments – particularly those in the developed world

---

soil degradation, for which the solution is a thorough-going land reform and rural development programme - i.e., the opposite of the extremely meagre efforts the South African government is making (less than 1% arable land redistribution during the first term of ANC rule, 1994-99, and an even slower pace since). But more generally, to ascribe environmental destruction to 'growth in poverty' is, implicitly, to blame the victims: the masses whose poverty has worsened in part because of corporate-led globalisation.

51. Most African societies require upliftment from majority poverty/ starvation levels to basic-needs survival levels, so as to achieve the human right to food, clean water and sanitation, electricity and very simple household appliances, housing, simple clothing, good public health, primary and secondary education, childcare, roads and safe public transport, and other simple services, as well as gainful employment. For a rise in living standards to translate into 'massive potential for growth in the entire international economy' is highly dubious, and would entirely depend upon Africa's input-output framework for goods and services. Very few of the desperately-required basic needs listed above would logically be satisfied by imports.

52. As argued above, the case Nepad makes concerning the alleged threat to 'the sustainability of the globalisation process' - in paragraphs 28-38 - is unconvincing. The more profound threats to Western prosperity - most likely associated with international financial crisis, dire environmental damage or debilitating oil shortages - go unremarked upon in Nepad.

53. The technological explanation, as well as the word partnership, is fundamentally apolitical, and disguises the reality of dramatic changes in class relations, especially the resurgent power of US and EU capital in relation to working classes there and across the world (as reflected in pro-corporate state 'partnerships' and the decline of the social wage during the Reagan, Thatcher and Kohl administrations).

– have, in partnership with the private sector, played an important role in shaping its form, content and course.

40. The case for the role of national authorities and private institutions in guiding the globalisation agenda along a sustainable path and, therefore, one in which its benefits are more equally spread, remains strong.[54] Experience shows that, despite the unparalleled opportunities that globalisation has offered to some previously poor countries, there is nothing inherent in the process that automatically reduces poverty and inequality.[55]

41. What is needed is a commitment on the part of governments, the private sector and other institutions of civil society, to the genuine integration of all nations into the global economy and body politic.[56] This requires the recognition of global interdependence in respect of production and demand, the environmental base that sustains the planet, cross-border migration, a global financial architecture that rewards good socio-economic management, and global governance that recognises partnership among all peoples.[57] We hold that it is within the capacity of the international community to

---

54. Still, the case is a purely moral one up to this point, as other arguments do not bear scrutiny.

55. Again, due to necessary conditions associated with globalisation such as the debt burden, declining terms of trade and *compradorisation*, and all the power relations thereby entailed, it would be more accurate to assert that 'there is much inherent in the process that automatically increases poverty and inequality.'

56. The alternative case is that the responsibility of the world's citizens is to disempower the main agents of corporate-dominated globalisation (multilateral agencies, transnational corporations and imperialist states), and to allow the space for national authorities to *de*globalise, in order to better serve the interests of their citizenries.

57. Each feature in this sentence is controversial: 'global interdependence in respect of production and demand' is a social construct which can easily be changed, as happened from the 1920s-40s, depending upon circumstances. Protecting 'the environmental base that sustains the planet' is crucial - however, such protection will primarily depend upon the United States, EU and Japan reducing the emission of global warming gasses, and reducing pressure (mainly via their own transnational corporations) on trade in environmentally-fragile resources. There is little or nothing that can be done via the Kyoto Protocol or similar conventions if the balance of forces in the United States is not amenable. The same basic problem also

create fair and just conditions in which Africa can participate effectively in the global economy and body politic.[58]

---

holds true for 'cross-border migration, a global financial architecture that rewards good socio-economic management' and many other issues. The United Nations (or any other vehicle of 'global governance') may recognise 'partnerships among all peoples.' But such sentiments have so far proved useless at getting the most powerful rogue nations – especially the United States – to recognise landmine treaties, the World Court, the legacy of racism, its United Nations arrears, or any number of other human rights obligations.

It could be argued, thus, that the appropriate role for Africans is, therefore, not to engage in illusory global-governance exercises through a United Nations system that is debilitatingly compromised: geopolitically, by virtue of the Security Council power relations; and socio-economically, through its ideological proximity to the Bretton Woods system. The role for genuine African leaders, activists and humanists, is to establish much more durable and trust-building people-to-people partnerships with the aim of intensifying the lobbying capacity of progressive advocacy forces in the West and across the world.

The best example of this kind of internationalist people's partnership is the 1998-2001 alliance between the Treatment Action Campaign and the Aids Coalition to Unleash Power (ACT UP) in the United States, joined subsequently by many other organisations across the world. In spite of the extremely uncooperative Aids policies of the South African government, international people's solidarity and protest succeeded in forcing the pharmaceutical corporations and the US government to back down from blatantly imperialist positions. But to embrace this successful model of solidarity would require a commitment to the *globalisation of people* – instead of Nepad's commitment to the *globalisation of capital.*

58. The term 'international community' is just as studiously apolitical, and hence pernicious, as the rest of the analysis of globalisation offered in Nepad. While several audiences – the governments of the US, EU and Japan, the G-8 as a group, the Bretton Woods institutions' leaders, senior UN officials and the World Economic Forum – gave Nepad their endorsement during 2001, it would be naive to think that this was going to be anything more substantial than mere diplomacy. None of the substantial problems associated with trade, debt, investment or aid – all requiring far more than 'marginal concessions' (paragraph 5 above) – will be seriously addressed in the near future given prevailing power relations and material interests.

To argue otherwise is both to harbour dangerous and fundamentally disempowering illusions, and to refute evidence that mounts daily:

- the ongoing decline of aid/GDP ratios;

III. THE NEW POLITICAL WILL OF AFRICAN LEADERS

42. The *New Partnership for Africa's Development* recognises that there have been attempts in the past to set out continent-wide development programmes. For a variety of reasons, both internal and external, including questionable leadership and ownership by Africans themselves, these have been less than successful.[59]

- the IMF/World Bank refusal to engage in substantive debt cancellation, and to withdraw its neo-liberal conditionality power and proclivities;
- growing protectionist tendencies in the United States, reflected in part in the early-2002 imposition of massive tariffs on imported steel;
- the insistence of the European Union that virtually all essential services be opened up for privatisation as part of its General Agreement on Trade in Services demands of South Africa and other countries;
- the Doha WTO Summit's refusal to make substantive changes in trade rules.

Where Doha made a minor concession, on intellectual property rights associated with public health emergencies, it was merely a confirmation of Gatt-era exemptions. Overall, Doha opened up for future negotiation many objectionable new areas of transnational corporate interference in Third World economies and societies.

59. As noted earlier, the problems of 'questionable leadership and African ownership' remain very serious. The most respected South African newspaper, the *Mail & Guardian*, has repeatedly questioned Mbeki's 'fitness' to lead, for multiple reasons, chief amongst which was his refusal to provide anti-retroviral drugs to people living with HIV/Aids. Influenced by Aids-dissidents he believes that 'a virus cannot cause a syndrome,' and that the Aids pandemic is primarily a function of poverty. The cruel insanity of Pretoria's policies included refusing an inexpensive drug, Nevirapine, to tens of thousands of pregnant HIV+ women each year who, as a result, needlessly transmitted HIV to their infants. Even after a reversal on that point in April 2002, the need to roll out a treatment regime to all HIV+ South Africans in need of antiretrovirals remains far off, due largely to the president's Aids-denialism.

The governments of Nigeria and Algeria have been characterised by extreme militarism, resulting in regular massacres of innocent people and high levels of social unrest. Tens of thousands of people have been killed in Algeria because Bouteflika's predecessors refused to recognise an election won by a Muslim party, which subsequently became extremist and terrorist; Pretoria sold Algeria millions of dollars worth of arms.

Another African leader who has a high-profile role in promoting Nepad (e.g. at the World Economic Forum in 2001), Tanzania's Benjamin Mkapa, oversees a state whose most recent elections were discredited and where police killed hundreds of protesters. The Tanzanian government's obeisance to the interests of transnational corporations was emblematised in 2001 by the repression of families protesting a World Bank-backed transnational corporate mining firm, whose expansion of diggings coincided with the government's murder of dozens of small-scale miners.

On the other hand, progressive leadership by Obasanjo was demonstrated at least twice recently, when he rejected a role for the International Monetary Fund in running the Nigerian economy (which has been interpreted as his desire for fiscal laxity in the run-up to an election), and when he led a surprise revolt against Pretoria's capitulation to US-European pressure at the World Conference Against Racism. The latter issue was the demand for reparations that are due the continent as compensation for slavery and colonialism. The South African host delegation was reportedly furious at Obasanjo's outburst because it nearly scuppered a final conference resolution.

As for African 'ownership,' it bears repeating that the first systematic attempt to sell Nepad (then the *Millennial African Recovery Plan*) to Africans on the African continent was in February 2001 in Mali, at a time when the chief executive officers of the IMF and World Bank, Horst Koehler and James Wolfensohn, were also visiting. Prior presentations of the African-'owned' plan during 2000 were to Bill Clinton in May in Washington, the G-8 in Tokyo in July, the UN in New York in September, a high-profile private meeting in Pretoria with Wolfensohn in November, a European Union meeting in Portugal in December, and the World Economic Forum in January 2001.

At the latter site, the South African presidential website provides the giveaway information in Mbeki's prepared speech: 'It is significant that in a sense the first formal briefing on the progress in developing this programme is taking place at the World Economic Forum meeting. The success of its implementation would require the buy-in from members of this exciting and vibrant forum!'

Commented former ANC councillor Trevor Ngwane (*Business Day*, 5 February 2001),

> This sounds suspiciously like June 1996, when the Growth, Employment and Redistribution policy was launched prior to public debate, to parliamentary enquiry, to consultations with the people affected. And the exclusive club of Davos fatcats who use Third World leaders like Mbeki as figleafs will probably give the New Programme exactly the same support they have given Gear: currency speculation, capital flight, refusal to invest, free-trade deals filled with last-minute Northern protectionism, and pressure on our government not to provide desperately-needed cheap drugs

However, there is today a new set of circumstances, which lend themselves to integrated practical implementation.

43. The new phase of globalisation coincided with the reshaping of international relations in the aftermath of the Cold War. This is associated with the emergence of new concepts of security and self-interest, which encompass the right to development and the eradication of poverty.[60] Democracy and state legitimacy have been redefined to include accountable government, a culture of human rights and popular participation as central elements.[61]

44. Significantly, the numbers of democratically elected leaders are on the increase.[62] Through their actions, they have

---

to ward off HIV. Does Africa need a spruced-up continuation of the discredited policies of the World Bank, IMF and WTO, which have destroyed so many lives and subjugated so many states to the dictates of the multinational corporations and of imperialism?

As for 'attempts in the past to set out continent-wide development programmes,' the main 'external' forces opposing a genuine strategy for Africa – e.g., the *Lagos Plan of Action* and *African Alternative Framework to Structural Adjustment Programmes* – were the Bretton Woods institutions and the major Western governments – the same group which Nepad begs for a partnership. Other African initiatives were more progressive than Nepad, and do not deserve the latter's sneering dismissal without a robust analysis of why they were undermined.

60. While it is true that progressive initiatives are being made, e.g. through the UN Human Rights Commission, to 'encompass the right to development and the eradication of poverty,' these have not had any impact beyond rhetoric – just as the constitutional rights to water, housing, healthcare, education and dignity did not halt the deprivation of the South African masses or even the state's concerted efforts, continuing into 2002, to cut off water, sanitation and electricity to deeply impoverished residents who could not afford their bills. Rather than relying, abstractly, upon 'new concepts of security and self-interest,' the only way to make human rights a reality is to engage in grassroots struggles, which necessarily include global-local linkages against the neo-liberal dictates of the Bretton Woods institutions.

61. This is wishful thinking. Most African states are ruled by venal elites who know that their survival depends upon *denying* good governance to their citizenry.

62. The main wave of post-nationalist regimes was elected or came to power in popular uprisings between 1988 and 1995 (often in the wake of serious IMF riots). Their records in power, and subsequent democratisation processes, have been nearly universally unsatisfactory.

declared that the hopes of Africa's peoples for a better life can no longer rest on the magnanimity of others.

45. Across the continent, democracy is spreading, backed by the African Union (AU), which has shown a new resolve to deal with conflicts and censure deviation from the norm.[63] These efforts are reinforced by voices in civil society, including associations of women, youth and the independent media.[64] In addition, African governments are much more resolute about regional and continental goals of economic cooperation and integration. This serves both to consolidate the gains of the economic turnaround and to reinforce the advantages of mutual interdependence.[65]

---

63. In reality, the African Union was sponsored by the relatively wealthy Libyan dictator Moammar Qaddafy, in his eccentric quest for relevance, as the Organisation of African Unity fell apart due to member-states' arrears. The AU has done nothing to punish 'deviation from the norm' in relation to one of the most notorious contemporary slides into dictatorship, Zimbabwe's. Within six weeks of Nepad's launch, SADC foreign ministers meeting in Harare gave Mugabe a clean bill of health to continue his tyrannical oppression of rural and urban Zimbabweans, in spite of hearing evidence of more than 26,000 human rights violations in 2001 alone and seeing irrefutable signs of an unfree, unfair presidential election in 2002. In Zambia, the endorsement by African states - including the SADC observer mission, and especially Zimbabwe - of the deeply flawed, hotly-contested December 2001 election, reportedly rife with electoral irregularities, is another example of deviation from the norm, becoming the norm.

64. In many cases, these voices are the decisive pressure-points on selfish elites - as in the case of brave Zambians who demonstrated in 2001 for Frederick Chiluba to stand down after his maximum term-length has expired. Yet working-class and popular civil society voices are invariably dismissed when in their quest for democracy, they request solidarity from neighbouring African elites. Zimbabwe democracy activists learned this from Pretoria in 2001 when they demanded 'smart sanctions' against the Mugabe regime. The South African government was first and loudest to reject the request, even after it was made more explicitly in January 2002 once several Zimbabwean generals threatened a coup in the event of an opposition electoral victory.

65. This was disproved by angry regional opposition to South African domination of Southern Africa's economy, and especially by Pretoria's imposition of the SA-EU Free Trade Agreement on the region without sufficient consultation. Indeed, in recent years, Zimbabwe and Zambia both imposed new, high tariffs against South African imports, as they found their economies being deindustrialised. Regional cooperation in

46. The changed conditions in Africa have already been recognised by governments across the world.[66] The United Nations Millennium Declaration, adopted in September 2000, confirms the global community's readiness to support Africa's efforts to address the continent's underdevelopment and marginalisation. The Declaration emphasises support for the prevention of conflict and the establishment of conditions of stability and democracy on the continent, as well as for the key challenges of eradicating poverty and disease. The Declaration further points to the global community's commitment to enhance resource flows to Africa, by improving aid, trade and debt relationships between Africa and the rest of the world, and by increasing private capital flows to the continent. It is now important to translate these commitments into reality.[67]

47. The *New Partnership for Africa's Development* centres around African ownership and management. Through this programme, African leaders are setting an agenda for the renewal of the continent. The agenda is based on national and regional priorities and development plans that must be prepared through participatory processes involving the people.[68] We believe that while African leaders derive their

---

Southern Africa was also reflected in Pretoria's ongoing brutal treatment of regional immigrants (e.g., at the notorious Lindela repatriation camp). The problem appears to be worsening. In December 2001, decisions were taken by South Africa to expel 15,000 undocumented guest Zimbabwean farmworkers, and by Mozambique to arrest and in many cases expel hundreds of Zimbabweans and even South Africans for alleged (but mainly imagined) immigration violations.

66. All indications are that, measured by donor aid ratios, and Western respect for African governments' economic requests (e.g. at Doha in November 2001, or repeatedly in debt renegotiations), the opposite is more factual. Disregard for Africa's plight was confirmed in two panicky analyses by four top World Bank officials published in the *Financial Times* in October 2001. In the wake of the September 11 terrorist attacks, they begged their readers to not ignore Africa, and pledged support for Nepad. There is a real danger that aside from posturing about Zimbabwe sanctions and democracy, the Bush Administration will allow Africa to fall entirely off its radar screen.

67. Perhaps the realisation in this sentence, even though left undeveloped, suggests the true significance of the UN Millennium Declaration.

68. In reality, there is probably no African ruling elite which has such a commitment.

mandates from their people, it is their role to articulate these plans as well as lead the processes of implementation on behalf of their people.[69]

48. The programme is a new framework of interaction with the rest of the world, including the industrialised countries and multilateral organisations. It is based on the agenda set by African peoples through their own initiatives and of their own volition, to shape their own destiny.[70]

49. To achieve these objectives, African leaders will take joint responsibility for the following:

- Strengthening mechanisms for conflict prevention, management and resolution at the regional and continental levels, and to ensure that these mechanisms are used to restore and maintain peace;[71]

Pretoria offers the prime example. In June 1996, Mbeki held a press conference to promote his homegrown structural adjustment programme (*Gear*) and confirmed the veracity of finance minister Manuel's boast to the press: 'the programme is non-negotiable.' Added Mbeki, 'Just call me a Thatcherite.' Regular mass protests against *Gear* have not persuaded Pretoria to reopen the neo-liberal policy to negotiation.

69. This is logical in theory, under conditions of thoroughgoing democracy. But because Nepad is essentially uncritical of Africa's contemporary ruling elites, with no analysis about how they came to power and what tricks are used to remain in power, in practice the assumption of mandated leadership is both incorrect and profoundly delusionary.

70. Everything in this paragraph is untrue. Nepad offers nothing new, and the document represents the work not of African peoples but of a handful of elite technicians from South Africa (including an author of *Gear*), Nigeria, Algeria, Senegal and Egypt. Objectively, its core presumptions, proposals and processes contradict the interests of most African peoples.

71. These are ambitious and potentially progressive commitments. However, the generally dismal record in this area leads to the questions: are the existing mechanisms worth 'strengthening'; or are the continent's ruling classes so profoundly undemocratic and prone to internecine warfare that their own elite-dominated institutions offer little or no hope?

There is a profound questionmark over the AU, given not only its origins with Qaddafy, but the financial unsustainability and uselessness of its predecessor - with the possible exception of the December 1999 Seattle WTO summit, where objections by the OAU Caucus to the process and anticipated outcomes managed to sabotage the meeting.

Emblematic of problematic regional peacekeeping is the Southern African Development Community's uneven initiatives since 1998.

Extraordinary inconsistencies arose during interventions in the Democratic Republic of the Congo (DRC) and Lesotho, in part because of Pretoria's own mixed signals.

In the first case, the former Zaire had been liberated from rule by the dictator Mobutu Sese Seko in 1996 by a guerrilla force led by Laurent Kabila. A crucial component was regional geopolitics, through which Kabila received logistical and military support from the governments of Rwanda, Uganda and Zimbabwe, as well as from at least one North American mining firm anxious to exploit the country's great mineral wealth. At the instigation of Robert Mugabe, Kabila's application for DRC membership in SADC was successful. But when in 1998, Rwanda and Uganda withdrew their support from the DRC government and instead transferred troops to promote pro-Tutsi rebel factions, Kabila called for SADC's help. In July, South African defense minister Joe Modise initially agreed to a formal SADC military intervention, but then switched positions and, on principle, refused to participate in a SADC military alliance - consisting of Zimbabwe, Namibia and Angola - to prop up the controversial government.

(The rationale for the support that Zimbabwe, Angola and Namibia have given the unelected DRC governments of Kabila and Kabila Jr. was analysed by a United Nations agency in November 2001, and was found to be based on mercenary-type looting of minerals. Similar allegations arose about the occupation of the DRC's eastern provinces by troops from Rwanda, Burundi and Uganda. Meanwhile, an estimated three million civilian lives were lost.)

However, reversing its principles in September 1998, Pretoria decided to intervene in Lesotho to unilaterally prop up the controversial government. (Botswana was later drawn in to make it appear based on a SADC mandate.) The Maseru government had, effectively, been overthrown in a coup following a controversial parliamentary election. That election gave the main opposition party just one out of 80 seats in a first-past-the-post system, notwithstanding the opposition's winning more than a third of the vote, leading to riots in Maseru and a loss of loyalty by the armed forces. The military mission was itself botched. Maseru was razed by anti-government protesters, who then turned to explicitly anti-South African rioting. Meanwhile, the SA National Defense Force murdered dozens of Basotho soldiers - some sleeping - at the Katse Dam because of an alleged (highly implausible) threat that it would be blown up by army rebels. (Subsequently, the anomalous British-style parliamentary system has been reformed, but ongoing personality conflicts and sharp feuding within the major parties promise further political crises, including the 2002 election.)

In sum, SADC's peacekeeping function has been the source of great disappointment. The organisation's entire senior secretariat was fired during the late 1990s as a result of a corruption scandal. In theory, it is possible to strengthen SADC peacekeeping capacity through an infusion

- Promoting and protecting democracy and human rights in their respective countries and regions, by developing clear standards of accountability, transparency and participatory governance at the national and sub-national levels;[72]

- Restoring and maintaining macroeconomic stability, especially by developing appropriate standards and targets for fiscal and monetary policies, and introducing appropriate institutional frameworks to achieve these standards;[73]

- Instituting transparent legal and regulatory frameworks for financial markets and auditing of private companies and the public sector;[74]

---

of donor funds and clarity on rules of engagement, but this has not worked in the past, in part because there is little genuine will by regional leaders to work together when their geopolitical interests so obviously diverge. And it is the regional aspirant-hegemonic role of South Africa, ranging from military to economic to political terrains, that provides such strong grounds to doubt SADC's potential.

72. These are noble aims, and correlate to demands from progressive civil society throughout Africa.

73. This phraseology - especially the words 'macroeconomic stability' - is invidious. Virtually all structural adjustment programmes in Africa generated instability (Zimbabwe is one of the most tragic examples). Is Pretoria able to make a convincing case based on its own experience? The South African government's determined, neo-liberal fiscal and monetary strategies - maintaining the budget-deficit/GDP radio at a target of less than 3% and imposing high real interest rates to reduce inflation to below 6% - were, along with trade liberalisation, contributing factors to the loss of more than 10% of formal sector jobs during the first seven years of ANC rule (the worst ever recorded in an industrialised country outside war and the Great Depression). Financial liberalisation was responsible for two crashes of the currency of 30% over several weeks (early 1996 and mid-1998) and the 60% crash that occurred during the 2000-01 period when Nepad was being prepared. The use of weasel-words like 'macroeconomic stability' disguises the actual process, which is imposition of Washington's agenda, typically leading to macroeconomic instability and sustained misery.

74. These provisions sound innocuous, and should be incorporated into standard capitalist operating routines. However, it should be borne in mind that the most forceful demands for financial 'transparency' were made by Washington during the 1997-99 emerging markets crisis because New York, London and Frankfurt banks complained vociferously about being caught with loans to South Korean, Thai and Indonesian firms whose books did not properly reflect their full indebtedness. In that respect,

> - Revitalising and extend the provision of education, technical training and health services, with high priority given to tackling HIV/Aids, malaria and other communicable diseases;[75]

---

the transparency demand from Washington was a form of 'blaming the victim,' because the Western banks were generally allowed to both claim a degree of innocence, and also then utilise the muscle of the Bretton Woods institutions to more forcefully close down firms and banks across East Asia on grounds of transparency. The core complaint from progressive experts in these countries is that the premature bankruptcies and the sale of assets - often to transnational corporations - at huge discounts together meant that gains made over previous decades in establishing a productive national base were unnecessarily reversed. Additionally, with increased transparency in public accounts (e.g. rapid reporting of foreign exchange reserves), international financial speculators have a great deal more information and hence leverage with which to roil currency markets.

To illustrate the complexity, the South African Reserve Bank recently backtracked from transparency in releasing financial information. Its failure to install an appropriate financial regulatory framework is a national scandal, both because of the crash of several badly-run small banks, and because the larger financial institutions systematically 'redline' (discriminate against) desegregating and black areas. A law was finally proposed to force disclosure of such practices, but was not forcefully implemented by either the Housing and Finance Ministries or the Reserve Bank.

Moreover, in relation to private-sector auditing, although some improvements were made during the post-apartheid era, South Africa is no model for the rest of the continent. Its firms are notorious for transfer-pricing - i.e., changing invoices to make it appear that imported inputs are more expensive - to overseas allies, which is of particular concern given the penetration of South African companies throughout Africa since the early 1990s. In the mining sector, Swiss intermediaries helped profits to be channeled externally as a result, and firms like Anglo American Corporation shifted funds into foreign accounts on spurious grounds. Such scandals were never addressed by the ANC government. The outflow of capital was identified in the South African business media during the course of the rand's crash in late 2001, but was never explicitly tackled by the neo-liberal Reserve Bank and Finance Ministry.

75. For most countries, whose real per capita spending on education and health has fallen - sometimes precipitously - over the past two decades, this would be welcome. Too often, the goals of alleged 'macroeconomic stability' and tightened budget-deficit targets outweighed education and health spending for large segments of the population who, for all effective purposes, were redundant to the employment needs of Africa's shrinking capitalist sector.

As a result, South Africa led the way in recent years in denying education and healthcare to its rural masses. Although some minor improvements in

- Promoting the role of women in social and economic development by reinforcing their capacity in the domains of education and training; by the development of revenue-generating activities through facilitating access to credit; and by assuring their participation in the political and economic life of African countries;[76]

---

school facilities were made and a few clinics were built in peripheral areas, the overall policy was to retain the main apartheid-era inequalities, and amplify these by permitting schools in wealthy, urban areas to augment ongoing grants with their own student fees (hence making it difficult for low-income families to enroll their children). In the field of healthcare, the shift to private-sector provision grew dramatically during the late 1990s, under the rubric of 'managed care' which, again, had the effect of denying access to lower-income sections of the society.

Most notoriously, until April 2002, the South African government repeatedly refused to save the lives of tens of thousands of babies and rape survivors by providing anti-retroviral drugs. Refusal of comprehensive treatment so as to prolong the lives of millions of HIV+ citizens continues. The most common official explanation was 'unaffordability,' notwithstanding the capacity that the state had to either manufacture generic versions of these drugs or import the generic drugs from countries like Brazil, India or Thailand that had more effective health programmes and pharmaceutical manufacturers. (To do so would have offended the transnational corporations, which showed their displeasure with the mere option of parallel imports and compulsory licensing by suing the South African government from 1998-2001, until massive South African and international popular pressure forced the corporations to withdraw.)

'Tackling HIV/Aids' was not merely a low priority in government, due to the lack of financial return on prolonging people's lives. It correlated to the Anglo American Corporation's mid-2001 decision to make available anti-retroviral drugs to their senior managers but not to ordinary workers (all workers had been promised the drugs in April 2001). Tragically, such public-private cost-benefit analyses of South African workers' lives were ultimately determinant in the fight against Aids. (In the United States and other northern countries, where the cost-benefit analysis was different, HIV+ status became merely a chronic illness, rather than a certain fatality, thanks to anti-retroviral drugs.) Even more tragically, since South Africa's mass workforce is amongst the continent's highest-paid, it is logical to expect that South African-type cost-benefit analyses applied elsewhere in Africa would be even less forgiving.

76. Rhetoric of this sort, while pleasing, has been uttered sufficiently – with no results – that cynicism has set in amongst women's groups. For example, from 'Women-in-Development' to 'Gender-and-Development' at the World Bank during the 1980s, a conceptual shift from mainstreaming women into existing capitalist structures evolved into a more nuanced

- Building the capacity of the states in Africa to set and enforce the legal framework, as well as maintaining law and order;[77]

---

concern with gender relations and women's empowerment. But little good that did most African women, who suffered ever more extreme oppression because of the Bank's promotion of neo-liberal economic policies - the same policies Nepad promotes. The problem was not merely the lack of an effective social safety net, even in countries like Ghana that were pilot projects for Bank programmes to mitigate the effects of adjustment, which were in reality ineffectual whitewash exercises. The problems of African women's oppression also stem from the way in which existing patriarchal relations - from traditional, colonial-era and migrancy-related oppressions - were amplified by increasing stress on the economy generated by neo-liberalism. The stress took the form of the shutting down of industries that had supplied both men and women with at least some reliable formal income; budget cuts (and the introduction of cost-recovery utilisation fees) for basic state services; and the shift of as much productive land as possible away from food destined for the local consumption market, towards cash crops for export or game farms for wealthy tourists.

The World Bank's 1995 global strategy to recognise and address these problems through an expansion of microlending to women, as parroted by Nepad, was a *chimera*. Even the world's model microcredit scheme for women, the Grameen Bank in Bangladesh, began suffering crippling default rates due in part to excessively high interest rates and brutal debt collection methods, leaving the entire world's microcredit industry - 7,000 organisations serving 25 million clients - 'alarmed,' according to a November 2001 *Wall Street Journal* report. Similarly in South Africa, there was enormous hype over women's microcredit during the 1990s, but the industry collapsed in 1998-99 when interest rates soared due to the financial crisis caused, in turn, by financial liberalisation and currency speculation. Pretoria neo-liberals hence no longer speak with such great enthusiasm about microcredit in South Africa, and indeed recently the government even threatened to refuse the microcredit industry the most important mainstay of their business: a stop-order system to assure repayment from civil servant salaries prior to the salaries being paid. In hundreds of thousands of cases, civil servants were left with such tiny paychecks that they were unable to feed and house themselves.

77. Regrettably, the capacities of states to enforce legal contracts (especially where transnational corporations were concerned) and to police the population were amongst the very few areas where increased resources were made available during the structural adjustment era. Complex investment-insurance schemes proliferated, not only from Washington but also within Africa. But without internally-generated economic dynamism, however, these improvements in the enforcement of capitalist property relations did not realise their anticipated investment benefits. It would be naive and misleading for Nepad to oversell this strategy.

- Promoting the development of infrastructure, agriculture and its diversification into agro-industries and manufacturing to serve both domestic and export markets.[78]

IV. APPEAL TO THE PEOPLES OF AFRICA

50. The African Renaissance project, which should allow our continent, plundered for centuries to take its rightful place in the world, depends on the building of a strong and competitive economy as the world moves towards greater liberalisation and competition.[79]

51. The *New Partnership for Africa's Development* will be successful only if it is owned by the African peoples united in their diversity.[80]

---

78. The objective of 'diversification into agro-industries and manufacturing' is essential. The tradition of neo-liberalism has been to downplay the development of internal markets in favour of mythical export-led growth. The mandate that more economic balance should be sought 'to serve both domestic and export markets' is potentially misleading given Nepad's overall orientation to, e.g., 'the genuine integration of all nations into the global economy' (paragraph 41). Nepad doesn't provide any evidence that *domestic* agriculture is taken seriously, and there is no proof that the export of food can eradicate poverty.

In South Africa's own case, the only successful manufacturing diversification occurred in highly vulnerable niche markets such as auto components and upmarket garments. Other heavy-industrial manufacturing outputs, including base metals and a few auto models, also rose in importance, but these successes had their own disadvantages, such as ongoing dependence on various state subsidies, lack of backward-forward linkage and environmental externalities which were not accounted for.

79. The *non sequitur* in this sentence is potentially debilitating. If Africa was plundered (generally by force) for centuries, thereby starting the 21st century from a position of artificial weakness, how can the 'African Renaissance project' realistically build 'a strong and competitive economy as the world moves towards greater liberalisation and competition' without compensation (e.g. massive reparations), and without significantly lower pressure to liberalise and to contribute to excessive international economic competition? Nepad innocently, continuously posits that Africa's increased participation in the world economy will be its saviour, yet provides no marketing data, realistic economic analysis or any other rationale aside from its authors' surrender to the inevitability of globalisation.

80. This is probably true; as is the converse. Since Nepad was formulated in Pretoria, with reference initially to Washington, Davos, and the G-7 instead of to Africa, it can never be 'owned' by the African peoples, and

52. Africa, impoverished by slavery, corruption and economic mismanagement is taking off in a difficult situation. However, if her enormous natural and human resources are properly harnessed and utilised, it could lead to equitable and sustainable growth of the continent as well as enhance its rapid integration into the world economy.[81]

53. This is why our peoples, in spite of the present difficulties must regain confidence in their genius and their capacity to face obstacles and be involved in the building of the new Africa. The present initiative is an expression of the commitment of Africa's leaders to translate the deep popular will into action.[82]

54. But the struggle they would be waging will be successful only if our peoples are the masters of their own destiny.[83]

---

it will not be successful. Likewise, the phraseology 'united in diversity' evaporates the struggles against local inequality and oppression.

81. All evidence thus far is that 'equitable and sustainable growth of the continent' and 'rapid integration into the world economy' are mutually exclusive. Although Africa's *share* of world trade has declined during the 1980s-90s, the *volume* of exports increased. So 'marginalisation' has occurred not because of *lack* of integration, but because other areas of the world - especially East Asia - moved to the export of manufactured goods while Africa's industrial potential declined, thanks to excessive deregulation associated with structural adjustment. Likewise, while integrating more rapidly into the world economy through the 1980s-90s' orientation toward 'export-led growth,' as demanded by Washington, Africa's ability to grow - either equitably and sustainably, or even inequitably - actually declined, in comparison to the period prior to structural adjustment.

82. Nepad could - but doesn't - document 'the deep popular will' to build a new Africa. That will certainly does exist in various civil society initiatives, most of which stand in explicit opposition to Nepad. Across the continent, varied grassroots organisations - community-based groups, HIV/Aids support organisations, traditional and ethnic-based movements, progressive churches, women's and youth clubs, environmental groups and many others - have joined trade unionists and radical intellectuals in diverse struggles against neo-liberalism and for democracy. Many of the strongest expressions of popular will exist in South Africa, for even the ANC's Alliance partners reject the same policies of alleged 'macroeconomic stability' (fiscal and monetary austerity) and privatisation which Nepad promotes.

83. The struggles that Africans *are* already waging *do* have the objective of controlling their own destiny, which requires a genuine break with - not accommodation to - the *compradorism* and imperialism (a.k.a. 'partnership' and 'globalisation') advocated in Nepad.

55. This is why the political leaders of the continent appeal to all the peoples of Africa, in all their diversity, to become aware of the seriousness of the situation and the need to mobilise themselves in order to put an end to further marginalisation of the continent and ensure its development by bridging the gap with the developed countries.[84]

56. We are, therefore, asking the African peoples to take up the challenge of mobilising in support of the implementation of this initiative by setting up, at all levels, structures for organisation, mobilisation and action.[85]

57. The leaders of the continent are aware of the fact that the true genius of a people is measured by its capacity for bold and imaginative thinking, and determination in support of their development.[86]

---

84. The hypocrisy in this passage is breathtaking. Africans falling further into poverty as a result of leadership *compradorism* and globalisation do not need to 'become aware of the seriousness of the situation,' as much as do the elite rulers who generally live in luxury, at great distance from the masses. And when Africans in progressive civil society organisations express 'the need to mobilise themselves,' they are nearly invariably met with repression from the ruling elites.

85. This is empty rhetoric: Nepad contains no suggested actions to be taken by the African peoples, no organisational resources, and no civil-society implementation plan. The document itself was available only through obscure internet websites and until April 2002 there were no leadership-catalysed discussions of Nepad within civil-society organisations in South Africa itself – which is perhaps partly explained by the fact that the ANC's Alliance partners were firmly opposing central neo-liberal Nepad economic and infrastructure provisions in mass protests simultaneous to Pretoria's attempt to sell these in international and a few continental venues.

86. In reality, Nepad cannot, by any stretch, be termed 'bold' or 'imaginative.' The document's central characteristics are the rehash of mild-mannered pro-globalisation rhetoric and the promotion of tired, unsuccessful economic conditions – especially alleged 'macroeconomic stability' targets for fiscal and monetary austerity, and privatisation of infrastructure – that have been imposed by Washington on Africa for at least two decades. Even the strong pro-democracy, good-governance rhetoric has become badly worn, as Washington and donor governments repeatedly reward authoritarian regimes with aid – most of which is spent in home countries or on outrageous expatriate salaries – that should instead be going directly to the masses through progressive civil society organisations. The alleged African leadership commitment to good

58. We must not relent in implementing this ambitious programme of building sound and resilient economies, and democratic societies. In this respect, the African leaders are convinced that Africa, a continent whose development process has been marked by false starts and failures will succeed with this initiative.[87]

V. PROGRAMME OF ACTION: THE STRATEGY FOR ACHIEVING SUSTAINABLE DEVELOPMENT IN THE 21ST CENTURY

59. The *New Partnership for Africa's Development* differs in its approach and strategy from all previous plans and initiatives in support of Africa's development, although the problems to be addressed remain largely the same.[88]

60. The *New Partnership for Africa's Development* is envisaged as a long-term vision of an African-owned and African-led development programme.[89]

61. The Action Programme includes the top priorities structured in the same way as the strategy outlined and these priorities

---

government has been exposed through repeated, ongoing 'Old Boys Club' missions - such as those by SADC to Zimbabwe in late 2001 - that turn a blind eye to blatant repression.

87. There is a dangerous degree of false *bravado* in Nepad, for if leaders are 'convinced' that the initiative will succeed, and if it is instead yet another 'false start and failure,' where will that leave self-confidence? Even if Nepad was not an objectionable rehashing of prior false starts and failures imposed on Africa by Washington, it would still warrant a greater degree of humility.

88. It is true that Nepad differs dramatically in approach and strategy from previous organic, progressive, African plans and initiatives, such as the Lagos Plan of Action, as noted above. But it is not discernibly different from existing Washington-imposed policies which have nearly universally failed. For that reason, as two leading Africa managers at the Bretton Woods institutions wrote in the *Financial Times* (7 October 2001), 'The IMF and the World Bank are doing everything possible to play a part' in Nepad.

89. It is true that 'an African-owned and African-led development programme' is required. But Nepad does not qualify, given the lack of real ownership from the document's outset, the dubious leadership offered by the continent's current ruling elites, and Nepad's recipe for ongoing *under*development along familiar lines.

may be revised from time to time by the Heads of State Implementation Committee. The Programme covers what needs to be done in the short term, despite the wide scope of the actions to be taken.

62. Although long-term funding, is envisaged under the initiative, the projects can, however, be expedited to help eradicate poverty in Africa and place African countries, both individually and collectively, on a path of sustainable growth and development and thus halt the marginalisation of Africa in the globalisation process.[90]

63. Although there are other urgent priorities, those selected here would have a catalytic effect for intervention in other priority areas in the future.[91]

64. While growth rates are important, they are not by themselves sufficient to enable African countries achieve the goal of poverty reduction. The challenge for Africa, therefore, is to develop the capacity to sustain growth at levels required to achieve poverty reduction and sustainable development. This, in turn depends on other factors such as infrastructure, capital accumulation, human capital, institutions, structural diversification, competitiveness, health and good stewardship of the environment.[92]

---

90. This is a terribly confusing and contradictory formulation, which begs for 'long-term funding' but claims simultaneously to be 'sustainable.' Moreover, the focus on *projects* is antithetical to the development of a genuine, well-constructed *programme* – based upon coherent, interlinked *policies* that in turn follow from a genuinely African development *philosophy* – for sustainable growth and development. In sum, the order of construction is backward.

91. This claim cannot be believed without coherence and interrelationships spelled out in a programmatic manner, something Nepad does not (at this stage) attempt.

92. There is, here, an annoying combination of progressive and neo-liberal objectives: infrastructure, human capital, institutions, structural diversification, health and good stewardship of the environment in the first category, and capital accumulation and competitiveness in the second. Objectively, neo-liberal policies have, during the past two decades, destroyed Africa's infrastructure, human capital, institutions, structural diversification, health and stewardship of the environment. The failure to come to grips with this contradiction is emblematic of Nepad's double-talk. And Nepad continually falls back upon discourses of commodification – e.g., 'human capital' – instead of human rights concepts.

65. The objective of the *New Partnership for Africa's Development* is, to provide an impetus to Africa's development by bridging existing gaps in priority sectors to enable the continent catch up with developed parts of the world.[93]

66. The new long-term vision will require massive and heavy investment to bridge existing gaps. The challenge ahead for Africa is to be able to raise the required funding under the best conditions possible. We therefore call on our development partners to assist in this endeavour.[94]

67. Long-Term Objective

- To eradicate poverty in Africa and to place African countries, both individually and collectively, on a path of sustainable growth and development and thus halt the marginalisation of Africa in the globalisation process;[95]
- To promote the role of women in all activities.[96]

---

93. The objective is worthwhile. The main economic features of Nepad - entailing more open trade and investment relations - will, however, probably exacerbate the continent's deterioration in relation to developed parts of the world.

94. The bottom-line aim of Nepad is finally apparent, in begging for the required funding under the best conditions possible. If this is 'the challenge ahead for Africa,' compared to the popular removal of undemocratic regimes and establishment of well-balanced, self-reliant economies that meet everyone's basic needs, end gender inequity and restore the environment, then Nepad is little more than an appeal to the West for a last chance to undergird the *status quo* - and consequently should be rejected by people of conscience in the West.

95. As noted earlier, poverty and 'marginalisation' arise not from African countries' failure to take advantage of 'the globalisation process,' but on the contrary *because* features of international economic integration - especially declining terms of trade, the debt trap, multinational corporate looting through transfer-pricing, and the role of *compradors* - systematically impoverish Africa and make sustainable growth and development impossible.

96. The pro-women add-on, as the second long-term objective, is not matched by any concrete commitments to gender equality in Nepad, suggesting that it is a contentless, politically-correct gesture of window-dressing, probably required by donor 'partners.' The natural gender concerns of Africa's patriarchal leaders are reflected in the fact that virtually none have lifted a finger to improve women's conditions in substantive ways during the era of structural adjustment. For example, only South Africa offers reproductive rights to women, yet even there, the

68. Goals

- To achieve and sustain an average gross domestic product (GDP) growth rate of above 7 per cent per annum for the next 15 years;[97]
- To ensure that the continent achieves the agreed International Development Goals (IDGs), which are:[98]

  - To reduce the proportion of people living in extreme poverty by half between 1990 and 2015;

  - To enrol all children of school age in primary schools by 2015;[99]

  - To make progress towards gender equality and empowering women by eliminating gender disparities in the enrolment in primary and secondary education by 2005;[100]

---

lack of public health facilities in low-income rural areas means that only a few tens of thousands of unwanted pregnancies are terminated each year. To make matters far worse, Pretoria's stark refusal to provide generalised access to anti-retroviral drugs to rape survivors and HIV+ pregnant women, was one of the most indefensible acts of aggression against women in Africa.. To add insult to injury, less than two months after the launch of Nepad, the government appealed a lower court judgment (requiring the Dept of Health reverse this specific onslaught on women and infants) at the Constitutional Court. Even after changing policy direction in April 2002, the government continued attempting to bat down the Constitutional Court decision.

97. By way of comparison, the *Growth, Employment and Redistribution* policy was launched in South Africa in June 1996, with the annual GDP growth prediction of 6%, to be sustainable by 2000. In reality, GDP grew by far less than *Gear* projected, and dipped below 2% at the outset of the 21st century.

98. All the following goals are admirable, no doubt, but they are not likely to be achieved if *status quo* strategies and power relations are simply accepted and codified as 'homegrown' African, as Nepad does.

99. As noted below, the double disincentives for primary school enrolment, namely cost-recovery provisions and exceedingly low state education budgets, are not explicitly addressed by Nepad, aside from an endorsement of community cost-sharing (which will probably exacerbate the situation) and a vague promise to 'Review levels of expenditure on education by African countries.'

100. One of the most important barriers to ending gender disparity in education has been the imposition of cost-recovery ('user-fee') provisions in most African primary and secondary school systems, usually by World

- To reduce infant and child mortality ratios by two-thirds between 1990 and 2015;[101]

- To reduce maternal mortality ratios by three-quarters between 1990 and 2015;

- To provide access for all who need reproductive health services by 2015;[102]

- To implement national strategies for sustainable development by 2005, so as to reverse the loss of environmental resources by 2015.[103]

Bank and IMF dictate. Nepad is silent on this extreme disincentive to female education.

101. The most crucial interventions towards this objective include the provision of free lifeline water/sanitation and electricity supplies, expansion of well-remunerated formal-sector employment, a stronger social security system (including a higher child support payment and a Basic Income Grant), and availability of free primary health care services such as free anti-retroviral drugs and related treatment for HIV+ pregnant women. Nepad is silent on all these, notwithstanding that they are all on the progressive political agenda in South Africa, perhaps in part because they have come to represent Pretoria's greatest potentials, and simultaneously its greatest failures.

102. This would be remarkable, but depending upon how 'reproductive health services' are defined (no doubt not to include reproductive rights such as safe access to abortion), will simply not happen in view of resistance by Catholic- or Muslim-dominated leaderships in many parts of Africa, and patriarchal control functions virtually everywhere else. However, it is certainly a laudable goal to articulate.

103. Notwithstanding South Africa's hosting role for the World Summit on Sustainable Development in August 2002, Pretoria overrode civil society objections in late 2001 by publicly conceding that its own sustainable development strategy would not be in place by the time of the Summit.

104. The following outcomes are all highly desirable, of course (although the export-led, competitiveness-oriented growth model is being universally questioned). What is important as a warning, however, is that the similar 1996 project for South Africa, *Gear*, also promised higher 'economic growth... increased employment [and a] reduction in poverty and inequality.' In reality, the homegrown policy delivered economic decline, increased unemployment and an increase in socio-economic polarisation - the opposite of growth, employment and redistribution. As for the promised 'diversification of productive activities' and 'increased African integration,' a warning is also due that *Gear*, augmented by free-trade deals with Europe and

69. The strategy has the following expected outcomes:[104]

- Economic growth and development and increased employment;
- Reduction in poverty and inequality;
- Diversification of productive activities, enhanced international competitiveness and increased exports;
- Increased African integration.

70. Realising that unless something new and radical is done, Africa will not achieve the IDGs and the 7 per cent annual GDP growth rate, the African Heads of State propose the programme described below.[105] The programme is anchored on key themes and is supported by detailed programmes of action.

A. CONDITIONS FOR SUSTAINABLE DEVELOPMENT[106]

• The Peace, Security, Democracy, and Political Governance Initiative

71. African leaders have learnt from their own experiences that peace, security, democracy, good governance, human

---

the US, generated *less* diversification, and increased regional *dis*integration. Southern Africa after a generation of neo-liberalism is more dependent upon raw materials and is much less industrialised and economically integrated than before. The main integration that has occurred is the domineering role of Johannesburg capital in Southern Africa, as South Africa's regional trade surplus soared since 1994, leading to plant closure and mass unemployment in the manufacturing sectors of neighbours such as Zimbabwe and Zambia.

105. There is nothing in Nepad that can be described as new, much less 'radical.' The latter term derives from the Latin, 'root,' which would require much more profound commitment to challenging global, regional, national, local and household inequalities than Africa's elite leaders – and their supporters in the Bretton Woods institutions, G-7 and UN – will ever contemplate.

106. The section contains three subthemes into which sustainable development 'conditions' are summarised: The Peace, Security, Democracy, and Political Governance Initiative; The Economic and Corporate Governance Initiative; and Sub-Regional and Regional Approaches to Development. As argued below, the breadth (and lack of depth) of the first, the narrowness of the second and the lack of convincing information in the third together suggest that the Nepad authors are not yet serious about confronting the many political-economic biases in Africa that will prevent sustainable development.

rights and sound economic management are conditions for sustainable development.[107] They are making a pledge to work, both individually and collectively, to promote these principles in their countries, sub-regions and the continent.[108]

(i) Peace and Security Initiative

72. The Peace and Security Initiative consists of three elements as follows:

- Promoting long-term conditions for development and security;[109]

- Building the capacity of African institutions for early warning, as well as enhancing African institutions' capacity to prevent, manage and resolve conflicts;[110]

- Institutionalising commitment to the core values of the *New Partnership for Africa's Development* through the leadership.[111]

---

107. Aside from Nepad failing to show evidence that African leaders have learned that peace, security, democracy, good governance, and human rights promote sustainability - because more counterevidence than evidence exists - the adjective 'sound' raises the same problems associated with 'macroeconomic stability,' as noted above. It is hard to show that there has been any economic payoff to the vast majority of South African people from the imposition of allegedly sound policies.

108. Crucially, Nepad offers no guarantee, beyond a non-binding 'pledge,' that African signatories will actually abide by the document's provisions.

109. The only way to establish long-term conditions for development and security is to go to the foundations of Africa's economic problems. Through sophistry and word play, which are apparently required to both appease the major international institutions and donors on the one hand and unscrupulous African leaders on the other, Nepad systematically avoids grappling with the roots of Africa's problems. Those roots are today most powerfully intertwined as *compradorism* and imperialism (i.e., 'partnership' and 'globalisation').

110. The 'early warning' systems of economic breakdown, human misery and ecological destruction, exist all over Africa already, in the experiences of ordinary people. Were Nepad serious about institution-building to these ends, it would address the question of how to better reflect their reality through democratised media, improved lateral communications and promotion of democratic mass organisations, all of which African leaders have shown they are wont to repress.

111. The *top-down* process of establishing peace, security, democracy, good governance, human rights and sound economic management has most

73. Long-term conditions for ensuring peace and security in Africa require policy measures to address the political and social vulnerabilities on which conflict is premised.[112] These are dealt with by the Political and Economic Governance Initiatives, the Capital Flows and Market Access Initiatives and the Human Development Initiative.

74. Efforts to build Africa's capacity to manage all aspects of conflict must focus on the means necessary to strengthen existing regional and sub-regional institutions,[113] especially in four key areas:

- Prevention, management and resolution of conflict;[114]

---

often failed in Africa, via previous experiences of donor conditionality. A much more thorough-going, genuinely radical restructuring of society and economy is required, that nurtures the creativity of the mass of African producers, the grassroots leadership and mutual-support systems of women, the intrinsic democratic norms of progressive civil society organisations, and the enthusiasm of the youth. Were Nepad serious about its core values, the focus would be on unleashing the power of the people, through removing the barriers to genuine people-centred development, which are too often found in the ways that African leaders reproduce their systems of rule, as part of the reproduction of Africa's disempowered role in the international division of labour.

112. This is absolutely true; yet Nepad offers policies that lead to the *opposite* results as are allegedly desired.

113. The regional institutions have generally proven themselves incapable of these tasks. The fundamental change required would entail scrapping most existing institutions - which are in many cases incurably corrupt and inefficient - and building ones that are in the image of the African people, not pale reflections of Western colonial- and neo-liberal-era models.

114. The most important issues in conflict prevention are all off the Nepad agenda:

a) reconfiguring state boundaries in a manner that is not reliant upon the 1885 Berlin conference between the imperial powers, but that instead reflects functional, geographically-coherent and potentially ethnically-sensitive boundaries;

b) rejigging economic policies so that they achieve growth, sustainable inward industrialisation, and environmentally responsible production and distribution systems, instead of the debt-driven, conflict-generating over-exporting of raw materials that require territorial domination and environmental destruction; and

- Peacemaking, peacekeeping and peace enforcement;

- Post-conflict reconciliation, rehabilitation and reconstruction;

- Combating the illicit proliferation of small arms, light weapons and landmines.[115]

75. The leadership of the *New Partnership for Africa's Development* will consider, within six months of its establishment, setting out detailed and costed measures required in each of the four areas above. The exercise will also include actions required of partners, and the nature and sources of financing such activities.[116]

76. The envisaged Heads of State Forum will serve as a platform for the *New Partnership for Africa's Development* leadership to seek to enhance the capacity of African institutions to promote peace and security on the continent, to share experience and to mobilise collective action. The Forum will ensure that the principles and commitments implicit in the initiative are fulfilled.[117]

---

c) reducing the scope for monopolistic control of the state by ruling parties without reference to opposition parties, freedom of expression and of the press, minority groups, and mass-popular interests.

115. With the exception of landmines, which South Africa once made and laid prolifically, Pretoria still takes great pride in arms exports. While small arms are a major problem, so too are large-scale weapons, such as the R66 billion in inappropriate offensive weapons that Pretoria contracted to purchase on the basis of specious, wildly inaccurate projections of job-creating 'offsets' in South Africa that cannot materialise. Were Nepad's authors serious about weapons proliferation, cancellation of Africa's single-largest arms deal would be the logical place to start.

116. The six-month deadline passed on 23 March 2002 without such documentation emerging. The discussion in Nigeria in March 2002 included more vague commitments to peace and security, unburdened by details or by anything resembling a genuine system of accountability.

117. The main institutional problem here is that the states most requiring intervention - those with collapsed or 'failed' governments (e.g., in West Africa or the Horn of Africa) - are not part of the Forum. Aside from a few examples in which regional peacekeeping was attempted, generally unsuccessfully (e.g. through the West African Ecomog), African heads of states have been notoriously unwilling to make consistent *collective* interventions on behalf of political stability. To illustrate, when, in mid-1998, the Southern African Development Community was split by debates over the merits of interventions in the Democratic Republic of the Congo

77. Aware of that requirement, Africans must make all efforts to find a lasting solution to existing conflicts, strengthen their internal security and promote peace among the countries.[118]

78. At the Lusaka Summit, the African Union decided to take drastic measures in reviving the organs responsible for conflict prevention and resolution.[119]

(ii) Democracy and Political Governance Initiative

79. It is now generally acknowledged that development is impossible in the absence of true democracy, respect for human rights, peace and good governance. With the *New Partnership for Africa's Development*, Africa undertakes to respect the global standards of democracy, which core components include political pluralism, allowing for the existence of several political parties and workers' unions, fair, open, free and democratic elections periodically organised to enable the populace choose their leaders freely.[120]

---

and Lesotho (both under threat of military take-over), Pretoria proved to be the most fickle and inconsistent of the participating governments. It initially opposed intervention on behalf of the threatened Kabila regime but soon thereafter invaded Lesotho to restore an overthrown government.

118. Although 'strengthen internal stability' might serve as an excuse for increasing the repressive apparatus within undemocratic regimes, these are useful sentiments. But in reality, the cases of election-related conflicts in Congo-Brazzaville, Madagascar, Zambia and Zimbabwe – all within six months of the launch of Nepad – suggest that African heads of state are entirely willing to support the political *status quo* even when illegitimate government is manifestly the main cause of internal conflict. There was no hesitation by any African head of state (with the exception of Senegal's Wade on Zimbabwe) to accept the self-declared victors in these stolen elections, even though conflict and insecurity are going to worsen in many of these sites, and even though the legitimacy of Nepad itself comes under question.

119. There is no evidence that the 'drastic' revival of such organs is being attempted, or that the existing structures can be made effective, without changes in the attitudes and interests of participating regimes.

120. These are vital first-cut objectives, albeit of a purely bourgeois-democratic character. Far-reaching radical-participatory democratic objectives are apparently off Nepad's agenda.

But to reiterate, the most important test cases of bourgeois democracy, in Congo-Brazzaville, Madagascar, Zambia and Zimbabwe quickly proved the mettle of Africa's leaders. African leaders, especially from Pretoria,

80. The purpose of the Democracy and Governance Initiative is to contribute to strengthening the political and administrative framework of participating countries, in line with the principles of democracy, transparency, accountability, integrity, respect for human rights and promotion of the rule of law.[121] It is strengthened by and supports the Economic Governance Initiative, with which it shares key features, and taken together will contribute to harnessing the energies of the continent towards development and poverty eradication.[122]

81. The Initiative consists of the following elements:

- A series of commitments by participating countries to create or consolidate basic governance processes and practices;[123]

---

turned a blind eye to undemocratic processes in all settings and codified the outcomes of elections stolen by the ruling parties. South Africa, for example, refused to consider even mild 'smart sanctions' against Zimbabwe's leaders, even though these were explicitly requested by the democratic opposition.

121. These are valid aims and ambitions, and have been promoted by progressive civil society organisations for many years. But virtually all cut against the grain of most existing African heads of state and ruling parties.

122. Again, under the structural internal and external constraints Africa faces, achieving both together is virtually impossible. The inappropriate conflation of democracy and free markets neglects evidence that only one or the other is possible in the short-term.

123. Such 'commitments' could easily have been enumerated in this document, but have not been. A standard listing of governance commitments would have started with free and fair elections and moved to more detailed provisions, such as:

- **greater accountability (financial and political) of public officials, including politicians and civil servants;**
- **transparency in governmental procedures and processes;**
- **a concerted attack on corruption;**
- **predictability in governmental behaviour and in the political system;**
- **rationality in governmental decisions;**
- **competent auditing of governmental transactions;**
- **drastic curbing of bureaucratic red tape**
- **elimination of unnecessary administrative controls, to plug avenues for rent-seeking;**

- An undertaking by participating countries to take the lead in supporting initiatives that foster good governance;[124]

- The institutionalisation of commitments through the *New Partnership for Africa's Development* leadership to ensure that the core values of the initiative are abided by.[125]

82. The *New Partnership for Africa's Development* states will also undertake a series of commitments towards meeting basic standards of good governance and democratic behaviour while, at the same time, giving support to each other. Participating states will be supported in undertaking such

---

- free flow of information;
- encouragement of a culture of public debate;
- institution of a system of checks and balances within the governmental structure;
- decentralisation of government;
- respect for human rights;
- judicial autonomy and the rule of law;
- establishment of a reliable legal framework;
- protection of property;
- enforcement of contracts;
- capacity-building for technocrats; and
- consultation and participation with all affected stakeholders.

(This list is from Mkandawire, T. and C. Soludo (2000), *Our Continent, our Future:: African Perspectives on Structural Adjustment*, Dakar, Codesria; Ottawa, IDRC; and Trenton, Africa World Press, p.47.)

124. With Pretoria as the key catalyst of Nepad, expectations for leadership were lowered when in March 2002 the Cabinet agreed with the South African Observer Delegation that the Zimbabwean elections were 'legitimate' and 'credible' (even if they were not free and fair).

125. Nepad contains no meaningful sanctions or punishment for violating core democratic principles, rendering the ideas worthless, mere window-dressing, as demonstrated in various settings (Congo-Brazzaville, Madagascar, Zambia, Zimbabwe) just months after Nepad's launch. And as a reflection of the lack of serious commitment to governance by another key Nepad spokesperson, Benjamin Mkapa presided over elections in Tanzania in 2001 which, in April 2002, were revealed by an investigation to have been massively flawed due to police violence against people of Zanzibar and other parts of Tanzania. Neither disciplinary procedures nor self-expulsion from Nepad were considered.

desired institutional reforms where required. Within six months of its institutionalisation, the *New Partnership for Africa's Development* leadership will identify recommendations on appropriate diagnostic and assessment tools, in support of compliance with the shared goals of good governance, as well as to identify institutional weaknesses and to seek resources and expertise for addressing these weaknesses.[126]

83. In order to strengthen political governance and build capacity to meet these commitments, the *New Partnership for Africa's Development* leadership will undertake a process of targeted capacity-building initiatives. These institutional reforms will focus on:

- Administrative and civil services;
- Strengthening parliamentary oversight;
- Promoting participatory decision-making;
- Adopting effective measures to combat corruption and embezzlement;
- Undertaking judicial reforms.[127]

---

126. The phraseology employed here offers grounds for pessimism: 'leadership,' 'recommendations,' 'appropriate diagnostic and assessment tools,' 'institutional weaknesses,' 'resources and expertise for addressing these weaknesses.' In reality, most African elites run extremely undemocratic regimes. Even one of the best-case examples, South Africa, has recently exhibited bizarre leadership paranoia, for example, in permitting the use of state resources for internecine ruling party intrigue, as in the case of three business leaders allegedly plotting to overthrow the president. South Africa's democratic parliament also suffered a debilitating deterioration in its ability to conduct critical oversight, when its Public Accounts Committee was reduced to farce while carrying out a multi-billion dollar arms-deal investigation, due to blind ruling-party loyalty.

127. These are important ambitions, for across Africa all these institutional bulwarks of any effective state remain extremely weak or corrupted by ruling-party pressure. However, the only genuine guarantee of accountability in state-society relations is civil-society oversight, which goes unmentioned here. Below, the weaknesses in Nepad's conception of civil society are explored.

Moreover, the record of 1980s-90s governance according to the dictates of the Washington Consensus, with which Nepad concurs, is that the administrative and civil services were crippled under the pressure of fiscal constraints; parliaments were denuded of the possibility of

84. Countries participating in the initiative will take the lead in supporting and building institutions and initiatives that protect these commitments. They will dedicate their efforts towards creating and strengthening national, sub-regional and continental structures that support good governance.[128] The Heads of State Forum on the *New Partnership for Africa's Development* will serve as a mechanism through which the leadership of the *New Partnership for Africa's Development* will periodically monitor and assess the progress made by African countries in meeting their commitment towards achieving good governance and social reforms.[129] The Forum will also provide a platform for countries to share experiences with a view to fostering good governance and democratic practices.

---

meaningful dissent against neo-liberalism; participatory decision-making occurred in name only; corruption and embezzlement were aided and abetted by incoming foreign-currency loans and Washington-dictated financial liberalisation; and judicial reforms were invariably geared to strengthening property rights instead of human rights.

128. Unfortunately, key Nepad founder-governments have been either unsuccessful or unwilling to assure improved governance in even the procedural aspects of democracy. This is particularly embarrassing in Algeria, where a lost election was simply not recognised by the current ruling party; and in Nigeria, which continues to manifest numerous problems in ordinary democratic governance.

Even in South Africa, the past few years have witnessed centralisation of power extended to the point where virtually all major cities' mayors, as well as provincial premiers, are chosen by a small team from the ruling party executive, often with very controversial results. The same party passed national legislation in February 2002 to encourage minority parties to 'cross the floor' with more than 10% of their elected representatives (a figure arrived at so as to hurt the opposition while effectively disallowing defections from the ruling party). The objective was to draw one of the opposition parties - the New National Party which had imposed apartheid in 1948 - into an alliance. When in March 2002 the Zimbabwe elections were evidently rigged, according to unbiased observers (e.g., from the SADC parliamentary forum and a variety of NGOs), the South African ruling party's observer team overrode the minority parties in parliament so as to conclude otherwise. In short, respect for the basics of good governance is often lacking amongst the rulers of South Africa's own ruling party.

129. The commitment to 'monitor and assess' is the closest that Nepad comes to acknowledging that there are, in fact, no provisions (aside from self-disqualification) for disapproval and punishment envisaged in the programme.

• The Economic and Corporate Governance Initiative

85. State capacity-building is a critical aspect of creating conditions for development.[130] The State has a major role to play in promoting economic growth and development, and in the implementation of poverty reduction programmes. However, the reality is that many governments lack the capacity to fulfil this role. As a consequence, many countries lack the necessary policy and regulatory frameworks for private sector-led growth. They also lack the capacity to implement programmes even when funding is available.[131]

87. It is for this reason that targeted capacity building should be given a high priority. Programmes in every area must

---

130. This is manifestly obvious. But it bears pointing out that the main Nepad authors in Pretoria desire capacity in some areas, but obviously not in others.

The challenge of building state developmental capacity in South Africa arose on two occasions in 2000-01, through citizen appeals to the courts that socio-economic and health capacity be improved. In the first case (Irene Grootboom v. the state, September 2000), the plaintiffs won their claim that the state (at national, provincial and municipal tiers) is obliged to provide shelter for the very poorest South Africans, but there was no corresponding change in housing policy - aside from Pretoria's counterproductive insistence during 2001 that to access a higher housing subsidy, beneficiaries would have to show substantial savings. In the second case (Treatment Action Campaign v. the state, December 2001), the plaintiffs won their claim that tens of thousands of infants' lives should be saved by state provision of anti-retroviral drugs to pregnant HIV+ women. Pretoria showed its commitment to state capacity building and citizen empowerment, by announcing a decision to appeal the case - not only on grounds that Pretoria didn't want to allocate funds to save the infants' lives, but also because it didn't believe that the courts had such a powerful policy-overview role, notwithstanding an explicit mandate to that effect in the socio-economic rights clauses within the South African constitution's Bill of Rights.

In sum, without any explicit change in the attitudes of Africa's governing classes, it is unlikely that referring state capacity-building exercises back to those same governments will result in any change.

131. This would be an appropriate place to identify and analyse various causes of state decapacitation in economic management: e.g., the neo-liberal ideology of market-centred development, and the systematic defunding and desubsidisation, deregulation, fragmentation,

corporatisation and privatisation of state functions (including even basic water provision) forced upon Africa by the Bretton Woods institutions over a two-decades long period. Nepad ignores these universal causes of state decapacitation, either because of diplomatic considerations (in its request for meagre, highly conditioned HIPC debt relief and more loans) or because the document's authors don't really have a serious critique of this kind of decapacitation.

The Nepad authors' failure to provide analysis or details about building state capacity and combating corporate malgovernance is probably no accident. Cases in point include South Africa's own deregulation and decapacitation of its financial regulatory apparatus, especially its 1985-95 dual exchange control system; its oversight and regulation of small banks (most of which went bankrupt during the late 1990s and early 2000s); and the urgent unmet need to compel its large banks to achieve more racial, geographic, class and gender equity in credit allocation. Pretoria's failure reflects both its commitment to neo-liberal economic ideology, and prevailing power relations: especially, the 'independence' (i.e. insulation from democratic oversight) of the Reserve Bank which remains under commercial bank ownership and whose board is heavily weighted towards banking and corporate interests. Likewise, ongoing malfeasance in corporate governance is not taken seriously in South Africa, as witnessed by numerous scandals in which the primary pressure point for reform is the neo-liberal daily business paper, while Pretoria agencies remain silent and prosecutions remain extremely rare. This is a crucial defect at the very heart of Nepad, given the highly expansive role of South African firms in the region, mainly in the banking, construction, mining, retail, tourism and brewery sectors.

To illustrate the very real danger of worsening corporate malgovernance, Pretoria did not engage in any public investigation or prosecution associated with the blatant corruption case now under prosecution in Lesotho, in which the largest South African construction companies bribed the head of the agency overseeing Africa's largest public-works project, the Lesotho Highlands Water Project. The World Bank played a vital role in maintaining the corrupt head of the agency, by writing a threatening letter to the Lesotho government in 1994, six years after the corruption began (and four years before it ended), requiring that the corrupt executive be retained in his position, and in 2001 refused to comply with a commitment it had made to assist Maseru with financial support for ongoing prosecution of the firms involved. The Bank has also failed to debar the companies associated with the corruption, which was first exposed in press investigations in mid-1999. In sum, the evidence suggested by this emblematic, high-profile, multi-million dollar case is that neither Pretoria nor Washington can be trusted to promote good governance and state capacity-building.

be preceded by an assessment of capacity, followed by the provision of appropriate support.

Objective

88. To promote throughout the participating countries a set of concrete and time-bound programmes aimed at enhancing the quality of economic and public financial management as well as corporate governance.

Actions

89. A Task Force from Ministries of Finance and Central Banks will be commissioned to review economic and corporate governance practices in the various countries and regions, and make recommendations on appropriate standards and codes of good practice for consideration by the Heads of State Implementation Committee within six months.[132]

90. The Implementation Committee will refer its recommendations to African states for implementation.[133]

91. The Implementation Committee will give high priority to public financial management. Countries will develop a programme for improving public financial management and targets, and assessment mechanisms will also be set.[134]

Although South Africa is making some progress in relation to financial management and corporate governance, certainly in relation to the apartheid era, there are enormous gaps. Repeated financial bankruptcies and corporate scandals have regularly brought systematic irregularities in South African capitalism to light.

132. By May 2002, there was no record of this objective having been achieved, notwithstanding the request by Mbeki himself (in August 2001) that the region's central banks make it a high priority.

133. Were Nepad serious about building state capacity and improving corporate governance, it would not leave the entire process up to African states, which in turn remain unduly influenced by the deregulatory-oriented Bretton Woods institutions. A genuine effort would empower ordinary citizens to insist upon participatory roles in state capacity-building, through means such as the Porto Alegre participatory budgeting (as one well-known example). Nepad offers no mechanisms to this end.

134. There is no question that, because of the structural tendency towards building patronage-oriented regimes dominated by powerful politicians, financial management across Africa is beset by inefficiency and corruption. Yet too often, the real barriers to raising revenues and providing financial resources lie in neo-liberal ideology and programmatic dictates. Evidence

92. The Heads of State Implementation Committee will mobilise resources for capacity building to enable all countries to comply with the mutually agreed minimum standards and codes of conduct.[135]

---

includes the drive across Africa to lower tax and tariff rates associated with deregulatory regimes, vain attempts to attract foreign direct investment, and the mindless adoption of decentralisation, which in practice entails more responsibilities at lower levels of government but with fewer resources. Thus the codewords 'public financial management' probably refer to the desire of Nepad's authors to centralise financial and fiscal power while decentralising responsibilities.

In South Africa, this arrangement has done enormous harm to both local-level democracy and to municipal financial affairs. Recent problems have included:

- the head of the political party (whether African National Congress or Democratic Alliance) now chooses the mayor in the major metropolitan areas;
- the consolidation of newly demarcated municipalities, from 843 in 1994 to 284 in 2001, which had limited redistributive benefits but crippling impacts on local democracy in areas where constituents and councillors alike must now travel many kilometres to the new central municipal headquarters;
- dramatic declines in central-to-local grants for operating and maintenance expenses on infrastructure during the 1990s (by an average of 85% in real terms);
- growing 'unfunded mandates' to provincial and municipal governments;
- provisions to prohibit municipalities from borrowing and from raising property tax rates (notwithstanding huge apartheid deficits and unparalleled wealth/property/income inequality); and
- recent legislation that harshly penalises municipal managers for overspending on social and municipal services - in spite of a (laudable) ruling-party political mandate that municipalities offer a free lifeline amount of basic services such as water and electricity to all citizens.

135. To the extent that these resources will be mobilised via the same Washington financial agencies, the African Development Bank and donors who are already compelling African states to decapacitate, they will be contradictory in nature. If the South African case is indicative, an elite cadre will be established within the civil service, and paid vast sums more than their colleagues, so as to compete with other private and donor-sector employers of skilled financial managers.

• Sub-Regional and Regional Approaches to Development

93. Most African countries are small, both in terms of population and per capita incomes. As a consequence of limited markets, they do not offer attractive returns to potential investors, while progress in diversifying production and exports is retarded. This limits investment in essential infrastructure that depends on economies of scale for viability.[136]

94. These economic conditions point to the need for African countries to pool their resources and enhance regional development and economic integration on the continent, in order to improve international competitiveness.[137] The five subregional economic groupings of the continent must, therefore, be strengthened.

95. The *New Partnership for Africa's Development* focuses on the provision of essential regional public goods (such as transport, energy, water, ICT, disease eradication, environmental preservation, and provision of regional research capacity), as well as the promotion of intra-African trade and investments. The focus will be on rationalising the institutional framework for economic integration, by identifying common projects compatible with integrated country and regional development programmes, and on the harmonisation of economic and investment policies and practices.[138] There needs to be co-ordination of national sector policies and effective monitoring of regional decisions.

---

136. There is a great deal of truth in this comment. But other profound causes of insufficient markets could also have been noted, were the Nepad authors inclined. Declining living standards, destruction of Keynesian demand-stimulation, and excessive deregulation of tariffs and other industrial-policy tools are also very much to blame for the lack of buying power and competitive capacity which together have wrecked Africa's manufacturing base. However, these very real factors are not to be identified as problems in Nepad, and are not on its agenda for resolution.

137. Ideally, the first objective of regional integration would not be to improve 'international competitiveness.' Africa needs integration not so as to become an export platform, but primarily so as to meet the socio-economic and environmental needs of its citizenries.

138. With a focus on 'rationalising the institutional framework,' rather than on the more profound dilemma of regional production/consumption complementarities, the anticipated 'economic integration' will not be achieved. Examples of an excessive emphasis on institutional issues, to the

96. The *New Partnership for Africa's Development* will give priority to the capacity building in order to enhance the effectiveness of existing regional structures and the rationalisation of existing regional organisations. The African Development Bank must play a leading role in financing regional studies, programmes and projects.[139]

97. The sectors covered by the current Programme include the following priority areas:

(i) Infrastructure, especially information and communications technology (ICT) and energy

(ii) Human resources, including education, skills development, and reversing the brain drain

(iii) Health

(iv) Agriculture

(v) Access to the markets of developed countries for African exports

98. For each sector, however, the objective is to bridge existing gaps between Africa and the developed countries so as to improve the continent's international competitiveness and to enable her to participate in the globalisation process.[140] The special circumstances of African island and land-locked states will also be addressed in this context.

---

neglect of *content* in regional economic development, are South Africa's Spatial Development Initiatives (SDIs). These are allegedly 'common projects compatible with integrated country and regional development programmes,' and they attempt to harmonise 'economic and investment policies and practices.' But the SDIs to date – whether within the region, such as the Maputo Corridor, or simply within South Africa – have been extremely disappointing, particularly insofar as promises of trickle-down benefits to local communities have been systematically broken.

139. The African Development Bank, an aid-dependent institution, lends in inappropriate hard currency, fails to grant debt cancellation, parrots Washington's neo-liberal philosophy, and nearly went bankrupt during the late 1990s, as senior management went into hiding. Its failure to perform in the interests of Africa's poor and working people requires a genuine cost-benefit audit to determine whether it can be salvaged or requires replacement by a genuine people's development bank.

140. As noted before, if the objective is merely 'to improve the continent's international competitiveness and to enable her to participate in the globalisation process,' there will be two problems: a) Africa is already too

B. SECTORAL PRIORITIES

• Bridging the Infrastructure Gap

(i) All Infrastructure Sectors

99. The infrastructures considered include roads, highways, airports, seaports, railways, waterways, and telecommunication facilities.[141] However, only sub-regional or continental infrastructures will be the focus of the Plan.

100. Infrastructure is one of the major parameters of economic growth, and solutions should be found to permit Africa to rise to the level of developed countries in terms of the accumulation of material and human capital.[142]

101. If Africa had the same basic infrastructure as developed countries, it would be in a more favourable position to focus on production and improving productivity for international competition.[143] The structural gap in infrastructure constitutes a very serious handicap to economic growth and poverty reduction. Improved infrastructure, including the cost and reliability of services, would benefit both Africa and the

---

far behind the rest of the world to catch up on the terms of 'globalisation,' and b) to reduce the objective of development to international competitiveness will necessarily mean leaving out the masses of Africans who are not 'competitive.'

141. It makes little sense to isolate electricity and water/sanitation bulk supply systems from this list, but they are dealt with separately below.

142. The most important question is whether the 'level of developed countries' - particularly in relation to highways and airports - is necessary and desirable, for it implies the adoption in Africa of unsustainable, ecologically-damaging and socially-questionable Northern-style automobile and truck density, and the expansion of pollution/energy-intensive air transport.

143. As it stands (and as Nepad soon acknowledges), most of Africa's infrastructure is *already* biased towards improving the continent's international competitiveness, as a result of the rail, road, shipping and air-transport links between the continent and its former colonial powers. Indeed, the 'competitiveness' of Africa's raw material exports has been one of the reasons for the continent's *underdevelopment,* and Nepad should therefore have stressed infrastructure for internal coherence, not for exacerbating the export-led bias of Africa's economies.

international community, which would be able to obtain African goods and services more cheaply.[144]

102. In many African countries, the colonial powers built the infrastructure to foster exportation of African raw materials and importation of industrial goods into Africa.[145]

103. We recognise also that if infrastructure is to improve in Africa, private foreign finance is essential to complement the two major funding methods, namely credit and aid.[146]

104. The Infrastructure Initiative comprises elements that are common to all the infrastructure sectors. It also includes elements that are sector-specific.

105. Objectives

- To improve access to and affordability and reliability of infrastructure services for both firms and households;[147]

---

144. The excessively 'cheap' (in all senses of the word) character of African raw materials is one of the systematic causes of the continent's economic problems, as terms-of-trade data convincingly show.

145. This is the essential problem with Africa's economy: its debilitating bias is its export-led character, inherited from extractive-colonialism and exacerbated during neocolonialism and neo-liberalism. Nepad simply amplifies this bias.

146. Investment by foreign firms in Africa's infrastructure has many untenable characteristics, as discussed below, which can be summarised as:

- **inappropriate tariffing that observes only short-run costs (not longer-term benefits or positive externalities achieved by unprofitable provision to the masses, e.g., through state subsidies or cross-subsidisation);**
- **inappropriate hard-currency inputs for many features of infrastructure development (labour, local materials) which do not require hard currency;**
- **repatriation of profits to Northern centres (in hard currency), thus draining Africa's scarce foreign exchange reserves;**
- **use of overpriced Northern consultants and employees; and**
- **reliance upon inappropriate Northern technology for which the need to import expensive (hard-currency denominated) maintenance support and spare parts ensures Africa's ongoing dependency.**

147. Such an objective should be endorsed. However, if the means to achieve it include public-private partnerships, Nepad owes its readers an

- To enhance regional co-operation and trade through expanded cross-border development of infrastructure;[148]
- To increase financial investments in infrastructure by lowering risks facing private investors, especially in the area of policy and regulatory frameworks;[149]

---

explanation of the profit motive in privatised infrastructure. Supplying to most of Africa at the 30%+ profit (remitted in hard currency) required by the typical infrastructure investor is unaffordable to the average, much less lower-income consumer.

Even in relatively low-risk South Africa, one investment fund sponsored by the African Development Bank in 1997 projected before-tax internal rates of return (IRRs) of 26-27% over the fund's '15-year life in constant US dollar terms,' assuming that '10% of all investments will fail; 50% of all investments will generate an IRR of 30%; and 40% of all investments will generate an IRR of 35%.' To earn such high rates of return on infrastructure investments that are often long-term in nature (often forty years before full social and economic returns on investment are realised), and on top of that to compress the high earnings into the early stages of investment (on average 7.5 years, given that this particular fund was to be shut down after 15 years), and to do so using a wide range of social infrastructure investments, implies an extremely high cost-recovery burden for direct infrastructure recipients, or dramatic cost reductions at the level of the enterprise. Amongst 'potential project pipeline' investments were the hotly debated Nelspruit water treatment, Eskom electricity transmission lines, Empangeni water management, and Telkom's partial privatisation, all of which entailed infrastructure aimed at bringing low-income people into the economy, and none of which proved sustainable. (African Development Bank (1997), 'Investment Proposal: South Africa Infrastructure Investment Fund,' ADB Private Sector Unit, Abidjan.)

148. This is also admirable, but if the vehicles chosen include those that South Africa has been promoting – i.e., the Spatial Development Initiatives – then extreme uneven development can be expected: the nature of the projects is usually resource-extractive, and the existing regional power relations in some parts of Africa are overwhelmingly biased towards domination by a sub-hegemon (South Africa and Nigeria). The phrase 'Africa's yankees' is often used of South Africans in Southern Africa. 'Subimperialism' is a genuine problem.

149. The privatisation of infrastructure requires higher regulatory barriers and tougher public policy, not lower and weaker regulations and policies as implied. South Africa is a case in point, in areas such as telecommunications where the 30% foreign investors (from Texas and Malaysia) have regularly attempted to cheat the public on fixed-line costs and roll-out of lines to millions of people who were denied access during apartheid, according to the national regulator. Policy has swung backward

- To build adequate knowledge and skills in technology and engineering with a view to installing, operating and maintaining 'hard' infrastructure networks in Africa.[150]

106. Actions

- With the assistance of sector-specialised agencies, put in place policy and legislative frameworks to encourage competition.[151] At the same time, introduce new regulatory frameworks as well as build capacity for regulators, so as to promote policy and regulatory harmonisation in order to facilitate cross-border interaction and market enlargement;[152]

---

and forward, and the regulator has been disempowered on occasion, precisely because of the desire by the neo-liberal faction of government to 'lower risks facing private investors.' The Texan/Malaysian firm has even publicly threatened to sell its stake in Telkom because of a strong regulator, in a debate that will continue.

150. Some infrastructure is enormously complex, costly and difficult to maintain (e.g. telephony), while others (e.g. postal services, roads, and the like) are relatively easy. Nepad fails to distinguish between these, and to rank priorities for infrastructure that would help unveil who benefits and at what cost to the national coffers.

151. The introduction of 'competition' implies privatisation of infrastructure. Yet the case for privatisation is not made within Nepad, either on the basis of past experiences or contemporary logic. This is extremely unsatisfying, given that most infrastructure is of a 'natural monopoly' type, for which competition is unsuitable. Such natural monopolies include roads and railroads, telephone land lines (including optic-fibre), water and sewage reticulation systems, electricity transmission, ports and the like. Nepad cannot make a case for competition in these areas; there is, in contrast, an extremely strong case, based on the public-good and merit-good factors, for *state* control and non-profit operation, including cross-subsidisation to enhance affordability for poor consumers (which is also anathema to the private sector).

152. The problem of 'captive regulation' remains profound where states are weak and multinational corporations have extraordinary capacity. The failure of South Africa to establish effective regulation in crucial, life-and-death sectors undergoing privatisation, such as water and passenger transport, and the ineffectiveness of the National Electricity Regulator, together suggest that the one example of a strong regulator (in the telecommunications sector) is the exception that proves the rule.

- Increase investment in infrastructure, especially refurbishment, and improve system maintenance practices that will sustain infrastructure;[153]

- Initiate the development of training institutions and networks which can develop and produce high-skill technicians and engineers in all infrastructure sectors;[154]

- Promote community and user involvement in infrastructure construction, maintenance and management, especially in poor urban and rural areas, in collaboration with the *New Partnership for Africa's Development* Governance Initiatives;[155]

- Work with the African Development Bank and other development finance institutions on the continent to

---

153. Costs, returns on investment and other crucial information are missing. The reluctance of foreign donors, private investors and states to invest in infrastructure to date cannot simply be willed away. As for maintenance, South Africa is one of the best examples of how quickly a commitment to fiscal austerity can undermine the budget for public-works maintenance. It is widely recognised in government that the backlog on refurbishing state-owned buildings, roads, bridges and many other state assets rose dramatically after 1994, *as a matter of policy*.

154. This is important, but Nepad owes its readers an explanation of why such training institutions, which used to exist in greater quantities, were subsequently defunded, along with most state tertiary education, and how that condition can be reversed.

155. Community participation in infrastructure is, in principle, a useful strategy. But in practice under neo-liberalism, it has had the effect of placing financial and technical obligations that are the responsibility of the state in most civilised societies, onto the shoulders of impoverished communities.

In South Africa, the effect of requiring a greater role for communities in administering full cost-recovery rural water schemes, was to leave most of them broken due to lack of community affordability. This philosophy already prevails in many African settings, notwithstanding the extreme poverty, on mainly ideological grounds of full cost-recovery. The World Bank insists that African governments which aim to supply rural villages in desperate need of water and sanitation supplies, must follow the following neo-liberal formula: 'Promote increased capital cost recovery from users. An upfront cash contribution based on their willingness-to-pay is required from users to demonstrate demand and develop community capacity to administer funds and tariffs. Ensure 100% recovery of operation and maintenance costs.' (World Bank (2000), 'Sourcebook on Community Driven Development in the Africa Region: Community Action Programs,' Africa Region, Washington, DC, 17 March, Annex 2.)

mobilise sustainable financing especially through multilateral processes, institutions and donor governments, with a view to securing grant and concessional finance to mitigate medium term risks;[156]

- Promote PPPs as a promising vehicle for attracting private investors, and focus public funding on the pressing needs of the poor, by building capacity to implement and monitor such agreements;[157]

---

156. Financing is one of Nepad's Achilles Heels, because existing institutions and processes are so destructive. The African Development Bank is an example of a failed institution. The World Bank's own internal assessments of African lending (e.g. the Wappenhans Report) are shocking, with a majority of projects considered failures. There is no logic to the African Development Bank and World Bank process of lending in hard currency for developmental goods and services – e.g., rural education – whose components are nearly entirely based on locally-sourced inputs (not requiring hard currency repayment). Many donor agencies, especially US AID, suffer from the same problem, of lending in extremely expensive hard currency – repayable with high effective interest rates as the value of African currencies falls – for projects with few foreign inputs. The hard currency is then utilised, in part, for import of luxury goods by African elites. If countries attempt to put on luxury goods import taxes (as did Zimbabwe in 1998), the International Monetary Fund and World Trade Organisation force the countries to remove them.

Will 'concessional' loans solve Africa's financing problems? The existing external financing for most of Africa is already highly concessional, in the form of World Bank International Development Administration loans at 0.75% or lower interest rate. But those cheap loans, repayable in hard currency, did not stop Africa from falling into an extremely painful and durable debt crisis. Servicing the full debt is truly impossible, and the payment of a 'sustainable' 20% of export earnings, as determined by the Bretton Woods institutions and Paris Club creditor/donor cartels, has drained Africa of desperately-needed resources.

The more important financing challenges are establishing institutions and regulations, including effective exchange controls, that would allow for the circulation and reinvestment of Africa's existing financial resources, too many of which are frittered away in speculative projects, luxury real estate development and capital flight via African branches of foreign banks (typically headquartered in London and Paris) and by corrupt, *comprador* local banks.

157. The record of PPPs in South Africa doesn't foster optimism. In virtually all sectors of public asset disposal or contracting of public services, controversies have become debilitating:

- in water and sanitation, unacceptable problems recently emerged in key pilot projects run by the world's biggest water companies - e.g., the Eastern Cape town of Nkonkobe sued to cancel its disadvantageous long-term contract with Suez due to overpricing and underservicing (including ongoing use of the 'bucket system' of sanitation); the KwaZulu-Natal town of Dolphin Coast where Sauer demanded - and won - a renegotiation of its contract in order to raise tariffs because profits were insufficient; and the Mpumalanga city of Nelspruit where Biwater was sharply criticised for failing to extend services and cutting off services to low-income residents;
- in electricity, privatisation of generation is being planned and commercialisation of the state utility Eskom - with the intention of selling a stake to private shareholders this year - has already led to: higher tariffs for lower-income residential customers (as cross-subsidies came under attack); to the rejection by Eskom in both 2001 and 2002 of the ruling party's campaign promise of free electricity; to a slowdown in the extension of the electricity grid to low-income rural residents; and to the disconnection of tens of thousands of households who had fallen into arrears on inflated bills;
- in fixed-line telecommunications, the cost of local phone calls skyrocketed as cross-subsidisation from long-distance (especially international) calls was phased out; hundreds of thousands of disconnections have occurred due to unaffordability (termed 'churning' of lines); a second fixed-line operator was first discouraged then encouraged under pressure from competing commercial interests (ensuring ongoing confusion as to regulatory intention); and attempts to cap fixed-line pricing by the state regulator were rejected by the Texan/Malaysian partnership through a court challenge and a threat to sell their 30% share of the telecommunications company;
- in cellular telecommunications, a collusion pact exists between the two main operators, and persistent allegations of corruption (of state officials) stymied the introduction of a third operator;
- in transport, unsatisfactory privatisation and corporatisation have included toll roads which local residents cannot afford; private 'kombi' taxi transport (increasingly dangerous due to profit pressures); a corporatised rail service (which shut down many unprofitable but socially useful feeder routes) and the apparent breakdown in April 2002 of an agreement with the main trade union (Satawu) *not* to privatise key lines (as one *quid pro quo* for Satawu accepting 8,000 job cuts); air transport (the first state airline privatisation, of Sun Air, led to a quick bankruptcy, and South African Airway's disastrous mismanagement and the bankruptcy of its 20% Swiss shareholder required renationalisation in November 2001), and the airports themselves (where substantial security problems emerged repeatedly even in the wake of the September 2001 terrorist attacks);

- In addition to these common issues, the following are sector-specific strategies for the different types of infrastructure.

(ii) Bridging the Digital Divide: Investing in Information and Communication Technologies

107. Information and Communication Technologies (ICTs), driven by the convergence of computers, telecommunications and traditional media, are crucial for the knowledge-based economy of the future. Rapid advances in technology and the diminishing cost of acquiring the new ICT tools have opened new windows of opportunity for African countries to accelerate economic growth and development. The goals of achieving a Common Market and an African Union can benefit immensely from the revolution in information technology. In addition to fostering intra-regional trade, the use of ICTs could also accelerate Africa's integration into the global economy.[158]

- in ports, unsuccessful high-profile attempts were made from 1996-2002 to establish a public-private partnership for construction and management of a new deep harbour and container terminal at Port Elizabeth's Coega location (repeatedly delayed by the failure of government to establish a viable business plan and core tenant);
- in other PPPs, ranging from the Post Office (where the New Zealand service had to be fired for mismanagement of corporatisation), to forests (which attracted few or no bidders for state forests), to the state's holiday resorts (which were initially sold to a consortium that included trade unions, in a deal that fell apart when Malaysian partners backed out).

The 'needs of the poor' were the last priority in virtually all of these privatisation and corporatisation experiences.

158. As noted already, the faith in ICT is misplaced. The 'convergence of computers, telecommunications and traditional media' offers little ground for optimism in relation to African development and democracy, because *existing power relations - especially North-South information flows, cultural norms and values, and consumption processes - are being strengthened in the process.* As is evident from even cursory examination of the roles of major high-tech corporations (Microsoft, General Electric, etc) in the mass media, *there is even less of a propensity for the Northern mass media to cover the issues facing Africa with seriousness and sympathy.*

The convergence of these technologies in Africa has not yet taken root, but to the extent they do, it is just as likely that biased public broadcasting and politicians on the one hand, and large-corporate private media plus wealthy business elites on the other, will continue to subvert democracy and development. The 'rapid advances in technology' and 'diminishing

108. Intensive use of ICTs can bring, unprecedented comparative advantages to the continent.[159] It can:

- Provide an impetus to the democratisation process and good governance;[160]

- Facilitate the integration of Africa into the new information society, using its cultural diversity as a leverage;[161]

---

cost of ICT tools' are together excessively hyped, because dependency relations (in parts and maintenance, as well as in content provision), obsolescence of existing investments, foreign-exchange shortages, and crashing African currencies together mean that reliance upon high-tech solutions can do more harm than good, and just as easily close rather than open the windows of opportunity.

Moreover, while promotion of *appropriate* intra-regional trade is a notable objective, it is just as likely that *inappropriate* trade - controlled especially from centres of African affluence such as Johannesburg - will be enhanced, and will in turn worsen the continent's uneven development. And the merits of 'accelerating Africa's integration into the global economy' have yet to be demonstrated, given the problems of falling terms of trade and dramatic capital flight from Africa to international 'hot money' centres.

159. Nepad provides no convincing evidence that alleged 'comparative advantages' will come to Africa. The most important evidence is to the contrary, namely the efforts of South African ICT leaders Didata and rand-billionaire inventor Mark Shuttlesworth to relocate their businesses offshore, along with the vast bulk of their financial assets. Comparative *disadvantages* will, instead, be more likely to increase, the more Africa relates to the world economy via ICT-driven integration.

160. There are certainly instances whereby ICTs can assist social movements for human rights and democratisation, most notably in the cases of China during the Tianenmen Square crisis of 1988-89, and in Zimbabwe during the 2000-02 era when electoral-based opposition was strongest. However, because in both cases state authorities were capable of repressing democratic organisations and restoring their own hegemony over the media (including ICT functions), it is not wise to raise expectations that ICT will inexorably lead to democratisation and good governance. Much more important are political power relations, which, as noted above, Nepad is apparently incapable of changing for the better.

161. There is no information provided as to how highly-fragmented African cultures can become a source of leverage. During past waves of technological change, the opposite occurred: Africa was looted more and more effectively thanks to military conquest, the diffusion of electricity, rail and air transport, and the rise of mass media through television and radio. There are, additionally, so many uncompetitive aspects of

- ICTs can be helpful tools for a wide range of applications, such as remote sensing and environmental, agricultural and infrastructural planning;[162]

- The existing complementarities can be better utilised to provide training that would allow for the production of a critical mass of professionals on the use of ICTs;[163]

- In the research sector, we can establish African programmes as well as technological exchange programmes capable of meeting the continent's specific needs, with particular regard to the fight against illiteracy;[164]

- ICTs can be used to identify and exploit opportunities for trade, investment and finance;[165]

African culture - some of which are socially beneficial, others of which are repressive, patriarchal and superstitious - that instead of acting as leverage, it is just as likely that existing cultural modes will serve as an anchor to Africa's economic advance in the information age.

162. This is true, but in the process, ICTs enhance the power of those who are already powerful. Nepad offers no hope for changing such power relations, which are currently exploitative and parasitical in nature, and indeed on the contrary, promotes the *expanded* roles of transnational corporations and the Bretton Woods institutions.

163. This is another worthwhile ambition, but the legacy of brain drain in Africa - which Nepad ineffectively addresses below - suggests that unless the underlying conditions are changed dramatically, training African ICT professionals will not necessarily result in an upgrade of African-based capacity. Various modes of 'bonding' recipients of training have been used in parts of the continent, but it is telling that in South Africa, nothing has been done to halt either outward brain drain or inward brain drain from other African countries.

164. The suggestion is, again, laudable, but the harsh reality of opportunity costs suggests that *either* African governments focus their scarce resources on ending illiteracy, *or* they push those resources into training an elite in ICT skills. Doing *both* would be ideal, but there is no evidence in Nepad to suggest that this can be achieved.

165. Under certain circumstances whereby states maintain control or investment (e.g. as in the case of Botswana's diamond policies), this objective is not unreasonable. However, liberalised African states are less and less capable of imposing such controls. The main ways in which the 'opportunities' of trade, investment and finance will, instead, continue *underdeveloping* Africa, are capital flight, transfer pricing and financial speculation. These are simply not addressed in Nepad.

- Can be used to establish regional distance learning and health education programmes to improve the situation in the health and education sectors;[166]

- In conflict management and control of pandemic diseases, ICTs will help towards the organisation of an efficient early warning mechanism by providing the tools for constant monitoring of tension spots.[167]

109. In Africa, poor ICT infrastructure, combined with weak policy and regulatory frameworks and limited human resources, has resulted in inadequate access to affordable telephones, broadcasting, computers and the Internet.[168] African

---

166. The limitations of ICTs are so great as to be cost/skills-prohibitive, when it comes to penetration into distant, impoverished rural areas. The application of ICTs has, according to various studies, simply not been economically sustainable where they are needed most. Even South Africa's own late-1990s Universal Services Agency programme of rolling out telephony and internet connectivity to low-income areas via 'telecentres,' is widely acknowledged as a failure because of the government's insistence upon cost recovery. Also illustrative about that case was the failure of the programme to integrate with the health and education sectors, which might have been the basis for additional recurrent-financing support. Once again, where there are enormous ambitions to change the ICT landscape of Africa, the inability of the South African government to do so at home - largely because of the neo-liberal philosophy of financial sustainability without sufficient subsidies - is a bad omen for the continent.

167. This is, again, a laudable objective, and one that has proven effective in some pandemics such as isolated Central African outbreaks of Ebola. However, even in South Africa, epidemics such as HIV/Aids, cholera and diarrhoea have been identified with a degree of rigour - in part through ICT - yet public policy has been extremely ineffective in curbing mortality and morbidity. In such cases, the main problem has been that people's human rights to healthcare (especially antiretroviral drugs) and sufficient clean drinking water have been determined to be too expensive for a government obsessed with meeting artificial fiscal deficit targets.

168. This sentence is tautological. More appropriate would be an assessment of prerequisite infrastructure (especially electricity), the high costs of equipment and training in relation to African incomes, foreign-exchange unavailability in many circumstances, the lack of economy of scales, and the systematic weakening of African states during the past two decades. But because these underlying prerequisite conditions are not likely to change, given prevailing socio-economic circumstances, it is easier for Nepad to blame the lack of African ICT infrastructure upon the lack of African ICT infrastructure.

teledensity remains below one line per 100 people. Service costs are also high: the connection cost in Africa averages 20 per cent of GDP per capita, compared with the world average of 9 per cent, and 1 per cent for high-income countries. Africa has been unable to capitalise on ICT as a tool in enhancing livelihoods and creating new business opportunities, and cross-border linkages within the continent and with global markets have been constrained. Though many countries in Africa have started ICT policy reforms, service penetration, quality or tariffs have not yet improved.[169]

110. Objectives

- To double teledensity to two lines per 100 people by 2005, with an adequate level of access for households;[170]

- To lower the cost and improve reliability of service;[171]

- To achieve e-readiness for all countries in Africa;[172]

---

169. There must be reasons that existing strategies - which are generally based on private-sector initiative - have not overcome the constraints noted. There is nothing in Nepad to suggest that the limits to market constraints are recognised or that any strategy will be adopted to change the market-related conditions. Such strategies have worked in many other settings, and if tried seriously in Africa could make the difference between continuing underdevelopment of ICTs, and moving towards universal access. These include free open source software, compulsory licensing, public access and public ownership of the infrastructure.

170. It is hard to see where, aside from penetration of some cellphone markets that are only now being set up, the doubling of teledensity can be achieved *without a dramatic change in the income of Africans*. A particularly important barrier remains the difficulty of achieving increased coverage through cross-subsidisation under circumstances when corporatisation and privatisation erode all internal subsidies. In South Africa, the evidence for this problem exists in the partially-privatised South African parastatal Telkom, which has raised local-call costs, dramatically lowered internal subsidies, and 'churned' (cut off) hundreds of thousands of new customers.

171. While evidence suggests that private telephone operators are more reliable - in part because of new non-fixed-line technology - it is only through state provision that *prices* to consumers are typically lowered. Virtually all experiences are that in telephony, the private sector increases prices (even where it might have lowered costs).

172. The objective is valid and indeed viable, but requires much more attention to prerequisite technologies in many African settings, ranging from electricity to reliable telephone lines. Obviously these are the objectives of Nepad, but as discussed, there is no basis for believing that

- To develop and produce a pool of ICT-proficient youth and students from which Africa can draw trainee ICT engineers, programmers and software developers;[173]

- To develop local content software, based especially on Africa's cultural legacy.[174]

111. Actions[175]

- Work with regional agencies such as the African Telecommunications Union and Africa Connection to design model policy and legislation for telecommunications reform, and protocols and templates for e-readiness assessments;

- Work with the regional agencies to build regulatory capacity;

- Establish a network of training and research institutions to build high-level manpower;

- Promote and accelerate existing projects to connect schools and youth centres;

- Work with development finance institutions in Africa, multilateral initiatives (G-8 DotForce, UN Task Force) and bilateral donors to establish financial mechanisms to mitigate and reduce sector risks.

---

these will be achieved given the strongly market-oriented characteristics of the programme.

173. This is a valid objective, but as noted, there is no basis in Nepad to believe that the brain drain won't continue, or indeed be exacerbated.

174. There are no details in Nepad to suggest that this is anything other than romantic rhetoric. The opposite effect of ICT penetration on African culture can be expected: its extinction under the pressures of Western consumerism. This, indeed, has been the effect across the world on local cultures, as a previous round of ICTs - television, radio and film - promoted US and European values and consumption norms, to the detriment of organic, non-commercial culture.

175. The actions listed here certainly have potential, and should be pursued. But many of them, especially the G-8 DotForce, are still based upon the World Bank 'Global Knowledge' ideology that attempts to commodify information. And there is no basis for believing that accomplishing these actions will generate any of the grandiose results that are claimed in preceding paragraphs.

(iii) Energy

112. Objectives

- Energy plays a critical role in the development process, first as a domestic necessity but also as a factor of production whose cost directly affects prices of other goods and services, and the competitiveness of enterprises. Given the uneven distribution of these resources on the continent, it is recommended that the search for abundant and cheap energy to focus on rationalising the territorial distribution of existing but unevenly allocated energy resources.[176] Furthermore,

176. The rationalisation of massive energy overcapacity in some parts of regions, and debilitating electricity shortages in others, makes sense. But it is crucial to analyse the context for the uneven development of energy resources in Africa and to understand the vehicles for redistribution.

Thus, imperial-sponsored geopolitical arrangements have allowed Nigerian and Angolan oil to flow to the West, no matter how environmentally destructive the process (e.g. to Ogoniland), or how undemocratic their regimes (e.g., mid-1990s attempts by Nelson Mandela to organise sanctions against the Abacha regime were foiled by the oil-dependent West). Nigeria's own brown-outs and petrol shortages demonstrate the irrationality of existing arrangements, which go unremarked upon in (and unchallenged by) Nepad. Likewise, the ability of a tiny Angolan elite to skim off the benefits of oil extraction for the purposes of personal accumulation are well known, but Nepad and African leaders avoid criticism of the extensive corruption associated with western oil companies' operations in Angola.

As for the process of energy-sector rehabilitation, if it is left to international energy corporations - e.g., the now-bankrupt Enron, which benefitted from US AID's power over the Mozambican government to win access to the Pande gas field - and the huge South African firm Eskom, the problems of uneven development will only intensify. Further environmental abuse and social upheaval will occur through World Bank-funded projects such as the Chad-Cameroon pipeline and Bujagali Dam in Uganda, as well as proposed hydroprojects at Epupa in Namibia and on the Zambezi River in Mozambique.

What Nepad appears incapable of doing is enquiring into the *utilisation* of Africa's energy, perhaps because South Africa's own controversial practices of extremely cheap electricity generation are crucial to Pretoria's export-led growth strategy. But South Africa consistently fails to incorporate the environmental, social and opportunity costs of the inexpensive power provided to large smelter operations (Mozal in Maputo, Alusaf in Richards Bay, Iscor at Saldanha, proposed Ferrostal smelters at Coega near Port Elizabeth, and many other existing and proposed aluminium, iron, stainless steel, platinum and zinc operations).

> Africa should strive to develop its solar energy resources which are abundantly available.[177]
>
> - To increase from 10 per cent to 35 per cent *or more*, access to reliable and affordable commercial energy supply by Africa's population in 20 years;[178]
>
> - To improve the reliability as well as lower the cost of energy supply to productive activities in order to enable economic growth of 6 per cent per annum;[179]

Nepad neglects to acknowledge the vast contribution that utilisation of this energy in South Africa makes to the problem of global warming. Nor does the document engage in analysis of the temporal benefits of delaying exploitation of non-renewable energy resources. Until Nepad considers the uses to which Africa's energy is put, it is impossible to engage in debate surrounding the merits of regional rationalisation.

177. There is enormous potential in solar energy, which should indeed be explored. However, the main problem associated with the application of solar energy in much of Africa - unremarked upon by Nepad but notorious for energy-development practitioners - is the low level of amps that can be obtained by virtually all the panels available through retail sources to individual households. While permitting a light and radio, the existing technology is not capable of allowing substitution of coal or firewood for cooking or heating. Maintenance and spare parts are also barriers to the widespread expansion of solar systems, and the energy-intensity of solar panel production processes has also been criticised.

178. In arguing for 'commercial' expansion, Nepad makes no provisions for the subsidisation that, in reality, will be required to accomplish this feat. The market simply is too small and affordability is too great a constraint to achieve that degree of expansion without massive subsidies. Nepad's failure to take this into explicit account merely reflects its utopian tendency to make unfulfillable promises.

179. Although through greater efficiencies and new technologies, it should be easier to lower the cost of electricity generation, Nepad fails to spell out the precise relationship of cheaper energy to the desired growth rate (which, as a trivial footnote, is a per cent lower than promoted in paragraph 70). As argued above, it is in part the reliance of South Africa's 'minerals-energy complex' upon cheap electricity that imposes barriers to less biased economic development and hence limits the country's growth, since South Africa has become far more dependent upon international minerals prices for its export revenues. (The seminal critique of South African economic development patterns during apartheid is by Ben Fine and Zav Rustomjee: *The Political Economy of South Africa: From Minerals-Energy Complex to Industrialisation*, Johannesburg, Wits University Press and London, Christopher Hirst.)

- To reverse environmental degradation that are associated with the use of traditional fuels in rural areas;[180]

- To exploit and develop the hydropower potential of river basins of Africa;[181]

---

180. The need to halt deforestation cannot be denied. But South Africa has itself failed to extend its own massive electricity surpluses (of more than a fifth of capacity) to rural households, half of whom still are without electricity, and the other half of whom either utilise solar power which is not capable of replacing fuelwood for cooking/heating purposes, or are unable to afford sufficient supplies at present tariff levels (at least R0.32 per kiloWatt hour) to substitute electricity for fuelwood.

Nepad fails to even mention the far more environmentally-destructive use of existing cheap electricity supplies for minerals smelting, which the post-apartheid economy has come to rely upon even more, thanks to the increased dependency of South Africa on the minerals-energy complex.

181. Nepad neglects to cite, much less rebut, the enormous controversies over new dams in Africa (e.g., Mohale, Maguge, Bujagali and Epupa):

- large dams in tropical settings have been identified as the cause of far higher global-warming gas emissions (due to decay of plant life) than other energy sources;
- displacement and socio-economic costs of large dams are very high (though rarely if ever incorporated into dam construction costs);
- downstream environmental implications are often severe;
- siltation and evaporation undermine the efficiency of dams;
- the economic benefits of large dams very rarely approach initial estimates; and
- there are a variety of other critiques of mega-dams and hydropower which emerged during the late 1990s from the World Commission on Dams, which ironically was chaired by South Africa's then-water minister, Kader Asmal. (Notably, Asmal's replacement, Ronnie Kasrils, stirred a controversy in 2001 by effectively disowning the commission's report when it came to applications in Southern Africa, and himself attracted sharp criticism for endorsing the Three Gorges Dam on the Yangtze River, which is considered the worst-ever attack by humans on nature.)

The critiques apply to Africa's existing mega-dams (e.g., on the Nile, Upper Volta, Zambezi and Orange Rivers). Zimbabwe/Zambia and South Africa's own ineffective management of dams and run-off systems - in the Zambezi, Save, Limpopo and Crocodile catchments - have been cited as contributing factors to Mozambique's deadly 2000-01 floods, even though the dams were meant to prevent flooding. In short, without some acknowledgement that large dams have had an often devastating impact on

- To integrate transmission grids and gas pipelines so as to facilitate crossborder energy flows;[182]

- To reform and harmonise petroleum regulations and legislation in the continent.[183]

113. Actions

- Establish an African Forum for Utility Regulation and establish regional regulatory associations;[184]

---

societies, environments and economies, Nepad encourages the repetition of the problems associated with reliance upon inappropriate hydropower.

182. The main sites for this sort of exercise appear to be Namibia and Mozambique, where the latter's Pande gas field is being integrated by Sasol into the South African energy grid, instead of providing cheap energy for impoverished Mozambicans. But questions are still needed about the manner in which additional excess capacity will be added, and the use to which it will be put, given the problem of excessively cheap electricity for smelting minerals and excessively expensive electricity for consumption by low-income households, as discussed above.

183. As noted above, the most important point in relation to Africa's petroleum industry is to consider not the regulations and legislation, but the character of production (e.g., Nigeria's environmentally and socially unsound practices) and distribution (e.g., from Angola and Nigeria to the United States, instead of into the country and region).

184. This idea is not necessarily new, nor deserving of the kinds of partnerships that exist between Northern agencies and African utilities at present. The case of the neo-liberal African Water Utilities Partnership is taken up below.

The South African corporatised energy utility, Eskom, has long held a vision of regional domination. Its first steps included relationships with the Renamo terrorist organisation during the late 1980s and early 1990s which opened the possibility of exploiting Cahorra Bassa hydropower in Mozambique. Eskom gradually supplied electricity to Zimbabwe, which had fallen into payment arrears; the Zimbabwe Electricity Supply Authority uses Eskom management to run the main thermal power plant at Hwange in what is viewed as a precursor to privatisation. Eskom's vision of a regional power grid extends to the notion - attractive in theory - of installing Congo River turbines in run-of-the-river settings (i.e., without the need for dams). Eskom engineers estimate that it would be economically viable to export power as far north as Italy and as far south as Cape Town. The problem, as discussed repeatedly above and below, is the subimperial character of these kinds of interventions, and the parallel problem of privatisation pressure on Eskom (from South Africa's Ministry of Finance). The bottom line for regional electricity utility coordination,

- Establish a task force to recommend priorities and implementation strategies for regional projects, including hydropower generation, transmission grids and gas pipelines;[185]

- Establish a task team to accelerate the development of energy supply to low-income housing;[186]

- Broaden the scope of the programme for biomass energy conservation from the Southern African Development Community (SADC) to the rest of the continent.[187]

(iv)Transport

114. Objectives[188]

- To reduce delays in cross-border movement of people, goods and services;

---

following water, is the opportunity for *profitable* sales. That opportunity cuts against the grain of service provision to low-income people.

185. A superior approach would be the establishment of regional strategies that have as a mandate not merely expanding energy supplies through additional projects, but rationalisation and more equitable sharing of existing generation capacities to promote more equitable and environmentally-appropriate development.

186. Electrification of low-cost houses would be a long-overdue step, since such a huge proportion of grid electricity generated in Sub-Saharan Africa is captured for the sake of extractive industries. This has been an especially acute problem in places like the Zambian copperbelt, the Zimbabwe-Zambia-Mozambique hydro-electricity catchment area, where a tiny fraction of rural people have access to the massive Zambezi hydro-electric generation, and even South Africa.

Unfortunately, however, the South African government's 1998 *White Paper* on electricity and Eskom's own business plan together militate against the supply of electricity to low-income households, on grounds that such supply is not 'cost-reflective' (the phrasing that both the policy and business plan rely upon to justify increasing commercialisation and eventual privatisation of Eskom). That remains the most fundamental problem across Africa, one which Nepad dare not concede, much less discuss.

187. This approach is a valid one, but like solar, is not considered sufficiently powerful to generate the levels of amps required to allow for substitution of traditional fuels.

188. These objectives are both valid and viable. However, in reality, severe limitations to intra-African transport have arisen due both to the market-led nature of transport and to African state policies that have

- To reduce waiting-time in ports;

- To promote economic activity and cross-border trade through improved land transport linkages;

- To increase air passenger and freight linkages across Africa's sub-regions.

115. Actions

- Establish customs and immigration task teams to harmonise border crossing and visa procedures;

---

proven extremely durable. South Africa, in particular, does not appear to be taking sufficient steps to rectify problems in these areas that are of its own making.

For example, an increasingly market-based philosophy to transport makes it unfeasible to break down spatial barriers effectively. Without sufficient state subsidies, attempts at gaining economies of scale in regional air transport arrangements - e.g., Air Afrique in West Africa and Alliance Air in Central Africa - were foiled, in part because South African Airways had predatory designs on the latter's Heathrow slot and therefore did not consider cooperation a genuine option, according to court documentation in a lawsuit against SAA. South Africa's post-apartheid government was similarly responsible for the termination of a decades-old passenger rail link between Southern Africa's two major cities, Johannesburg and Harare, because of a failure to cross-subsidise.

Most importantly, the authorship and leadership of Nepad comes from a country whose government's Home Affairs Department has a notoriously hostile relationship with immigrants from the rest of the continent, and whose people have fostered a world-class degree of xenophobia against alleged *makwerekwere* for stealing jobs - in a context where the post-apartheid government has adopted neo-liberal policies that resulted in approximately one-fifth of all jobs disappearing.

Although Pretoria did take the important step, in 1995, of giving permanent residence to hundreds of thousands of migrant workers who had lived in South Africa for many years, it did not subsequently relax any of the onerous visa requirements that contribute to the rise of illegal immigration. And the Department of Home Affairs and South African Police Service's own treatment of illegal aliens - from random arrests of dark-skinned people, to detention particularly in the notorious Lindela repatriation camp - suggests that key elements in the South African state will sabotage the intra-African components of Nepad. Rarely if ever have Nepad's leaders raised these issues as problems to be solved internally, and given that African state patronage systems are most acutely dependent upon control of borders, it is difficult to imagine similar problems being resolved elsewhere on the continent.

- Establish and nurture PPPs as well as grant concessions towards the construction, development and maintenance of ports, roads, railways and maritime transportation;[189]

- Promote harmonisation of transport modal standards and regulations, and the increased use of multimodal transport facilities;

- Work with the regional organisations to develop transport development corridors;[190]

- Promote PPPs in the rationalisation of the airline industry and build capacity for air traffic control.[191]

---

189. The role of PPPs in South African transport is highly contentious. As noted above, controversies have raged over toll roads, which are inordinately expensive for low-income people traveling on traditional migrant-labour routes; over rail rationalisation, especially closure of unprofitable trunk lines by Spoornet, leading to the death of numerous small towns dependent upon rail links; and over the establishment of highly-subsidised ports, especially at the Coega/Nqura deep-water harbour where R5 billion of state investments are planned to attract foreign capital for an Export Processing Zone which will create very few jobs. It may indeed be possible for private-sector entrepreneurs to assist in catalysing more effective transport arrangements, although South Africa's kombi taxi industry shows the myriad dangers of unregulated private control of a key transport mode. However, the fact that port, rail and road infrastructures are all characteristic of a natural monopoly (like electricity and telephone fixed-lines), means that it is against the public interest to turn these over to a private-sector monopoly for long-lease or fully privatised contracts.

190. The primary example of this kind of corridor is the Maputo Corridor linking Johannesburg to the sea. It consisted mainly of upgrades on roads paid for by expensive tolls. Two serious problems emerged for low-income people along the corridor: no provision was made for short trips along the corridor, and no alternative non-toll route was available; and the promised state roads and public works contracting/subcontracting opportunities for low-income people were, in reality, negligible. Moreover, the focus on transport development corridors concentrates economic activities in these narrow areas, to the neglect of people living away from the corridors.

191. As noted above, the extent to which the Private in PPPs becomes dominant is a guarantee of problems, as South African Airways demonstrated with its roles in the destruction of both a competitor (Sun Air) and an ally (Alliance Air). As court documents show in both cases, the drive for profitability led to predatory behaviour, leaving air transport consumers worse off in terms of choice.

(v) Water and Sanitation

116. Objectives

- To ensure sustainable access to safe and adequate clean water supply and sanitation, especially for the poor;[192]

---

192. This is an elemental objective. Without clean water, life itself is impossible. But beyond the rhetoric, there are reasons to doubt the seriousness of Nepad's commitment to provision of clean water.

Regional African evidence is presented in the next footnote. In particular, South Africa's own record is highly dubious. Promises by the ruling party of free lifeline water, made in the 1994 *Reconstruction and Development Programme* and the 2000 municipal elections campaign, were exemplary. But they are still not being taken seriously in most parts of the country, nor by key policy-makers in Pretoria.

Virtually all the lowest-income South Africans are still without a reliable, clean supply of tap water in their homes or yards. Although Pretoria claims that seven million people have been served by new communal-tap water schemes since the 1994 election, the reality is that a vast proportion of those schemes are not functioning anymore. The main reason that independent researchers have found for the breakdown of water schemes, is lack of affordability. (The alleged 'culture of non-payment' has regularly been refuted by objective surveys.)

One reflection of this problem is the recent finding, drawn from SA Human Sciences Research Council household surveys, that ten million of SA's 42 million people have suffered water cut-offs. The epicentre of the cholera epidemic that began in August 2000 - and that subsequently infected more than 130 000 people - was an area near the town of Empangeni, where a 17-year old free supply of water was converted to a metered system requiring a R51 (then US$7) connection fee, which thousands of residents could simply not afford. (Likewise, an estimated 40 000 diarrhoea deaths occur each year, unnecessarily, due to lack of clean, affordable water.)

As for sanitation, Pretoria has repeatedly conceded that since 1994 it has made practically no dent in the backlog of *18 million* people without decent sanitation. Again, excessive cost-recovery has been pinpointed as the main problem. Even in dense urban areas - many of which have hilly topography, high water tables and dolomitic soils - severe fiscal constraints mean that pit latrines are installed instead of water-borne sanitation, leading to extremely high E.coli counts.

In sum, water and sanitation is a sector in which the South African government brags about progress. In reality the South African experience has been so profoundly, self-consciously based upon neo-liberal policies, programmes and projects that it should instead be considered a disaster.

- To plan and manage water resources to become a basis for national and regional co-operation and development;[193]

While the recent commitments to free lifeline water may mitigate some damage in future, they are not being extended to South Africa's poorest people, who remain disconnected. In many cases where household water connections for low-income people do exist, arrears on water (or other municipal) bills have been used as grounds to disqualify households from receiving the free lifeline water. Water cut-offs still occur regularly, with the approval of Pretoria's water minister and leading bureaucrats.

193. In a variety of areas, African regional water programmes and related international coordination of water are already underway, *but generally according to neo-liberal principles* (with the close cooperation with or facilitation by the World Bank):

- the World Water Forum, co-chaired by the World Bank and UN Development Programme, which moved most decisively in its 2000 Hague meeting towards the commodification of water;
- the Global Water Partnership, which has the mandate of developing networks and knowledge for water resources management, and is based in Stockholm;
- the Water and Sanitation Program, a 20-year old partnership hosted by the World Bank, to improve the access of poor people to water and sanitation services;
- the Business Partnership for Development, hosted by the NGO Wateraid in London, to develop innovative mechanisms for ensuring that private water contracts serve the needs of the poor; and
- the International Program for Technological Research in Irrigation and Drainage, hosted by the FAO in Rome, which has the objective of developing innovative technologies for irrigation and drainage.

In relation to Africa in particular, the Water Utilities Partnership, also facilitated by the World Bank, issued a 'Kampala Statement' in March 2001. The Kampala Statement derives the problems of unaffordable access to clean water/sanitation services (WSS) by most Africans from one fundamental cause, namely, African bureaucrats get the prices 'wrong': 'The poor performance of a number of public utilities is rooted in a policy of repressed tariffs which leads to lack of investment, poor maintenance lagging coverage, and subsidised services reserved for the privileged who are connected to the network.' The mandate for full cost-recovery and an end to cross-subsidies - with meagre subsidies allegedly to be available for poor people at some future date - follow logically:

- 'the poor are willing and have the capacity to pay for services that are adapted to their needs'; and

- To systematically address and sustain ecosystems, biodiversity and wildlife;[194]

- 'an increased role of the private sector in Water/Sanitation/Services delivery has been a dominant feature of the reform processes of African countries as it has been recognised as a viable alternative to public service delivery and financial autonomy.'

  Yet in making the case for privatisation, the Kampala Statement notably neglects at least three aspects of water commodification and privatisation that have been responsible for disasters across the world, including South Africa (where several key pilot water privatisation schemes have failed):

- the high profit rate extractions, in hard currency, typically demanded by transnational corporations;
- the change in the incentive structure of water supply once private suppliers begin operating (especially in relation to pricing); and
- the difficulty of a private supplier recognising and internalising positive socio-environmental externalities.

Moreover, one of the most important issues associated with water resource management - abuse of water by large-scale agro-corporate irrigation and wealthy consumers - is barely remarked upon, and the word 'conservation' is only used once, in passing. Politically, the Kampala Statement is extremely naive - or disingenuous: 'Labour can also be a powerful ally in explaining the benefits of the reform to the general public. It is essential therefore that the utility workers themselves understand and appreciate the need for the reform.' The Kampala Statement's bottom line: 'an increased role of the private sector in WSS delivery has been a dominant feature of the reform processes of African countries as it has been recognised as a viable alternative to public service delivery and financial autonomy.' (Water Utilities Partnership [2001], 'Kampala Statement,' World Bank, Washington, DC, 14 March.)

194. Although South Africa's 1998 *Water Act* and key programmes such as 'Working for Water' have indeed moved to some extent towards an 'environmental reserve' for the preservation of biodiversity and the ecological integrity of river basins, there remain many areas of water-related environmental problems that are getting worse, not better:

- pollution of surface and ground water;
- the large forestry plantations which have expanded unsustainably across wetlands and water catchments;
- the acceptance in Pretoria of genetically modified plants and foodstuffs; and
- other manifestations of weak environmental stewardship.

- To co-operate on shared rivers among member states;[195]
- To effectively address the threat of climate change;[196]

---

195. South Africa's role in the Southern Africa region is particularly notable for lack of cooperation and unsustainable water development, as major controversies have arisen surrounding cross-border catchments and rivers:

- the repeated 2000-01 floodings of Mozambique can be attributed to lax South African environmental stewardship, such as the role of Mpumalanga forest plantations in changing water run-off patterns, and controversial dam release strategies in rivers upstream of Mozambique;
- Africa's largest dam system, the Lesotho Highlands Water Project (LHWP), drains water from the Senqu River for cross-catchment transfer to Johannesburg, but is enormously controversial on environmental, social and economic grounds;
- the LHWP will adversely affect water flows on the Orange River border between South African and Namibia, according to environmentalists; and
- periodic appeals are made to study prospects for the transfer of water from the Zambezi River to Gauteng Province in South Africa.

Rather than distorting natural water catchments so as to continue to allow Gauteng's hedonistic domestic and industrial consumers to waste water, Pretoria could have redirected human settlement patterns and new investment more appropriately to areas that have abundant water. Instead, in accordance with the neo-liberal, non-interventionist tradition of urban planning—it acquiesced to the inherited apartheid skews that have made Johannesburg the world's largest big city located nowhere near a major river.

Typifying the lack of concern about socio-hydroecological problems, Pretoria's 1995 *Urban Development Strategy* laid out policy principles which remain in place today: 'The country's largest cities are not excessively large by international standards, and the rates of growth of the various tiers also appear to be normal. Hence there appears to be little reason to favour policies which may artificially induce or restrain growth in a particular centre, region or tier.' Moreover, 'the growth rate is sufficiently normal to suggest that effective urban management is possible and there is, therefore, no justification for interventionist policies which attempt to prevent urbanisation.'

196. As discussed above, deriving energy from sources that generate global warming is highly controversial. The World Commission on Dams has recently documented the case that hydropower drawn from tropical dams causes very high levels of plant decay that last for years, often outstripping even coal-burning powerplants in C02 emissions per kiloWatt hour. Yet

- To ensure enhanced irrigation and rain-fed agriculture to improve agricultural production and food security.[197]

117. Actions

- Accelerate work on multipurpose water resource projects; for example, the SADC Water Secretariat's investigation of the utilisation of the Congo River, and the Nile Basin Initiative;[198]

- Establish a task team to make plans for mitigating the negative impact of climate change in Africa;[199]

---

the further development of hydropower is being planned, with large dams like Mohale (Lesotho), Maguga (Swaziland), Epupa (Namibia) and Bujagali (Uganda) blatantly violating Commission recommendations, including mitigation of global warming gas emissions.

197. Small-scale irrigation and rainwater harvesting systems can indeed support agriculture, but it must also be acknowledged that the twin goals of improving agricultural production and assuring food security are typically in conflict, because of the neo-liberal export-led growth model. It is no accident that, for example, during Zimbabwe's severe 1992 drought when maize production fell by more than 90%, the production of irrigated tobacco rose impressively. Corporate agribusiness too often has the resources necessary to pay both capital and recurrent charges for irrigation, leaving small farmers without sufficient irrigation. State policies exacerbate the bias, by prioritising the collection of foreign exchange through export-led cash crops, over the achievement of food security.

South Africa provides many examples of biased use of agricultural land, particularly in view of the historic apartheid-related subsidies to white farmers in the form of state irrigation schemes. It is notable that not only has there been practically no land reform - less than 2% of arable land - since 1994 because of the willing-seller/willing-buyer system adopted by Pretoria with the encouragement of the World Bank, but that progress in the expansion of irrigation to small black farmers has been even slower.

198. Unfortunately, the source of the Nile has already become the site of great controversy with the construction of the Bujagali Dam, and the Congo River remains fraught as a potential source of hydroelectricity given geopolitical problems.

199. As noted above, Pretoria has not rigorously tackled its own contribution to global warming, which - albeit not stemming in a major way from hydropower generation - is the worst in the world corrected for income and population size. Unfortunately, post-apartheid industrial policy remains premised upon the apartheid-era strategy of minerals extraction and beneficiation, which require vast amounts of electricity and whose impact has been to contribute to the glutting of already-saturated metals markets.

- Collaborate with the Global Environmental Sanitation Initiative (GESI) in promoting sanitary waste disposal methods and projects;[200]

- Support the UN Habitat programme on Water Conservation in African Cities.[201]

By way of mitigation, Pretoria has authorised the development of a Clean Development Mechanism prototype, in part designed by the World Bank, so that South Africa can help to pilot the idea of carbon trading. Consistent with the most questionable characteristic of the Kyoto Protocol, this effectively means that wealthy countries and transnational corporations can *buy* the right to continue destroying the environment. The alternative would be stronger treaties and agreements on the need to reduce the production of global warming gasses by moving to genuinely sustainable development strategies - which is off Pretoria's agenda and which will thus probably not feature in the Task Team's mandate.

200. As noted above, the South African government has been notably weak on its own sanitation initiatives, with deadly results. The continued failure to spend money on sanitation reflected, for example, an enormous requirement for co-payment by 'beneficiaries,' and hence another reflection of neo-liberal cost-recovery ideology driving public policy.

Moreover, the standards for sanitation have been extremely low, with Pretoria's main water policies dictating that lowest-income households will receive only a 'basic' Ventilated Improved Pit (VIP) latrine, even if they live in dense urban areas. VIPs rely on the soil on the site of the latrine to filter out contaminants from the water system, and treatment works for dealing with sludge off-site. Where the water table is high, such as in Cape Town, groundwater pollution due to pit latrines can be severe. In Winterveld, near Pretoria, the high water table allowed boreholes to serve as a reliable source of drinking water, yet the use of pit latrines by most residents resulted in dangerous groundwater exposure to biological contaminants such as fecal coliform bacteria and salmonella. On steep inclines, as in many residential areas of Natal, leakage to the surface can be expected, where people are directly exposed to the VIP sewage waste. Where the soil is excessively granular in character, even most of the bacterial contaminants that are filtered out well by most soils, along with the other contaminants, escape into groundwater. Even in wealthy Sandton, boreholes began to show lethal levels of E.coli in 2001, requiring the installation of expensive purification systems in households and schools. None of these environmental and public health considerations was taken into account by Pretoria's infrastructure planners, including the World Bank, in the early drafts (1994-96) which set policy directions.

201. Water conservation in African cities is desperately required where hedonistic consumption is the norm, typically by wealthy households and wasteful industries.

• Human Resource Development Initiative including reversing the Brain Drain

(i) Poverty Reduction

118. Objectives

- To provide focused leadership by prioritising poverty reduction in all the programmes and priorities of the *New Partnership for Africa's Development* as well as national macroeconomic and sectoral policies;[202]

Again, however, post-apartheid South Africa is one site to consider the opposite phenomenon, namely the refusal to promote tough 'demand-side management' conservation measures and instead promote construction of major supply-side water enhancements like the Lesotho Highlands Water Project's Mohale Dam for Johannesburg, and Skuifram Dam for Cape Town. In both cases, dam construction was chosen over the option of redirecting urbanisation patterns to more appropriate locations, and forcing wealthier Johannesburg and Cape Town residents and wasteful industries to conserve water. In both cases, community and environmental groups lobbied hard for demand-side management, but the Department of Water Affairs and Forestry in Pretoria overruled them, preferring to maintain relationships with the dam-building firms which were, at the very point decisions were being made, involved in corruption of authorities in the first major Lesotho Highlands Water Project dam. Instead of fast-rising household and industrial water tariffs that would have reflected the additional costs of dam building, most of the hedonistic and wasteful users of water in South Africa's largest cities have seen relatively low increases in their water bills. As even the World Bank was forced to admit, in an investigation of the Mohale Dam controversy, that whereas the overall cost of water had increased by 35% during the late 1990s, those Johannesburg households at the lowest tier consumption level were made to pay a 55% increase in tariffs, thus disproportionately paying the costs of building mega-dams whose benefits accrued largely to transnational corporate dam-building companies and to the hedonistic water users of Johannesburg.

202. This would be a laudable advance, but typically the stress on 'poverty reduction' is window-dressing for unchanged structural adjustment philosophy. Poverty reduction has also typically been incompatible with the privatisation of infrastructure.

In South Africa, where poverty has increased since 1994, attempts to 'prioritise poverty reduction' especially in 'national macroeconomic and sectoral programmes' such as the *Growth, Employment and Redistribution* programme were practically non-existent, aside from a small poverty-reduction fund which supports specific once-off interventions (such as job-creation through the removal of alien-invasive plants in both low- and higher-income areas).

- To give special attention to the reduction of poverty among women;[203]

- To ensure empowerment of the poor in poverty reduction strategies;[204]

- To support existing poverty reduction initiatives at the multilateral level, such as the Comprehensive Development Framework of the World Bank and the Poverty Reduction Strategy approach linked to the HIPC debt relief initiative.[205]

---

203. As noted above, women have been the main victims of the turn to neo-liberalism across Africa. Pretoria's own record includes grand vows about meeting women's socio-economic needs, but in reality, the establishment of national, well-funded programmes for women has been rare. Examples of Pretoria's approach to women's poverty include:

- a huge cut in the child support grant in 1996 (originally 44% but reduced to a 26% cut after church and social movement protests);
- the persistent failure of the state – as codified in even the Constitutional Court in 1999 – to give women (like Irene Grootboom and her fellow Wallacedene squatter camp residents) vital constitutionally-guaranteed services like housing;
- the failure (until April 2002) to give HIV+ pregnant women Nevirapine to prevent transmission to their infants and to give rape survivors anti-retroviral drugs; and
- the continuation of traditional-authority control over the fate of many aspects of rural women's lives.

204. This would be desirable, but if the process by which Nepad was drafted and consulted is any indication, the poor will be last to be empowered, and to participate in the formulations of programmes. This is not a new problem, of course, because the systematic *dis*empowerment of poor South Africans in the misnamed *Growth, Employment and Redistribution* programme (June 1996) was also confirmed by the process: 17 economists drafted the document, which was presented at the last moment to a few groups which have impoverished constituents (e.g. the Congress of South African Trade Unions and the SA Communist Party), but which were told by finance minister Manuel that the document was 'non-negotiable.' A similar phenomenon has been found in Poverty Reduction Strategy Programmes, as discussed below.

205. These type of initiatives have been termed by the Jubilee South movement as 'a cruel hoax.' They are fundamentally committed to maintaining existing power relations and the neo-liberal economic philosophy. They include only very slight adjustments to debt loads, and in return require lowest-income countries to further liberalise.

According to a May 2002 report by Jubilee Research in London (http://www.jubilee2000uk.org), 'the World Bank has admitted that its own Heavily Indebted Poor Countries (HIPC) Initiative is failing.' Because of overoptimistic export scenarios,

> the average ratio of debt to exports in 2001 for the 24 countries considered is now estimated to have been a staggering 280%, almost twice the levels deemed 'sustainable' by the World Bank and IMF. Even the four countries which had already passed Completion Point are estimated to have a Net Present Value of debt to export ratio of 156%. In total, 8 to 10 of the 20 countries which were between Decision Point and Completion Point at the time of writing can no longer expected to have a NPV of debt to exports at Completion Point of less than 150% (Benin, Burkina Faso, Chad, Ethiopia, The Gambia, Guinea-Bissau, Malawi, Rwanda, Senegal, and Zambia.)... For the first time, the World Bank is now admitting that its own initiative is failing: 31 out of the 42 HIPC countries are being failed by the initiative even according to the World Bank criteria.

Yet, the report continues, under the leadership of South African finance minister Manuel, 'The Development Committee of the World Bank has even gone so far as to say that the HIPC initiative is making 'sustained progress' in their Communique following their 21st April [20020] meeting in Washington. Such self-delusion is almost unbelievable.'

The additional costs of HIPC are also becoming evident. In Southern Africa, Mozambique's HIPC requirements included quintupling cost-recovery charges (user fees) at public health clinics, privatisation of urban and rural water supply systems, and the simultaneous liberalisation and privatisation of its largest agro-industry, cashew-nut processing, which destroyed the industry. President Chissano publicly complained about the low levels of debt cancellation and the pressure he was under to inappropriately liberalise the economy by the Bretton Woods institutions.

The South African government had a major role in creating the conditions for Mozambique's suffering. During apartheid, Pretoria sponsored the Renamo terrorist activities that caused an estimated million deaths and wiped out the majority of formal economic activity. Yet aside from the questionable Mozal aluminum mega-project investment – highly profitable to the main owners (Gencor in London and Pretoria's Industrial Development Corporation), South Africa's main post-apartheid contribution has been lending to Mozambique for self-interested reasons. The loans were used in Eskom's repair of electricity transmission lines destroyed by Renamo, and in the resettlement of Afrikaner farmers who could not adapt to South African democracy and who aimed to establish an apartheid-type enclave in Mozambique thanks to loans by the Development Bank of Southern Africa. Nelson Mandela's government did cancel illegitimate apartheid-era debt owed by Namibia, but refused to do the same for Mozambique.

119. Actions

- Require that country plans prepared for initiatives in this programme of action assess their poverty reduction impact, both before and after implementation;[206]
- Work with the World Bank, the International Monetary Fund (IMF), the ADB, and the United Nations (UN) agencies to accelerate implementation and adoption of the Comprehensive Development Framework, the Poverty Reduction Strategy and related approaches;[207]

As for the PRSPs, Jubilee South's Pan-African Declaration on Poverty Reduction Strategy Programmes in Kampala (May 2001, http://www.jubileesouth.net) criticised 'structural adjustment programmes (SAPs) in their various guises, particularly as based on the feminisation of adjustment to the further detriment of women and children.' Given that 'the World Bank and IMF are facing a deepening crisis of legitimacy,' the two institutions 'introduced PRSPs mainly as a public relations exercise to demonstrate a supposedly new-found concern for the poverty in the poorest countries of the South, and to prove that they have a genuine desire to see the people of these countries 'participating' in finding solutions to their poverty.' The Declaration argued that,

PRSPs represent nothing other than yet another attempt by the World Bank and the IMF to continue imposing their structural adjustment programmes on the people of our countries. In fact, the PRSPs will result in an even more comprehensive control by the IMF and World Bank - not only over financial and economic policies but over every aspect and detail of all our national policies and programmes. This will entrench the continuation of IMF and World Bank control over our countries, and contribute to the continuation of the global power relations, in which the rich overwhelmingly concentrated in the North dominate the South and the whole world.

206. This would be an improvement, but once again the record of Pretoria is wanting. As one reflection of failure to publicise or monitor poverty, the *Growth, Employment and Redistribution* programme contained all manner of detailed targets for budget deficit ratios, inflation and investment - which are of greatest concern to bankers who monitor state populism and spending - but *no* statistics for poverty reduction or redistribution. Notwithstanding criticism on this point, the Reserve Bank continued to neglect the collection of such statistics or the targeting of poverty and inequality.

207. A more appropriate approach would be to follow the lead of Jubilee South's 'Pan-African Declaration on PRSPs':

...on the basis of the long, deep and painful experiences of SAPs in our countries, we reject:

- **SAPs in any form or with any cosmetic 'adjustments';**
- **PRSPs as the latest version of structural adjustment;**
- **HIPC initiative as debt 'relief';**
- **all SAP-HIPC-PRSP conditionalities in order to be granted debt 'relief';**
- **'relief' of only a portion of debt and continued repayment of the remaining debt which will simply ensure continued control and domination;**
- **any attempt to use our organisations to legitimise structural adjustment, HIPCs, PRSPs or debt 'relief';**
- **any further role or interference of the World Bank or IMF in our countries; and**
- **any further loans to finance HIV-Aids programmes which only serve to further indebt our countries, which increase our dependence on the institutional finance institutions, while millions of our people continue to suffer and die in the pandemic in our countries.**

On the basis of our review in this workshop of a number of experiences of PRSPs in countries in Africa (and Latin America) and on the basis of in-depth analysis and wide-ranging discussion, we note that:

- **PRSPs are located within the IMF and World Bank macro-economic framework and this is not open for debate. The poverty programmes are expected to be consistent with the neo-liberal paradigm including privatisation, deregulation, budgetary constraints and trade and financial liberalisation. Yet these have exacerbated economic and social crises in our countries.**
- **They focus only on internal factors and ignore the role of international/ global factors and forces in creating economic crises and poverty in our countries.**
- **The only aspects of our realities that are open to consultation are those 'outside' the macro-economic realm, and even the realisation of these is actively contradicted by the requirements and constraints of the macro-economic prescriptions.**
- **The neo-liberal paradigm is also not acceptable because it fails to explicitly locate programmes to tackle poverty and subordination within effective gender equity perspectives and gender frameworks. Mere gender 'mainstreaming' is totally insufficient as a remedy.**
- **The World Bank and IMF are manoeuvering to regain their legitimacy by offering poverty 'reduction' and debt 'relief' whereas we demand full release from all debt bondage and the total eradication of poverty.**
- **These so-called poverty programmes have been imposed on countries in a manner which ignores and replaces existing anti-poverty and**

- Establish a gender task team to ensure that the specific issues faced by poor women are addressed in the poverty reduction strategies, of the *New Partnership for Africa's Development*;[208]

- Establish a task team to accelerate the adoption of participatory and decentralised processes for the provision of infrastructural and social services.[209]

---

national development programmes. As such, they are an external intervention with little or no regard for national dynamics, and are an unacceptable intrusion. But they cannot easily be ignored given that countries have to implement these programmes as an additional conditionality even for the much criticised HIPC debt 'relief.'

The experiences of the functioning of PRSPs in our countries raise a number of additional concerns with regard to the involvement of organisations of civil society:

- The PRSPs are not based on real people's participation and ownership, or decision-making. To the contrary, there is no intention of taking civil society perspectives seriously; but to keep participation to mere public relations legitimisation;
- The lack of genuine commitment to participation is further manifested in the failure to provide full and timeous access to all necessary information, limiting the capacity of civil society to make meaningful contributions.
- The PRSPs have been introduced according to pre-set external schedules which in most countries has resulted in an altogether inadequate time period for an effective participatory process.
- In addition to all the constraints placed on governments and civil society organisations in formulating PRSPs, the World Bank and IMF retain the right to veto the final programmes. This reflects the ultimate mockery of the threadbare claim that the PRSPs are based on 'national ownership.'
- An additional serious concern is the way in which PRSPs are being used by the World Bank and IMF, both directly and indirectly, to co-opt NGOs to 'monitor' their own governments on behalf of these institutions.

208. As noted above, all evidence to date is that pro-women provisions such as these are simply not taken seriously, and have been reduced to lip service in documents, to meet the typical requirements of international donors which are themselves mainly interested in lip-service feminism.

209. Any such genuine efforts are welcome, obviously. But typically 'decentralisation' has become a byword for the passing of responsibilities to lower tiers of government, with fewer resources. As hinted at above,

(ii) Bridging the Education Gap

120. Objectives

- To work with donors and multilateral institutions to ensure that the IDG of achieving universal primary education by 2015 is realised;[210]

- To work for improvements in curriculum development, quality improvements and access to ICT;[211]

---

the field of water provision is typical. Even in South Africa, 'participation' occurred in neo-liberal water projects that relied on full-cost recovery, without options for recurrent subsidies to support low-income people's consumption. When a 'free' lifeline water promise was made by the ruling party in 2000, in the wake of an embarrassing and costly cholera outbreak, government bureaucrats ensured that the national politicians' promises were accompanied by no additional funding to allow municipalities to implement the free water. In both cases, an extremely high failure rate resulted.

210. The World Bank is an especially unreliable agency. The lead it took in April 2002 on education is disturbing given its damaging role across Africa during the 1980s and 1990s. During two decades of structural adjustment programmes, typically drafted in and imposed from Washington in exchange for new loans (used mainly to pay the interest on old loans), the Bank's double financial attack on the education system was top-down in the form of lower budgetary allocations for education, and bottom up in the form of user-fee requirements. The latter typically had a severe gender bias, as impoverished families scraping together fees would ordinarily invest in their sons' educations, ahead of their daughters. Official donor agencies by and large agreed with these schemes. It was only in 2000 when the US Congress expressly prohibited the World Bank and IMF from imposing user-fee requirements in education, that this damaging neo-liberal philosophy began to wane. But with the Bretton Woods institutions and donor countries together refusing to cancel debt – so that they can retain financial and fiscal control over Africa – the progress in this area is illusory, and in most countries the payment of foreign debt (often contracted decades before by dictators) outstrips the education budget.

Even in post-apartheid South Africa, where education is the largest budget item (at more than 20% of state spending), repayment of apartheid-era debt came very close to education in monetary terms, and compelled the authorities to increase user fees via decentralising individual schools' budgets. Inequality between schools in wealthy and poor areas has sharply increased, as a result.

211. These are fine objectives, but the likelihood of meeting them is slim, especially in low-income rural areas, under circumstances in which the broader macroeconomic, fiscal and infrastructural constraints discussed above are likely to remain.

- To expand access to secondary education and improve its relevance to Africa's development;[212]

- Promote networks of specialised research and higher education institutions.[213]

121. Actions

- Review current initiatives jointly with the United Nations Educational, Scientific and Cultural Organisation (UNESCO) and other major international donors;[214]

- Review levels of expenditure on education by African countries, and lead the process of developing norms and standards for government expenditure on education;[215]

- Set up a task force to accelerate the introduction of ICT in primary schools;[216]

212. This is a laudable objective, but will require specific increases in capital expenditure for secondary schools and recurrent expenditure for teachers' salaries, neither of which have been available in budgets determined in Washington. The World Bank's April 2002 commitment to education is based on primary (not secondary) schools so this power relationship is likely to continue. There is no indication in Nepad of how to get out of Washington's grip, and indeed Nepad generally allows for the tightening of Washington conditionality, and promotes the Washington Consensus institutions and ideology.

213. The emphasis on higher education is welcomed, especially after a decade in which the Bretton Woods institutions systematically downgraded universities from entitlements for qualified students, to a mode of elite-class reproduction, by insisting on subsidy cuts and extremely expensive student fees.

214. The international donors have generally been part of the problem in getting increased expenditures and different policies (e.g. moving away from user fees). This would have been an opportunity to have Nepad make the point that donor-driven education programmes will now be taken back by African societies, but it does not do so.

215. This would have been an opportunity for Nepad to commit to an *increase* in African educational expenditures, but it does not do so.

216. The lack of telephony and electricity in Africa make this commitment extremely hollow. South Africa is notable for failing to provide telephones and electricity (much less ICT) in a large proportion of its rural schools.

- Set up a task force to review and put forward proposals for the research capacity needed in each region of the continent.[217]

122. The key problems in education in Africa are the poor facilities and inadequate systems under which the vast majority of Africans receive their training. Africans who have had the opportunity of obtaining training elsewhere in the world have demonstrated their ability to compete successfully.[218]

123. The plan supports the immediate strengthening of the university system across Africa, including the creation of specialised universities where needed, building on available African teaching staff. The need to establish and strengthen institutes of technology is especially emphasised.[219]

---

217. Such a proposal might start by recognising existing research institutions and official national bodies, which themselves are generally in dire need of refunding. To move to the subregional level in a context of systematic disinvestment in research, is like trying to stroll before learning to crawl.

218. This paragraph contains no explicit 'actions,' aside from the tragic implication that to 'compete' requires an escape from Africa.

219. Strengthening tertiary education would be laudable. However, Pretoria's own higher-education restructuring is indicative of a neo-liberal orientation to universities and technical colleges, which stresses:

- an often irrational desire to rationalise above all else;
- the defunding of university budgets;
- the internal restructuring of universities in a neo-liberal manner (particularly in relation to outsourcing);
- the rise of for-profit 'universities' and foreign (especially Australian) institutions whose students seek emigration opportunities; and
- the collapse of many of the historically black universities.

Together these suggest that Pretoria has contributed to problems that will now have to be solved by Nepad, yet there is nothing in Nepad to provide any confidence that a more progressive, less neo-liberal, approach will prevail.

(iii) Reversing the Brain Drain

124. Objectives

- To reverse the brain drain and turn it into a 'brain gain' for Africa[220]

- To build and retain within the continent critical human capacities for Africa's development[221]

- To develop strategies for utilising the scientific and technological know-how and skills of Africans in the diaspora for the development of Africa

125. Actions

- Create the necessary political, social and economic conditions in Africa that would serve as incentives to curb the brain drain and attract much-needed investment.[222]

- Establish a reliable data base on the brain drain both to determine the magnitude of the problem, and to promote networking and collaboration between experts in the country–of–origin and those in the diaspora.[223]

---

220. This would be an impressive accomplishment. However, one of the most important aspects of preventing human-capital flight is to prevent financial-capital flight. The latter lubricates the former. The relaxation of exchange controls across Africa during the 1980s-90s has made the latter possible. Pretoria embodies the problem, because of decisions in 1995 to end the financial rand mechanism, in 1996 to allow R750 000 in individual offshore financial repatriation, and in 1998 to allow the country's largest companies to delist their financial headquarters from Johannesburg to London. Nepad does not make the connection, and therefore it will not solve the brain drain problem. (Only in paragraph 148 does capital flight appear, and exchange controls are never mentioned as a policy option that would serve as a barrier to capital flight.)

221. Again, this is a laudable objective, but no concrete strategies yet exist for doing so.

222. The use of the carrot in Nepad follows the deregulation of commerce and investment over a period of two decades. This was the period that the brain drain increased most dramatically. In contrast, there are a variety of appropriate 'sticks,' ranging from exchange controls to the bonding of students who receive publicly-subsidised education, so that they work within the country to pay back their debt to society.

223. This is a worthwhile initiative which, thanks to the internet, should be easy to carry out. But its danger is that it will increase opportunities for

- Develop scientific and technical networks to channel the repatriation of scientific knowledge to the home country, and establish cooperation between those abroad and at home.[224]

- Ensure that the expertise of Africans living in the developed countries is utilised in the execution of some of the projects envisaged under the *New Partnership for Africa's Development*.

(iv) Health

126. Objectives

- To strengthen programmes for containing communicable diseases, so that they do not fall short of the scale required in order to reduce the burden of disease;[225]

- To have a secure health system that meets needs and supports disease control effectively;[226]

- To ensure the necessary support capacity for the sustainable development of an effective health care delivery system;[227]

---

brain drain and not brain gain, if resources continue to exist in Northern professional, scientific and academic communities, and not in Africa.

224. Again, this is a worthy suggestion at first blush, but runs the danger of uncritically celebrating the transfer of knowledge from exiled Africans, even in cases where Western norms and practices may be inappropriate.

225. This is a laudable objective, but as noted in the case of education, the last two decades have witnessed the systematic weakening of African health systems due to underfunding and the imposition of cost-recovery provisions. The result has been particularly onerous for women and girls, for whom the decline in health care utilisation rates is most damaging in both personal and social terms.

226. This is an appropriate objective. The same objective exists in many South African policies, but whether Aids or diarrhoea or TB or cholera, the associated support systems and socio-economic requirements - e.g. lifeline water and electricity - for meeting needs and curbing the main diseases are simply not being provided to people who are too poor to buy them on the market.

227. Maintaining health system subsidies especially for impoverished rural clinics is obviously vital. Unfortunately, Pretoria has performed very poorly in this regard since 1994, and the difficulty in getting even simple essential medicines at rural clinics is evidence of the state's lack of commitment to its poorest citizens.

- To empower the people of Africa to act to improve their own health and to achieve health literacy;[228]

- To successfully reduce the burden of disease on the poorest people in Africa;[229]

- To encourage cooperation between medical doctors and traditional practitioners.

127. Actions

- Strengthen Africa's participation in processes aimed at procuring affordable drugs, including those involving the international pharmaceutical companies and the international civil society, and explore the use of alternative delivery systems for essential drugs and supplies;[230]

---

228. This is a powerful sentiment. However, it is also sometimes used as an excuse to lower state responsibilities. In the most important such initiative in South Africa, the water minister has recently attempted to disguise the state's notorious (ongoing) failure to provide adequate sanitation services, using health education as a diversion.

229. To target the poorest would require a radical reorientation of the public-private combination of health services, as well as dramatic increases in water, electricity, nutritional and transport services (amongst others) to the poorest people. Nepad contains no information to suggest that this is a genuine objective, and indeed its orientation to public-private partnerships in the provision of infrastructure suggests that the poorest will actually be ignored.

Pretoria's own class-apartheid system of providing infrastructure on an 'affordable' basis includes an income-segregated process for accessing water, sanitation and electricity, for example.

230. Judicious use of drugs – 'treatment' – is one of the most crucial ways to address disease, and it is important to highlight drugs at the outset, alongside disease prevention. The single greatest advance in acquiring medicines at an affordable cost was the withdrawal (due to international public outrage) in April 2001 of 39 pharmaceutical companies, from a lawsuit against the South African government. The lawsuit, had it been successful, would have prevented Pretoria from implementing the 1997 Medicines Act provisions allowing for parallel import, compulsory licensing and generic production of lifesaving drugs. But in the year following that opportunity, Pretoria *failed to take advantage of the withdrawal* and made no efforts to activate the Medicines Act clauses.

If this is the leadership that Nepad offers Africans in the vital area of medicines access, then progress will be nonexistent. Nepad does not mention the options available through the Medicines Act, or the provisions in the World Trade Organisation's Trade in Intellectual

- Mobilise the resources required to build effective disease interventions and secure health systems:[231]

- Lead the campaign for increased international financial support for the struggle against HIV/Aids and other communicable diseases;[232]

- Join forces with other international agencies such as the WHO and donors to ensure support for the continent is increased by at least US $10 billion per annum;[233]

- Encourage African countries to give higher priority to health in their own budgets and to phase such increases in expenditure to a level to be mutually determined;[234]

- Jointly mobilise resources for capacity-building in order to enable all African countries to improve their health infrastructures and management.

128. Africa is home to major endemic diseases. Bacteria and parasites carried by insects, the movement of people and other carriers thrive, favoured as they are by weak

---

Property (Trips) provisions which allow for patent violation in the event of a medical emergency.

231. The 'resources required' are infinite, of course. But Nepad could attempt to specify ways in which the UN Global Fund (targeting Aids, malaria and TB) would be utilised in Africa. But Nepad doesn't specifically mention this fund, nor the long-standing debate over the Fund's need to prioritise the financing of treatment.

232. Ironically, finance minister Manuel announced at the February 2002 World Economic Forum that South Africa would not participate in the Global Fund. Pretoria's leadership on HIV/Aids will likely be as great a disaster for Africa as it is for South Africa.

233. The $10 billion reference apparently refers to the UN's attempt to raise money for the Global Fund to address health crisis in *all* parts of the world (not just Africa). The more funding received, the better – but Nepad does not engage in the heated debates about where such funds should be prioritised, and who should control them.

234. The 'mutual determination' of health budgets harks back to the structural adjustment era (1980s-present) in which budgets are determined in Washington. There is no indication in Nepad as to what sustainable health budgets are and should be, and in view of the systematic destruction of public health system capacity and the rise of private healthcare options for African ruling classes, the lack of detail and vague references to external funds is worrisome.

environmental policies and poor living conditions. One of the major impediments facing African development efforts is the widespread incidence of communicable diseases, in particular HIV/Aids, tuberculosis and malaria. Unless these epidemics are brought under control, real gains in human development will remain a pipe dream.[235]

129. In the health sector, Africa compares very poorly with the rest of the world. In 1997, child and juvenile death rates were 105 and 169 per 1000, as against 6 and 7 per 1000 respectively in developed countries. Life expectancy is 48.9 years, as against 77.7 years in developed countries. Only 16 doctors are available per 100 000 inhabitants against 253 in industrialised countries. Poverty, reflected in very low per capita incomes, is one of the major factors limiting the populations' capacity to address their health problems.[236]

130. Nutrition is an important ingredient of good health. The average daily intake of calories varies from 2384 in low-income countries to 2846 in middle-income countries to 3390 in the Organisation for Economic Co-operation and Development (OECD) countries.[237]

---

235. The only 'action' implied here is bringing the diseases under control. But Pretoria's failure to address HIV/Aids, in part by promoting dissident analysis in South Africa's Presidential Commission on Aids, and the ongoing cholera and diarrhoea epidemics caused mainly by lack of clean water, suggest that Nepad's own authors are not serious about these problems.

236. This is an obvious point, but contains no information about 'actions' to be taken. Moreover, the phraseology here implies that individuals are responsible for their health status, which takes the burden off the state. Given that individuals' incomes are so low in most of Africa and that health status indicators have fallen so quickly during the era of structural adjustment, the logical conclusion is that market-failure requires massive state intervention, but Nepad notably fails to promote this conclusion.

237. Again, this point cannot be contested, but Nepad contains no information about 'actions' to be taken. If nutrition was taken seriously as a component in Nepad, some additional state interventions in basic food markets and in food-related subsidisation would be on the agenda. But it is not.

131. Health, defined by the World Health Organisation (WHO) as a state of complete physical and mental well-being, contributes to increase in productivity and consequently to economic growth. The most obvious effects of health improvement on the working population are the reduction in lost working days due to sick leave, the increase in productivity, and the chance to get better paid jobs. Eventually, improvement in health and nutrition directly contributes to improved well-being as the spread of diseases is controlled, infant mortality rates are reduced, and life expectancy is higher. The link with poverty reduction is clearly established.[238]

• Agriculture

132. The majority of Africa's people live in rural areas. However, the agrarian systems are generally weak and unproductive. Coupled with external setbacks such as climatic uncertainty, biases in economic policy and instability in world commodity prices, these systems have held back agricultural supply and incomes in the rural areas, leading to poverty.[239]

---

238. This information is correct, but again contains no suggestions about 'actions' to be taken. For example, if externalities associated with healthcare, water, sanitation and electricity were incorporated into national and local economic strategies, then increased subsidies would be a logical way to translate those externalities into real economic gains, but Nepad is silent about such implications. Likewise, were the system of national accounts in African countries to be recalculated to take into account the health-poverty linkage, and especially to calculate the importance of women's (unpaid) labour in maintaining the health of the society, it might make it easier to better compensate healthworkers and women, and to improve their status. Again, Nepad shies away from any such conclusion, and the document's lip service to gender equity is unveiled as mere rhetoric, when opportunities to improve women's wellbeing, such as this example, are ignored.

239. There are many confused references in this sentence. Genuine 'external setbacks' include 'climatic uncertainty,' but scientific evidence suggests that severe climate change can be attributed in part to disturbances caused by global warming, which is endogenous (and can be prevented) not exogenous (and accidental). If global warming is one cause of declines in agricultural productivity generated by floods and droughts, Nepad should call on the advanced industrial countries for solidarity with victims of global warming, including compensation for agricultural losses. The idea of the North paying the South its 'ecological debt,' however, is

133. The urgent need to achieve food security in African countries requires that the problem of inadequate agricultural systems be addressed, so that food production can be increased and nutritional standards raised.[240]

---

not mentioned in Nepad - notwithstanding its rising importance in international debates over debt cancellation and reparations.

As for 'biases in economic policy,' this phrase was typically used during the 1980s across Africa, as a Washington-Consensus justification for removing both state-operated agricultural marketing systems and subsidies on foodstuffs in urban areas. The ending of the marketing boards and subsidies together contributed to enormous suffering and to declining nutritional intakes.

The issue of 'instability in world commodity prices' is misstated. The overall trendline in African agricultural exports is negative, with the only instability represented by how far and fast commodity prices decline. Since 1997, when East Asia went into crisis, for instance, the prices of raw materials (cash crops and minerals) fell very quickly, but the trend began in 1973 with no sign of reversal.

Worse, many African countries suffer from reliance upon a single product for at least 75% of their export earnings: Angola, Botswana, Burundi, Congo, Gabon, Guinea, Niger, Nigeria, Somalia, Uganda, and Zambia. The only countries which diversified their exports so that they claim at least 25% of their export earnings from more than four products are the Gambia, Lesotho, South Africa, Swaziland, Tanzania, and Zimbabwe. Generally, across Africa, four or fewer products make up three quarters of export revenues. More than three quarters of all Africa's trade is with developed countries.

The logical implication of this declining agricultural commodity price trend - sometimes unstable but mainly quite predictable - should be to end African countries' dependency upon export-led growth based on raw materials. However, while Nepad occasionally talks of industrial diversification, its logic is very much towards the *increase* of agricultural exports. Yet there is no guarantee that even if European Union and US tariffs and quotas on agricultural imports are lowered or even removed, the underlying negative price trend of commodity prices will change. On the contrary, such a process could easily lead to even greater reliance upon export-led growth, under the influence of small cartels of middle-men corporations, which would have negative effects upon 'incomes in the rural areas, leading to poverty.'

240. This analysis is purely of a supply-side character. In other words, the assumption is that if agricultural producers improve their productivity and bring more food to markets, nutrition will improve. There may be some grounds for hope, but the past quarter-century of falling agricultural prices have done nothing to improve nutrition, given that the 1980s-90s also decimated the effective demand of both urban and rural consumers.

134. Improvement in agricultural performance is a prerequisite of economic development on the continent. The resulting increase in rural peoples' purchasing power will also lead to higher effective demand for African industrial goods.[241] The induced dynamics would constitute a significant source of economic growth.

135. Productivity improvement in agriculture rests on the removal of a number of structural constraints affecting the sector. A key constraint is climatic uncertainty, which raises the risk factor facing intensive agriculture based on the significant

---

In other words, if Nepad places its entire nutritional emphasis on supply enhancements, especially in a context of even greater ambitions for export-led cash-crop growth, the effect on most Africans could be a *worse* not better nutritional status.

241. When the analysis now turns to demand-side issues, it assumes that the increase in supply-side output will generate increased incomes. In doing so it abstracts from the problem of the past two decades of supply-side agricultural policies, namely that when the IMF and World Bank persuaded all Third World countries to increase their output of agricultural products for the world market, the volume certainly increased, *but the gluts in world markets caused the prices of exports to fall far faster than the volume increases could compensate.* This was especially true in relation to terms of trade, because since 1980, the value of a basket of sub-Saharan export products has fallen by 50% compared to import prices of goods purchased from the North.

The question of which African countries will produce 'industrial goods' is also of interest, but is unexplored in Nepad. Unfortunately, in the case of appliances, clothing, footwear and furniture (which higher-income rural people would presumably purchase more of once their incomes rise), the small-scale production capacity of the two key Southern African countries, Zambia and Zimbabwe, was decimated by South Africa during the early 1990s. The problems of excessive trade liberalisation forced upon these countries by Washington, and South African exporters' economies of scale, were temporarily but ultimately unsuccessfully countered by higher trade barriers. However, in turn, as South Africa lifted its import tariffs in 1993-95 once the apartheid regime signed the General Agreement on Trade and Tariffs, several industries - electronics, other appliances, clothing and footwear - were also devastated by cheaper imports, especially from East Asia. The logical implication is that Africa needs continent-wide and regional-scale industrial policies that include the protection and rationalisation of infant industries, and an explicit strategy to lessen uneven regional development so that the 'bambezonke' polarisation that has characterised industry in Africa can be reversed. These sorts of interventions are, however, anathema to Nepad.

inflow of private investment. Consequently, governments must support the provision of irrigation equipments and develop arable lands when private agents are unwilling to do so.[242] The improvement of other rural infrastructure (roads, rural electrification, etc.) is also essential.[243]

136. The institutional environment for agriculture also significantly affects the sector's productivity and performance. Institutional support in the form of research centres and institutes, the provision of extension and support services, and agricultural trade fairs will further boost the production of marketable surpluses.[244] The regulatory framework for agriculture must

---

242. This is a very important statement, justifying enormous state interventions especially where (as in Zimbabwe) there were enormous tracts of underutilised land held by large-scale commercial farmers. As noted earlier, however, Pretoria has been probably Africa's *slowest* post-colonial government to implement either land reform or irrigation programmes for small-scale commercial farmers. Government policies often explicitly prohibit increased irrigation for key watersheds like the Orange River (which in turn justified the redirection of the Lesotho headwaters of the Senqu/Orange River to Johannesburg). It should be added that irrigation never justifies the construction of mega-dams.

243. It is *essential* to develop rural roads and electricity, yet Nepad promotes Public-Private Partnerships to do so *without disclosing the source of the effective demand required to make such development profitable.* As a result, Nepad will probably result in the continuing rural neglect that South Africa has witnessed since 1994. Road systems are in much worse repair today than in 1994, because as the Departments of Transport and Public Works admit, maintenance budgets have been systematically cut, leading to deeper rural impoverishment. Highways that have received new investment are invariably privatised toll roads linking urban centres.

Likewise, the rate of growth of rural electrification slowed dramatically during the late 1990s, as the failure of low-income people to afford extremely high tariffs led to much lower electricity usage than the state power company, Eskom, had estimated. In short, if Pretoria is a Nepad exemplar on rural roads and electricity, Africa has much to fear.

244. An increased state commitment to these kinds of support networks would be enormously helpful. Of course, however, the trend is that Africa's agricultural research capacity has withered under pressures of privatisation, budget cuts and deregulation, all of which Nepad implicitly endorses. In addition, the rising global problem of biopiracy includes the patenting of agricultural life forms which are unique to Africa. Nepad is silent about transnational corporate penetration of Africa's biogenetic pools, and indeed South Africa has been one of the least regulated and dangerous settings for the production of genetically-modified foodstuffs.

also be taken into account, including the encouragement of local community leadership in rural areas, and the involvement of these communities in policy and the provision of services.[245]

137. Too little attention has been paid by bilateral donors and multilateral institutions to the agriculture sector and rural development, where more than 70 per cent of the poor people in Africa reside. For example, in the World Bank lending portfolio, credits to agriculture amounted to 39 per cent in 1978, but dropped to 12 per cent in 1996 and even further to 7 per cent in 2000. The entire donor community must reverse such negative trends.[246]

• The Environment Initiative

138. It has been recognised that a healthy and productive environment is a prerequisite for the *New Partnership for Africa" Development*.[247] It is further recognised that the range

245. Without further details, the 'regulatory framework' described here appears consistent with deregulation and decentralisation, in which, typically, more responsibilities are transferred from central government to lower tiers, with fewer resources. Pretoria's own record of decentralising unfunded mandates (such as free water and electricity) to impoverished rural areas, offers worrisome precedents.

246. The World Bank switched its overall loan portfolio from projects into sectoral and structural adjustment loans during the 1980s, which explains some of the negative trends in the agricultural portfolio. But more importantly, Nepad should have referenced the early 1990s Wapenhans report finding on the efficacy of World Bank rural development lending, which was below 50% even in cases where Bank staff applauded their work in evaluations as 'highly satisfactory.' The point is, that if World Bank agricultural sector lending was extremely ineffective, and if World Bank hard-currency loans for land reform and agricultural microfinance (e.g. to Zimbabwe, which failed spectacularly) were used to purchase land or grant credit in local currency – *yet left the entire society with a hard-currency debt to repay, with ever-declining currency values thus making the interest rates prohibitively expensive* (even when they were IDA low-interest loans), then the opposite conclusion should be reached than the one Nepad arrives at. Declining World Bank credits to African agriculture is a positive not negative trend.

247. A 'healthy environment' means one that is not dying, and that is obviously a goal no one can object to. A 'productive environment' has many different kinds of meanings, which might include strip-mined soil or a toxic-saturated piece of land or a switch from homegrown seeds to

of issues necessary to nurture this environmental base is vast and complex, and that a systematic combination of initiatives is necessary in order to develop a coherent environmental programme. This will necessitate that choices be made, and particular issues be prioritised for initial interventions.[248]

139. It is also recognised that a core objective of the Environment Initiative must be to held in combating poverty and contributing to socio-economic development in Africa. It has been demonstrated in other parts of the world that measures taken to achieve a healthy environmental base can contribute greatly to employment, social and economic empowerment, and reduction of poverty.[249]

140. It should be mentioned, here, that Africa will host the World Summit on Sustainable Development in September 2002, and that environmental management form the basis of the Summit. In this regard, we propose that the event put particular emphasis on the deliberations on this theme in the *New Partnership for Africa's Development*.[250]

---

genetically-modified plants, all of which may be immensely productive of wealth - while destroying the resource for future generations.

248. Nepad shies away from naming, much less making, tough choices about the exploitation of Africa's wealth, versus the maintenance of ecological integrity.

249. Again, without details about such successes, this appears to be so-called 'greenwashing' rhetoric. The far more likely outcome of Nepad is intensified penetration of transnational capital, and the further degradation of the African environment. Pretoria's own current strategies for exploiting its cheap energy, and that of its neighbours, in places like Mozal, Pande, Coega and others, confirms that environmental concerns - *as well as sustainable economic development and job creation* - take a very low priority in planning.

250. This is a good proposal, of course, but the harsh reality is that the run-up to the WSSD has included a leaked G-8 Environment Ministers' report which does the opposite of what Nepad calls for. It promotes the WTO agenda of hyperliberalised trade, and dishonestly claims that this agenda is consistent with environmental protection. Well-regarded international NGOs such as Friends of the Earth and Greenpeace have already warned that the WSSD will drive standards even lower than the original Rio Earth Summit, and that the role of the United States in particular will limit the possibilities for any substantive changes that would benefit the African or indeed global environment. Pretoria's own intermediary hosting role in the WSSD debates, and its own weak environmental record, suggest that this paragraph is mere rhetoric.

141. The Environment Initiative has targeted eight sub-themes for priority interventions:

- Combating Desertification. Initial interventions are envisaged to rehabilitate degraded land and to address the factors that led to such degradation. Many of these steps will need to be labour intensive, along the lines of 'public works programmes', thereby contributing to the social development needs of the continent. The initial interventions will serve as best practices or prototypes for future interventions in this area;[251]

- Wetland Conservation. This involves implementation of African best practices on wetland conservation, where social and ecological benefits are derived from private sector investment in this area;[252]

- Invasive Alien Species. Partnerships are sought to prevent and control invasive alien species. These partnerships are critical for both the preservation of the eco systems and economic well-being. Major labour intensive initiatives are possible;[253]

---

251. Desertification is a terrible problem, and public-works type projects with high employment content would be most welcome. But one of the major factors behind desertification - overcrowding of areas beyond the ecological carrying capacity - should be immediately addressed here, in view of the fact that such overcrowding often has its roots in colonial (and apartheid) land acquisition, dispossession and forced removals. Neo-colonialism allowed land and migrant labour systems to continue virtually unchanged in both extractive and settler-colonial settings. The subsequent neo-liberal-era transition from food cropping to cash cropping (often monocrops or timber, with adverse ecological implications) and later to game farming, has put even greater pressure on those rural lands which host displacees.

252. The need to preserve and restore wetlands cannot be denied, in view of their degradation due to commercial agriculture and forestry, and their crucial role as sponges during times of excessive rainfall.

Again, however, Pretoria's own leadership in this area is highly dubious. The drive to convert Mpumalanga and KwaZulu-Natal wetlands into pulp-timber has destroyed many local eco-systems, according to environmentalists who have campaigned against the influence of huge agro-timber firms (Sappi and Mondi) over the Department of Water Affairs and Forestry.

253. In this one area, it is crucial to applaud Pretoria's leadership, through its Working for Water programme. However, concerns have been raised about the programme's extremely low wages and about the Department of

- Coastal Management. In protecting and utilising coastal resources to optimal effect, best practices are again suggested from which a broader programme can be drawn up;[254]

- Global Warming. The initial focus will be on monitoring and regulating the impact of climate change. Labour-intensive work is essential and critical to integrated fire management projects;[255]

- Cross-border Conservation Areas. This sub-theme seeks to build on the emerging initiatives, seeking partnerships across countries to boost conservation and tourism, and, therefore, create jobs;[256]

Water Affairs and Forestry's lack of institutional commitment to Working for Water, and thus its reliance on faddish donors.

254. The major debate over coastal and maritime management in South Africa is worth noting, namely how to deal with rapacious fishing industry businesses which would otherwise decimate the country's fish stocks. Internally, Pretoria has turned to a black-empowerment mode of authorising fishing permits, but in a relatively deregulatory context which has been taken advantage of by unscrupulous operators. In an international context, Pretoria should be praised for keeping Taiwanese, Spanish, Portuguese and other European operators out of local fishing waters. However, Pretoria has justified the expenditure of hundreds of millions of dollars on corvette ships and submarines based upon the need to patrol the boundary waters against such fishing fleets. (Radar and light aircraft are just as capable of monitoring and deterring illegal fishing).

There are concerns, as well, that although Pretoria has banned the use of 4x4 vehicles on sand dunes, other modes of rampant, environmentally-precarious coastal development continue unchecked, ranging from Cape Town across the luxury Garden Route, through the Eastern Cape and into the northern coasts of KwaZulu-Natal.

255. This note is a stunning cop-out on one of the world's most important issues. As noted above, South Africa leads the world on production of greenhouse gasses, corrected for income and population size. The 'monitoring' work on climate change is being done and should be expanded, but no details are offered on what 'regulating' means, much less on whether Pretoria will face up to its responsibility to *cut back* its contribution to global warming. The single detail – 'integrated fire management projects' – is highly unsatisfactory.

256. The cross-border conservation areas that Pretoria has put into effect, involving Botswana, Zimbabwe and Mozambique, appeared to be successful in their early stages. However, the Mozambican case was suddenly thrown into controversy in April 2002, as noted below.

- Environmental Governance. This relates to the securing of institutional, legal, planning, training and capacity-building requirements that underpin all of the above;[257]

- Financing. A carefully structured and fair system for financing is required.

142. The Environment Initiative has a distinct advantage in that many of the projects can start within relatively short time frames, and they also offer exceptionally good returns on investment in terms of creating the social and ecological base upon which the *New Partnership for Africa's Development* can thrive.[258]

• Culture

143. Culture is an integral part of development efforts on the continent. Consequently, it is essential to protect and effectively utilise indigenous knowledge that represents a major dimension of the continent's culture, and to share this knowledge for the benefit of humankind. The *New Partnership for Africa's Development* will give special attention to the protection and nurturing of indigenous knowledge, which includes tradition-based literacy, artistic and scientific works, inventions, scientific discoveries, designs, marks, names and symbols, undisclosed information and all other tradition-based

---

Moreover, the full context of these have to be considered, including whether the booming eco-tourism market is sustainable, whether the replacement of farmland for game park farming has unacceptable social costs (mainly to farmworkers), and whether conservation is being used in a paternalistic way – as was common in colonial times – to prevent a higher-value use of land by local inhabitants. Typically, villages that border game parks and other conservation initiatives in Africa are amongst the poorest, notwithstanding some programmes (e.g. Campfire) that attempt to mitigate the extreme inequality, in which some of the world's richest eco-tourists come for a quick period to view wild animals who occupy land traditionally used by peasants for survival, with virtually no trickle-down of the $1000+ spent per tourist per day.

257. There are many other environmental priorities not listed in the initiatives above, which also deserve training. The key problem, however, is to develop policies and programmes that are capable of achieving environmental justice, and to have appropriate training that involves communities, workers, environmentalists and experts in proper proportion.

258. Disappointingly, no details are provided as to which projects Nepad refers to.

innovations and creations resulting from intellectual activity in the industrial, scientific, literary or artistic fields. The term also includes genetic resources and associated knowledge.[259]

144. The *New Partnership for Africa's Development* leaders will take urgent steps to ensure that indigenous knowledge in Africa is protected through appropriate legislation. They will also promote its protection at the international level, by working closely with the World Intellectual Property Organisation (WIPO).[260]

• Science and Technology Platforms

145. Objectives[261]

- To promote cross-border co-operation and connectivity by utilising knowledge currently available in existing centres of excellence on the continent;

- To develop and adapt information collection and analysis capacity to support productive activities as well as for exports;

- To generate a critical mass of technological expertise in targeted areas that offer high growth potential, especially in biotechnology and natural sciences;

---

259. As noted above, the record of South Africa's own Department of Agriculture on genetically modified plant life is highly contentious.

260. It is important to have as an objective the protection of indigenous knowledge and other forms of what is often termed 'local content' from commodification, distortion and expropriation, and to thereby offer knowledge, culture and entertainment alternatives to mind-numbing international commercial processes. However, Nepad should address, frankly, how it will fight the formidable forces arrayed against any such effort, especially in the World Trade Organisation's TRIPS provisions, where local-content rules and regulations have been declared WTO-illegal. Nepad contains no information that would give confidence in African leaders ability to contest these one-sidedly 'free-trade' dynamics.

261. These objectives are excellent (to the extent that they are not simply tautological). For example, there are many such centres of organic research, especially where technologies are being adapted to local conditions. Nepad should identify these, and provide information about how they can be supported, particularly in light of the threat by transnational corporations to capture knowledge through TRIPS, ranging from new pharmaceutical products to development of software (to cite two issues that have been hotly contested in South Africa).

- To assimilate and adapt existing technologies to diversify manufacturing production.

146. Actions

- Establish regional co-operation on product standards development and dissemination, and on geographic information systems (GIS);[262]

- Develop networks among existing centres of excellence, especially through the Internet, for cross-border staff exchanges and training programmes, and develop schemes to assist displaced African scientists and researchers;[263]

- Work with UNESCO, the Food and Agriculture Organisation (FAO), and other international organisations to harness biotechnology in order to develop Africa's rich biodiversity and indigenous knowledge base by improving agricultural productivity and developing pharmaceutical products;[264]

- Expand geo-science research to enhance the exploitation of the mineral wealth of the African continent;[265]

262. This would be helpful, if Nepad clarified areas where the African regional standards - including GIS mapping - are notably different than those prevailing in international settings. It is not clear if the African standards would be higher or lower, or why they should be different, i.e., why Africa should have the burden of reinventing the wheel. If the provisions for science and technology in international standardisation systems reflect transnational corporate interests and agendas, this should be stated and clarified.

263. The difficulty in getting all appropriate researchers onto fast-speed internet connections should be obvious; and is discussed above in the section on ICT dissemination.

264. As noted above, Nepad should honestly confront the forces of transnational corporate capital that are already making such a strategy extremely difficult. If the strategy then entails a major attempt to acquire 'exemption' clauses from the WTO (as exists for medical emergencies in TRIPS), the need for organising international solidarity (as with ACT UP and Medicins sans Frontieres on anti-retroviral drug access) should be clearly stated. The FAO and UNESCO simply do not have sufficient power to protect Africa from voracious transnational corporations. In addition, Nepad's faith that biotechnology can be harnessed should be rejected, given its dangers and given the weak role of regulation in South Africa itself.

265. As noted above, this may or may not be a wise economic development strategy, and should not be so blithely promoted. If Nepad did ultimately advocate a more thorough-going exploitation of minerals, what conditions

- Establish and develop skills-based product engineering and quality control to support diversification in manufacturing.[266]

C. MOBILISING RESOURCES

• The Capital Flows Initiative

147. To achieve the estimated 7 per cent annual growth rate needed to meet the IDGs – particularly, the goal of reducing by half the proportion of Africans living in poverty by the year 2015 – Africa needs to fill an annual resource gap of 12 per cent of its GDP, or US$64 billion.[267] This will require

---

should prevail so that the existing processes of *under*development, caused by transnational mining capital, are not amplified? Nepad owes Africans an analysis of the international market conditions for minerals now and in the near future (very gloomy), the socio-environmental costs of mining (very high) and the potential for keeping non-renewable resources within African possession for longer, in the event that more productive and less environmentally-destructive extraction techniques emerge in coming years. Sustainable development, after all, is generally considered to entail a respect for future generations' inheritance of resources, rather than merely their 'enhanced exploitation' in the short run.

266. Diversification in manufacturing is a necessary ambition. However, aside from this suggestion that more skills are needed, there are no other hints in Nepad that the underlying processes that have led to African *de*industrialisation will be reversed.

267. Regrettably, Nepad offers no grounds for believing that the calculations of 7% growth, $64 billion in resource flows and halving the population of poor Africans living in poverty are anything more than thumbsuck guesses.

Recall the last set of thumbsucks within a medium-term economic strategy emanating from Pretoria: the June 1996 *Growth, Employment and Redistribution* document whose macroeconomic model combined those of the World Bank, Reserve Bank and several others in South Africa. The *Gear* model predicted that growth would reach a steady 6% by 2000, but instead - even after a positive 1%+ rejigging of growth figures by the official statistical agency - the rates of GDP increase from 1996-2000 were 3.2%, 1.7%, 0.7%, 1.9% and 3.0% (i.e., net negative per capita GDP growth). Manufacturing output in particular went sharply negative in 1998-99. Instead of achieving 126,000 new jobs in 1996, rising to 400,000 new jobs per year in 2000, as predicted in the June 1996 model, the actual job creation figure in 1996 was *negative* 71,000, and more than half a million jobs were lost in subsequent years. Poverty and inequality also soared during the late 1990s.

increased domestic savings, as well as improvements in the public revenue collection systems. However, the bulk of the needed resources will have to be obtained from outside the continent.[268] The *New Partnership for Africa's Development* focuses on debt reduction and ODA as complementary external resources required in the short to medium term, and addresses private capital flows as a longer-term concern. A basic principle of the Capital Flows Initiative is that improved governance is a necessary requirement for increased capital flows, so that participation in the Economic and Political Governance Initiatives is a prerequisite for participation in the Capital Flows Initiative.[269]

(i) Increasing domestic resource mobilisation

148. To achieve higher levels of growth and more effective poverty reduction, Africa needs to mobilise additional resources, both domestic and foreign. Domestic resources include national savings by firms and households, which need to

---

But perhaps of greatest importance in the comparison with Nepad, *Gear*'s ambitions for direct investment by both foreign and domestic capital were not only foiled, but during several years there was distinctly *negative* net investment by both foreigners and South Africans. In other words, the authors of both *Gear* and Nepad have some explaining to do, about how they vastly overestimated both the performance of the South African economy and interest by foreign/domestic investors, and why the same problem won't happen again. (The explanation must transcend blame upon the East Asian crisis, because all the negative trends were evident prior to mid-1997.)

268. This is a dubious proposition, given both existing international realities and the need for Africa to capture and recycle its own resources. Most African countries are net creditors to the North, if capital flight is taken into consideration. South African financial institutions have become a major part of this problem, given that from the early 1990s they opened offices in the Cayman Islands, Jersey, Guernsey, Panama, the Isle of Wight, Zurich and other hot-money centres.

269. As noted above, whether or not the various countries which have had unfree, unfair elections since 2001 - Tanzania, Madagascar, Zambia, Zimbabwe and Congo-Brazzaville, to name the highest profile - will disqualify themselves from participation in Nepad is beside the point. The unveiling of Nepad leaders Mbeki and Obsanjo as uncommitted to good political governance occurred in March 2002, when both went out of their way to give the impression that the Zimbabwe elections were 'legitimate.'

be substantially increased.[270] In addition, more effective tax collection is needed to increase public resources, as well as the rationalising of government expenditures. A significant proportion of their domestic savings is lost to African countries as a result of capital flight. This can only be reversed if African economies become attractive locations for residents to hold their wealth.[271] Therefore, there is also an urgent need to

270. This is no doubt true, but in the classical 20th century debate in economics over what comes first, income or savings, Nepad appears to be taking the typical monetarist route, which is to try to increase savings extraction (typically through higher interest rates) and then expect higher savings to translate into higher investment. That philosophy underpinned the monetary policy associated with the Washington Consensus during the 1980s and 1990s, and in most African and other Third World countries led to the adoption of the highest interest rates in recorded history by 'independent' central banks (typically under the thumb of Washington even when it came to appointment of top personnel). But savings typically did not increase, since financial liberalisation led to both capital flight and a string of banking-sector crises across Africa, and even where some new savings were drawn into formal financial institutions this was no guarantee of reinvestment in productive activities.

South Africa is a case in point, because of its wild deregulation of the financial sector beginning a decade before the country was liberated from apartheid. Unfortunately, instead of reregulating South African banks, the ruling party continued the deregulation: increased the interest rate (beginning in March 1995) to unprecedented real (after-inflation) levels; oversaw a string of important small/medium bank failures which left depositors without resources; failed to regulate the burgeoning microfinance sector and thus allowed the near-collapse of the industry (including runs on much larger banks with microfinance subsidiaries); and witnessed the *dis*saving of hundreds of thousands of working-class people whose bank savings accounts were too small for the major commercial banks to warrant holding. When the large banks closed offices in low-income areas, 'redlined' desegregating neighbourhoods and townships, terminated the bank accounts of low-income workers, and refused to open accounts of informal-sector workers (or anyone without a payslip), Pretoria watched idly, refusing to intervene. So in all respects, it is worrisome to see Nepad's emphasis on increasing savings as a strategy for investment, given the recent appalling performance of financial regulation in even the most sophisticated banking market, South Africa.

271. Since currency volatility and unsafe banking systems mean that in the near future, Africa will *not* be an attractive place for elites to hold money, there is only one solution to capital flight: controls. The controls need to occur in both the source country, as well as in the international financial markets. The latter markets – especially hot money centres like

create conditions that promote private sector investments by both domestic and foreign investors.[272] Furthermore, there are other resources which can be mobilised within Africa, while, at the same time, requesting the developed countries to pledge their Treasury Bills to finance the Plan. By so doing they would not directly commit their liquid assets.[273] Finally,

---

Zurich, Panama, the Cayman Islands, Bahamas and several others - were perpetually 'ungovernable,' it was always claimed. As a result, African capital flight money parked in the French, British, Belgian, Portuguese and South African bank subsidiaries located in hot money centres, were always alleged to be beyond regulation and repatriation. However, three events changed this conventional wisdom recently, which Nepad should logically have celebrated: a) the Swiss banks' looting of Holocaust victims' accounts was uncovered internally, and world opinion forced the banks to open their books; b) campaigns against the Odious Debt that has been owed by post-dictatorship countries as varied as the Philippines, Haiti, Nigeria and South Africa, have meant that some progress in identifying illegal capital flight is being made, and Swiss and London banks are being held to account for laundering Third World elites' stolen assets; and c) the terrorists responsible for the September 11 attacks on the United States have had their financial assets frozen in even the most obscure of the hot money centres, showing that if there is political will it is feasible to gain the transparency necessary to track much of Africa's stolen loot. The financial sanctions against Robert Mugabe and his Zanu elites may uncover more such information.

It is quite telling that Nepad neither mentions nor even considers, subliminally, the possibility of correcting capital flight by a) imposing exchange controls (e.g. of the sort Pretoria had in place until deregulation in 1995); and/or b) joining the global humanitarian campaigns to have dictators and corrupt elites return money that should actually be utilised for reinvestment within African societies and economies.

272. This same 'urgent need' has been articulated for decades, and every effort made to attract large-scale foreign investment has failed, with the notable exceptions of extremely corrupt governments in oil-rich Angola and Nigeria, which together have gathered the most foreign investment in Africa. Foreign investors in Africa have been notoriously *extractive* in orientation, only rarely putting down roots so as to accumulate capital in secondary and tertiary industries.

273. This particular innovation is only hinted at, and requires a great deal more information. If Nepad is suggesting that the Northern government bonds serve as guarantees, this is not dissimilar to existing World Bank/IMF financing, by which if Southern governments cannot repay their loans, they receive more Bretton Woods credits so as to pay the interest on old loans; the Bretton Woods institutions then go to Northern taxpayers for

we suggest the establishment of Special Drawing Rights for Africa.[274]

(ii) Debt Relief

149. The *New Partnership for Africa's Development* seeks the extension of debt relief beyond its current levels (based on debt 'sustainability'), which still require debt service payments amounting to a significant portion of the resource gap.[275] The long-term objective of the *New Partnership for Africa's Development* is to link debt relief with costed poverty reduction outcomes.[276] In the interim, debt service ceilings should be fixed as a proportion of fiscal revenue, with different ceilings for IDA and non-IDA countries.[277] To

top-up recapitalisations, which in turn lowers the share ownership in those institutions by Southern countries, which then have even less power to (allegedly) democratise the institutions. The Northern governments thus stand security, in effect, for more and more ineffectual lending to Southern countries. The entire system is kept afloat, to the great disadvantage of ordinary Africans and Third World peoples and environments, and Northern taxpayers. There is nothing particularly innovative in taking some of the taxpayer payments ahead of time as guarantees via bonds for further portfolio investments that cannot and ultimately will not be repaid.

274. The implication is that the IMF would have more power over African finance than it does already.

275. This departs fundamentally from the position of the main African civil society groups which work on debt issues, namely that there should be full debt cancellation plus reparations.

276. The problem of conditionalities on debt relief (or in Nepad's word, the 'link') is that the institutions with power to determine the linkages – the Bretton Woods institutions plus the major aid agencies – are not interested in poverty reduction (notwithstanding some new-found rhetoric). Institutionally, they are still interested mainly in liberalising Third World economies so as to improve prospects for Northern exporters, and promote export-led growth of Southern raw materials so as to lower input costs for Northern producers, at the same time as rolling over existing loans and aid programmes so that their own personnel stay busy.

277. These are artificial approaches to 'sustainability,' which reflect classical Washington-style attempts to shoehorn countries in very different situations, into a single formula. So many African countries have such variable sources of 'fiscal revenues,' with many deriving the bulk from donor countries, that the incentive structure will immediately go askew. The only such universal debt 'relief' formula that would work is total debt cancellation.

secure the full commitment of concessional resources – debt relief plus ODA – that Africa requires, the leadership of the *New Partnership for Africa's Development* will negotiate these arrangements with creditor governments.[278] Countries would engage with existing debt relief mechanisms – the HIPC and the Paris Club – before seeking recourse through the *New Partnership for Africa's Development.*[279] The Debt Initiative will require agreed poverty reduction strategies, debt strategies and participation in the Economic Governance Initiative to ensure that countries are able to absorb the extra resources.[280] In addition to seeking further debt relief through the interim debt strategy set out above, the *New Partnership for Africa's Development* leadership will establish a forum in which African countries will share experience and mobilise for the improvement of debt relief strategies.[281]

278. This suggests that leaders like Mbeki, Obsanjo and Bouteflika will suddenly adopt sufficiently powerful strategies and tactics to achieve remarkable negotiating outcomes that two decades of struggles have failed to achieve. Yet Nepad offers no clues about the power relationship changes that will be required to assure a positive outcome. Moreover, all prior evidence of renegotiation of South African, Nigerian and Algerian debt does not give confidence that Nepad's leaders have a record of success to build upon. The repayment of loans taken out by the odious apartheid and Abacha regimes, for instance, suggests that the South African and Nigerian governments are actually quite weak negotiators.

279. This chronology of debt-relief begging assures a degree of African disempowerment that the North will look upon favourably.

280. This is an extraordinary assumption, namely that Africans who are losing 20% and more of their export earnings to repaying illegitimate debt, won't know how to use that funding, at a time when budget cuts are still wreaking havoc across the continent's social sectors. While state capacity (e.g. the civil service) has certainly been devastated by the Bretton Woods institutions, there is no question but that restoration of subsidies on education and health (as two examples) would easily allow the rapid disbursement of additional resources.

281. This sentence is the one half-hearted attempt to suggest a collectivity of interest and power relations. But there is nothing in the behaviour of African ruling parties to date, to suggest that collective action will work under present circumstances. The last feeble effort of African ruling parties to protect their own self-interests was the OAU delegation's finding that the Zimbabwe election was legitimate, which was endorsed, in turn, by the South African and Nigerian governments. But a few tough words from Tony Blair and John Howard compelled the chastened Mbeki

150. Actions

- The *New Partnership for Africa's Development* heads of state will secure an agreement, negotiated with the international community, to provide further debt relief for countries participating in the *New Partnership for Africa's Development*, based on the principles outlined above.[282]

- The leadership of the *New Partnership for Africa's Development* will establish a forum in which African countries may share experiences and mobilise for the improvement of debt relief strategies. They will exchange ideas that may end the process of reform and qualification in the HIPC process.[283]

(iii) ODA Reforms

151. The *New Partnership for Africa's Development* seeks increased ODA flows in the medium term, as well as reform of the ODA delivery system, to ensure that flows are more effectively utilised by recipient African countries. The *New Partnership for Africa's Development* will establish an ODA forum of African countries so as to develop a common African position on ODA reform, and to engage with the Development Assistance Committee of the OECD (OECD/DAC) and other donors in developing a charter underpinning the development partnership. This charter will identify the Economic Governance Initiative as a prerequisite for enhancing African countries' capacity to utilise increased ODA flows, and will propose a complementary, independent assessment mechanism for monitoring donor performance. The *New Partnership for Africa's Development* will support a Poverty Reduction Strategy Paper (PRSP) Learning Group to engage in the PRSP process together with the IMF and the World Bank.[284]

---

and Obasanjo to agree that the 'legitimate' victor in the Zimbabwe election should be suspended from the Commonwealth for a year.

282. The World Bank, IMF and G-8 will no doubt be happy to extend the HIPC programme, so long as no African country takes the example of leaders of Zimbabwe and Argentina, and actually defaults, and so long as Nepad politicians continue to remove the default, repudiation and reparation options from the table.

283. The word 'may' reveals a) how onerous this 'reform' process really is; and b) the half-hearted character of the Nepad challenge to Washington.

284. Notably, in contrast, the leader of the respected NGO African Debt and Development Network (Afrodad) in Harare recently argued that 'aid

152. Actions[285]

- Constitute an ODA forum for developing a common African position on ODA reform, as a counterpart to the OECD/DAC structure;

- Engage, through the ODA forum, with donor agencies to establish a charter for the development partnership, which would embody the principles outlined above;

- Support ECA's efforts to establish a PRSP Learning Group;

- Establish an independent mechanism for assessing donor and recipient country performance.

(iv) The Private Capital Flows

153. The *New Partnership for Africa's Development* seeks to increase private capital flows to Africa, as an essential component of a sustainable long-term approach to filling the resource gap.[286]

---

is a tool to serve the commercial, political, economic and strategic interests of donor countries.' As a result, 'The donor creditor countries must keep all their aid and against it write off all the debt owed by poor African countries... The bottom line would be elimination of both aid and debt because they reinforce the power relations that are contributing to the imbalances in the world.' (Kapijimpanga, O. (2001), 'An Aid/Debt Trade-Off the Best Option,' in G.Ostravik (Ed), *The Reality of Aid Reality Check 2001*, Oslo, Norwegian Peoples Aid.)

See above for other critiques of aid and the PRSP process.

285. There is one Northern metaphor that captures the actions being contemplated: rearranging the deck chairs on the Titanic.

286. The issue of whether to support private capital flows to Africa is entirely dependent upon the character of capital accumulation that takes place as a result. It should be recalled that from the 1960s-early 1990s, the African National Congress called for *no* new fixed or portfolio capital flows to the apartheid regime. The reason was simple: transnational corporations and apartheid financiers were not only propping up the illegitimate government in Pretoria, but they were also making profits from oppression. Obviously with the change in government in 1994, South Africa was no longer a place to make profits from oppression, in the sense that the achievement of one-person, one-vote democracy was won. But just as obviously, there continued into the non-racial New South Africa many kinds of social relations that gave rise to enormously profitable investments during the height of apartheid: durable shopfloor racism, the migrant labour system, superexploitation of women, lax environmental and child labour regimes (especially in corporate farming), lax mining

154. The first priority is to address investors' perception of Africa as a 'high risk' continent, especially with regard to security of property rights, regulatory framework and markets.[287] Several key elements of the *New Partnership for Africa's Development* will help to lower these risks gradually, and include initiatives relating to peace and security, political and economic governance, infrastructure and poverty reduction. Interim risk mitigation measures will be put in place, including credit guarantee schemes and the strong regulatory and legislative frameworks. The next priority is the implementation of a Public-Private sector partnership (PPP) capacity-building programme through the African Development Bank and other regional development institutions, to assist national and sub-national governments in structuring and regulating transactions in the provision of infrastructural and social services.[288] The third priority is to promote the deepening of financial markets within countries, as well as cross-border harmonisation and integration, via a Financial Market Integration Task Force.[289]

---

regulations, dramatic cuts in corporate taxes (from 48% in 1994 to 30% in 1998) and a variety of other benefits to international capital.

Does capital accumulation take a fundamentally different form today in South Africa because the state is now controlled by a democratic government? Obviously the answer is yes and no. The same is true across Africa.

287. The single most important challenge to property rights in Africa, in recent years, has been the invasion of white-owned farmland in Zimbabwe. There are very good reasons, and some bad politics, behind the need for thorough-going land reform in Zimbabwe. Interestingly, Nepad authors saw Zimbabwe's constitutional property rights protections violated over an 18-month period in the wake of a failed willing-seller/willing-buyer land reform programme which Pretoria also adopted in 1994 (leading, similarly, to practically no land reform). The contradiction here, as in so many other places, is startling, yet Nepad makes no effort to resolve it.

288. The extent to which this privatisation capacity-building leads to actual outsourcing, management contracts and sale of public assets, remains to be seen. As noted above, international investor interest in South Africa's various post-1994 privatisations has been minimal, and South Africa is the strongest site on the continent for privatisation to find roots, given the large high-income population. In any event, for a variety of reasons noted above, the desirability of foreign investment in these sectors is highly dubious.

289. As noted above, the record of Pretoria in encouraging financial deepening was disastrous in relation to changing the distortions and biases – as well as protecting depositor funds – in some of the most

Initially, this will focus on the legislative and regulatory environment for the financial system.[290]

155. Actions

- Establish a task team to carry out audits of investment-related legislation and regulation, with a view to risk reduction and harmonisation within Africa;[291]

- Carry out a needs assessment of and feasibility study on financial instruments to mitigate risks associated with doing business in Africa;[292]

- Establish an initiative to enhance the capacity of countries to implement PPPs;[293]

- Establish a Financial Market Integration Task Force that will speed up financial market integration through the

---

important banks. The key barrier to achieving a more stable *and* equitable financial system is Pretoria's national Treasury, because its personnel are overwhelmingly neo-liberal in ideological orientation.

290. The South African legislative and regulatory environment became less onerous after 1994, leading to various financial disasters. In the sole area in which major lobbying for tighter regulation occurred, namely to halt discriminatory bank redlining, an extremely weak home mortgage disclosure bill was passed instead, with no changes whatsoever in financial sector consumer practices.

291. Notably, the enormous risks undertaken by African governments (and citizens and environments) in relation to the behaviour of transnational corporate capital - e.g., corruption, asset-stripping, transfer-pricing, the creation of dependency, the erasure of local culture, and the outflow of dividends and profits that far exceed inflows of new investment - are not flagged by Nepad.

292. To transfer investment risks from international capital back to home governments (e.g. through the World Bank's Multilateral Guarantee Agency programmes which are underwritten by Northern taxpayers) or even to African taxpayers, assumes that the merits of the investments made under such programmes are so enormous as to warrant the implicit subsidy. But this is yet to be proven.

293. Orders to privatise African infrastructure have been given by the Bretton Woods institutions for more than a decade. If countries have failed so far, it is either because the local power structure will not allow it, the assets are too run down to be of interest, or the potential new greenfield projects would operate at such a low level of maximum profitability so as to be unattractive. Whatever the reason, it is unlikely that the barrier has been 'capacity' problems in African governments.

establishment of an international standard legislative and regulatory framework and the creation of a single African trading platform.[294]

- Equally important, however, especially in the short to medium term, is the need for additional ODA and debt reduction. Additional ODA is required to enable least developed countries to achieve the international development goals, especially in the areas of primary education, health and poverty eradication. Further debt reduction is also crucial. The enhanced Highly Indebted Poor Countries (HIPC) debt relief initiative still leaves many countries within its scope with very high debt burdens, hence the need to direct more resources towards poverty reduction. In addition, there are countries not included in the HIPC that also require debt relief to release resources for poverty reduction.[295]

• The Market Access Initiative

(i) Diversification of Production

156. African economies are vulnerable because of their dependence on primary production and resource-based sectors, and their narrow export bases. There is an urgent need to diversify production and the logical starting point is to harness Africa's natural resource base.[296] Value added in agro-processing and mineral beneficiation must be increased and a broader capital

---

294. Given the weaknesses of African regulatory capacity and the fragility of most African banking systems (including South Africa's), this is an extremely dangerous proposition. 'Bigger' does not mean 'better' when it comes to bank regulation, and indeed it is most likely that both African and international banks will manipulate what are bound to be very weak cross-border financial regulations, as did the Bank of Credit and Commerce International a decade ago.

295. This point is interesting, and probably refers to Nigeria, which has (unsuccessfully) asked for debt cancellation in part because of the Odious Debt inheritance from prior military regimes.

296. It is absolutely true that diversification is urgently needed, but the *worst* place to start is the South African-style minerals beneficiation model, for all the reasons argued above. Instead, the best place to start is an economics strategy aimed at meeting people's needs for water, electricity, housing, public works opportunities, other consumption goods and many other examples of goods and services which also have economic benefits. This is the *opposite* of the industrial strategy pursued by the South African government.

goods sector developed, through a strategy of economic diversification based on inter-sectoral linkages.[297] Private enterprise must be supported, both micro-enterprises in the informal sector and small and medium enterprises in the manufacturing sector, which are principal engines of growth and development. Governments should remove constraints to business activity and encourage the creative talents of African entrepreneurs.[298]

157. Objectives[299]

- To improve the productivity of agriculture, with particular attention to smallscale and women farmers;

- To ensure food security for all people and increase the access of the poor to adequate food and nutrition;

- To promote measures against natural resource degradation and encourage production methods that are environmentally sustainable;

- To integrate the rural poor into the market economy and provide them with better access to export markets;

- To develop Africa into a net exporter of agricultural products;

- To become a strategic player in agricultural science and technology development.

297. The theory of economic linkage is correct, but it is highly dubious to begin this strategy from minerals and the capital goods sector, when so many basic needs goods can be more readily produced to meet needs, with more labour intensity and hence greater multipliers, and less foreign dependency and hence far less foreign debt.

298. While many patronage-based African states have extremely onerous regulatory constraints, the lifting of burdens is also associated with a power shift that disempowers workers and endangers environments. It is important to note that Pretoria's record of supporting black small business has been a dismal failure, as even the minister publicly acknowledges.

299. While all these objectives have merit, the unlikelihood of them being adopted and pursued with vigour is reflected in the fact that Pretoria's own rural people have heard them before (in various land and agriculture policy papers adopted since 1994). For the majority of low-income people, rural living conditions have become objectively worse since the neo-liberal restructuring of agriculture was pursued, and since the capacity of the state to intervene on behalf of its constituencies was denuded (as state marketing boards were privatised).

158. Actions

- At the African level:[300]

- Increase the security of water supply for agriculture by establishing small-scale irrigation facilities, improving local water management, and increasing the exchange of information and technical know-how with the international community;

- Improve land tenure security under traditional and modern forms of tenure, and promote necessary land reform;

- Foster regional, sub-regional, national and household food security through the development and management of increased production, transport, storage and marketing of food crops, as well as livestock and fisheries. Particular attention must also be given to the needs of the poor, as well as the establishment of early warning systems to monitor droughts and crop production;

- Enhance agricultural credit and financing schemes, and improve access to credit by small-scale and women farmers;

- Reduce the heavy urban bias of public spending in Africa by transferring resources from urban to rural activities.

- At the international level:[301]

- Develop new partnership schemes to address donor fatigue for individual, high-profile agricultural projects;

---

300. These are all important actions, but the likelihood of them being pursued is reflected in the fact that in South Africa, which is home to Africa's greatest rural contradictions, none of the suggestions listed has been pursued with any degree of vigour by Pretoria.

301. These action items are all of very marginal importance. The main reason that African rural incomes remain low in relation to international forces, is the double problem of glutted global markets (associated with the export-led growth strategies foisted upon all Third World countries since the early 1980s) and the extremely high share of final product costs that are attributed to transport and marketing, but that really reflect oligopolistic power relations in international agricultural markets.

Although South Africa did not participate in 'Development Box' advocacy at the Doha WTO ministerial summit, there were many more ambitious countries that tried to transcend the marginalism displayed in Nepad. Amongst them were Nigeria (others were Cuba, the Dominican Republic, El Salvador, Haiti, Honduras, India, Kenya, Nicaragua, Pakistan,

- Developing countries should assist Africa in carrying out and developing its research and development capabilities in agriculture;

- Promote access for African food and agricultural products, particularly processed products, to meet international markets by improving quality to meet the standards required by those markets;

- Support African networking with external partners in the areas of agricultural technology and know-how, extension services and rural infrastructure;

- Support investment in research in the areas of high-yield crops and durable preservation and storage methods;

- Provide support for building national and regional capacity for multilateral trade negotiations, including food sanitation and other agricultural trade regulations.

(ii) Mining

159. Objectives[302]

- To improve the quality of mineral resource information;

- To create a regulatory framework conducive to the development of the mining sector;

Peru, Senegal, Sri Lanka, Uganda, Venezuela and Zimbabwe). Together, they condemned global agricultural trade rules in a manner that shames the limited actions and objectives of Nepad:

These talks remain dominated by the EU on the one hand, and the US and Cairns group of exporting countries on the other. As a result, these negotiations have ignored developing country concerns about the problems our small subsistence farmers are facing... Since before Seattle, we have been pushing for a 'Development Box' to be included in the Agriculture Agreement, but our proposal has been sidelined. The WTO is supposed to ensure equity in trade, but the present agricultural trading system in practice legitimises the inequities, for instance, by allowing the dumping of agricultural products from the North. (Friends of the Development Box (2001), 'Press Statement,' Doha, 10 November.)

302. Aside from more 'efficient extraction,' there is nothing in these objectives to suggest any real changes in mining production are required. The mining sector is responsible for awesome environmental and social damage, and minerals have been subject to great degrees of market manipulation, not least of which is transfer pricing by international mining houses. Some of the worst cases of these problems are in South Africa, where aside from a minor degree of racial desegregation and a

- To establish best practices that will ensure efficient extraction of natural resources and minerals of high quality.

160. Actions

- At the African level:[303]

- Harmonise policies and regulations to ensure compliance with minimum levels of operational practices;

- Harmonise commitments to ensure reduction in the perceived investment risk in Africa;

---

mine workers' safety and health law, virtually nothing has changed in terms of social relations on the mines. The most important mining houses in Africa, namely Anglo American and Gencor/Billiton, have relisted their primary financial headquarters to London, which means that the profits and dividends associated with the main African mining houses do not stay on the continent. Changing these relationships should have been the basis for Nepad's mining sector objectives.

303. As noted above, these are extremely mild-mannered ambitions, and it behooves Nepad's authors to try to address much more profound problems in the mining sector, including the objective of assessing whether minerals and petroleum should *not* be mined in the short term, so that in future years, future generations have access to those resources in ways that might be much more beneficial than is immediate extraction. Issues associated with beneficiation were raised above, and relate to the relative merits of supplying high volumes of cheap energy to transnational mining corporations, versus using that energy for more eco-socially-beneficial domestic (household) purposes. Finally, the issue of blood diamonds and the various other minerals-related conflicts in western, central and southern Africa, all remind us that there is more to the geopolitics of mining than merely extraction issues. For Nepad to ignore controversies over blood diamonds, coltan, oil and other precious metals, is telling.

Notably, unlike in the agricultural section just above, the mining objectives *do not include any changes to international minerals markets.* This is extraordinary, not only for the reasons noted above. In three of the major mineral groups (diamonds, gold and platinum) that South Africa and other African countries have come to rely upon, as well as petroleum, there exist periodic price fluctuations and market manipulations that suggest a lack of genuine competition. With diamonds, Pretoria has been particularly complicit in allowing a monopolistic arrangement (DeBeers and the Central Selling Organisation) to continue and indeed amplify its powers through its private delisted status. By contrast in the United States DeBeers executives are unable even to visit as a result of their outstanding arrest orders for anti-competitive practices.

- Harmonise information sources on business opportunities for investments;

- Enhance collaboration for knowledge-sharing and value addition to natural resources;

- Enforce principles of value-addition (beneficiation) for investments in the African mining sector;

- Establish an African School of Mining System (for the development and production of education, skills and training at all levels). This could be achieved through collaboration among existing schools.

(iii) Manufacturing

161. Objectives[304]

- To increase the production, and improve the competitiveness and diversification of the domestic private sector, especially in the agroindustrial, mining and manufacturing sub-sectors, with potential for exports and employment creation;

- To establish organisations on national standards in African countries;

- To harmonise the technical regulatory frameworks of African countries.

162. Actions[305]

- At the African level:

- Develop new industries, or upgrade existing ones, where African countries have comparative advantages, including

304. There have been numerous efforts over the past two decades to move African manufacturing up the value chain, in part by exposing small-run manufacturers to international competition. But the results have nearly invariably included mass deindustrialisation of small African countries' light manufacturing sectors. Nepad offers no basis for believing that results will be any different in the current, more hostile international climate.

Other objectives, on standardisation and regulation, probably relate more to international manufacturers' need for protection from bootleg products, which Pretoria takes extremely seriously (to the extent that long delays are experienced at the main South African port, Durban, as customs officials pore over every imported container in search of counterfeits).

305. The entire set of actions - at African and international scales - boils down to expanding bureaucratic institutions and networks that allegedly help 'standardise' and 'harmonise' the manufacturing sector.

agro-based industries, energy and mineral resource-based industries;

- Acquire membership of the relevant international standards organisations. Active membership would give Africa a stronger voice in these bodies, and would enable African industry to participate meaningfully in the development of international standards. Membership would also result in the transfer copyright of international standards to the national associations;

- Establish national measurement institutions to ensure harmonisation with the international metrology system. Such activities will always remain the responsibility of government;

- Ensure that testing laboratories and certification organisations are set up to support the relevant national technical regulations. Such organisations should be established, as soon as possible, where they do not exist;

- Establish an accreditation infrastructure, such as the International Standards Organisation (ISO) system, which is acceptable internationally. Such an accreditation infrastructure can be nationally based where the industry is strong enough to maintain it, otherwise regional structures should be contemplated. Appropriate funding to ensure membership of international structures such as the

---

A less imaginative and bold programme for Africa's reindustrialisation has probably ever been put forth by Africans. There is nothing of the economic-linkage strategy that transcends banal neoclassical economic characterisations of 'comparative advantage.' Even where one action calls on Africa to 'develop new industries, or upgrade existing ones,' it is only 'where African countries have comparative advantages,' and there are no details provided whatsoever about how and where these new industries can emerge or revive. Taken together, the African and international actions proposed represent merely the advanced industrialised countries' trade-promotion agenda, via the WTO, for Africa to toe the line on 'standards, technical regulations, measurement, tractability and accreditation' and to do so through 'information-sharing' rather than anything so bold as an actual African industrial policy.

Likewise in South Africa, trade and industry minister Erwin is regularly criticised for not having an industrial policy, and his interventions in economic development projects have been understood to disproportionately favour – with enormous taxpayer subsidies – international capital. (See, e.g. http://www.coega.com for Erwin's largest industrial development zone, and http://www.coega.org for a critique.)

International Accreditation Forum (IAF) and the International Electrotechnical Commission (IEC) should be made available;

- Pursue mutual recognition of test and certification results with Africa's major trading partners. Generally, this will only be possible if the framework for standards, technical regulations, measurement, tractability and accreditation are in place and can be shown to meet international requirements.

– At the international level:

- Facilitate partnership through the development of mechanisms, such as joint business councils, for information-sharing between non-African and African firms, and for working towards the establishment of joint ventures and subcontracting arrangements;

- Assist in strengthening African training institutions for industrial development, particularly through the promotion of networking with international partners;

- Promote the transfer of new and appropriate technologies to African countries;

- Develop and accept a best-practice framework for technical regulations that meets both the requirements of the World Trade Organisation's Agreement on Technical Barriers to Trade (WTO/TBT) and the needs of Africa. The technical regulation frameworks of the developed countries may be too complex for many African countries;

- Establish Standards Bureaux, which would provide the industry and government with the necessary information on international, regional and national standards, thereby facilitating market access. These centres should be linked to the relevant international, regional and national standards information centres so that the latter can act as the national WTO/TBT Enquiry Points;

- Ensure the development of appropriate regional and national standards through the establishment of appropriate technical committee structures representing the stakeholders of the countries, as well as managing such committees in line with ISO/IEC Directives and WTO/TBT Agreement requirements.

(iv) Tourism

163. Objectives[306]

- To identify key 'anchor' projects at the national and sub-regional levels, which will generate significant spin-offs and assist in promoting interregional economic integration;

- To develop a regional marketing strategy;

- To develop a research capacity in tourism;

- To promote partnerships such as those formed via sub-regional bodies.

Examples include the Regional Tourism Organisation of Southern Africa (RETOSA), the Economic Community of West African States (ECOWAS) and the SADC.

164. Actions[307]

- At the African level:

- Forge co-operative partnerships to capture the benefits of shared knowledge, as well as provide a base for other countries to entering into tourist-related activities;

---

306. These are all reasonable as minor modifications to existing strategies, but do nothing to ensure that tourism translates into sustainable development, and that local people are beneficiaries in ways other than through meagre trickle-down, low-paid unskilled labour. The list of actions below, do have some provisions for community-based tourism, however they do nothing to assure Africans that *affordable access to local tourist facilities will be feasible.* Nepad appears to assume that all tourists are from outside the continent or are wealthy locals, for the strategy completely lacks any component oriented to democratising recreation.

307. The proposed actions appear benign. However, South Africa's domineering approach to subregional tourist initiatives is cause for concern. Zimbabwe's Victoria Falls is one example of the way the region is being utilised as merely a spin-off attraction for South African-centric tourism, to the detriment of other Zimbabwean features.

Another example is the South African role in the trans-frontier game park associated with apartheid-era tycoon Anton Rupert. The park stretches from Kruger on the eastern border of South Africa, into Mozambique, and up to Zimbabwe. But in spite of corruption by South African consultants to the Department of Environmental Affairs and Tourism, and an undercounting (by a factor of four) and lack of consultation of tens of thousands of affected Mozambican peasants whose villages will be removed, Rupert's 84th birthday occasioned the high-profile release of Kruger elephants into Mozambique, with dire consequences for

- Provide the African people with the capacity to be actively involved in sustainable tourism projects at the community level;

- Prioritise consumer safety and security issues;

- Market African tourism products, especially in adventure tourism, ecotourism and cultural tourism;

- Increase regional co-ordination of tourism initiatives in Africa for the expansion and increased diversity of products;

- Maximise our benefits from the strong interregional demand for tourism activities, by developing specialised consumer-targeted marketing campaigns.

(v) Services[308]

165. Services can constitute very important activities for African countries in particular those that are well equipped in the field of ICTs (téleservices).

(vi) Promoting the private sector

166. Objectives[309]

- To ensure a sound and conducive environment for private sector activities, with particular emphasis on domestic entrepreneurs;

---

local inhabitants. The multiple scandals emerged in April 2002, but are consistent with much of the Mpumalanga region's approach to tourism, including the attempted sale of huge national parks to Middle Eastern investors during the mid-1990s.

308. Measured as a percentage of GDP and with respect to employment, services have become the fastest-growing sector in many African countries. The Nepad authors' failure to generate anything more than an absurd reference to ICT suggests exceptionally sloppy preparatory work.

309. The emphasis on improving conditions for capital accumulation, with no similar provisions for 'third sector' (non-profit) enterprise, notwithstanding active cooperative movements and NGOs across Africa, unveils Nepad's biases.

Pretoria's own actions have been only somewhat successful, for after providing virtually all the 'sound and conducive' elements requested by big business – a 60% cut in the tax rate from 1994-98; freedom to take money out of the country, both through primary relisting in London and relaxation of exchange controls; a low and declining budget deficit; full respect for property rights; very little new corporate regulation; no efforts to address the legacies of wealth accumulated due to apartheid (e.g. by a

- To promote foreign direct investment and trade, with particular emphasis on exports;

- To develop micro, small and medium enterprises, including the informal sector.

***167. Actions*[310]**

- At the African level:

- Undertake measures to enhance the entrepreneurial, managerial and technical capacities of the private sector by supporting technology acquisition, production improvements, and training and skills development;

- Strengthen chambers of commerce, trade and professional associations, and their regional networks;

- Organise dialogue between the government and the private sector to develop a shared vision of economic development strategy and remove constraints to private sector development;

- Strengthen and encourage the growth of micro, small and medium-scale industries through appropriate technical support from service institutions and civil society, and improve access to capital by strengthening microfinancing schemes, with particular attention to women entrepreneurs.

---

wealth tax); and many other concessions – the largest firms in South Africa left for London. In the process they exported sufficient levels of profits and dividends to crash the value of the rand during 2000-01. Meanwhile, virtually no sustainable models of Black Economic Empowerment actually worked, given that most creative financing deals were established by merchant bankers – with the approval of the state – and crashed in mid-1998 when the stock market fell dramatically and interest rates soared. The small business sector was an even greater failure. In short, in spite of bending over backwards to generate *laissez faire* conditions that would assist private sector operators, Pretoria can claim mainly failures.

310. As in the case of manufacturing, none of the actions proposed amount to more than tinkering and institutional improvement. The extent to which such strategies have collapsed in South Africa is witnessed in the unseemly squabble by virtually all representatives of the private sector, who after years of attempting to pull together a non-racial business-interests grouping, still persistently fail.

- At the international level:

- Promote entrepreneurial development programmes for training managers of African firms;

- Provide technical assistance in relation to the development of an appropriate regulatory environment, promotion of small, medium and micro-enterprises and, establish micro-financing schemes for the African private sector.

(vii) Promoting African Exports

168. Objectives[311]

- To improve procedures for customs and drawback/rebate schemes;

- To tackle trade barriers in international trade through the improvement of standards;

- To increase intra-regional trade via promoting cross-border interaction among African firms;

- To improve Africa's negative image through conflict resolution and marketing;

- To deal with short-term skills shortages through appropriate firm-level incentives and training.

169. Actions

- At the African level:

- Promote intra-African trade with the aim of sourcing within Africa, imports formerly sourced from other parts of the world;

- Create marketing mechanisms and institutions to develop marketing strategies for African products;

---

311. What is most extraordinary about this list of extremely weak objectives, is that a grand rhetoric has emerged from Pretoria about changing the rules of world trade. Even minister Erwin has argued that the South must displace the North's 'dinosaur' industries: agriculture and manufacturing. Yet the extent of the objectives is merely to fiddle with marginal problems: 'customs and drawback/rebate schemes,' 'improvement of standards,' 'cross-border interaction among African firms,' 'improve Africa's negative image through conflict resolution and marketing,' and 'deal with short-term skills shortages.' There is nothing in Nepad to suggest that the new African exporter is ready to displace extinct Northerners in agriculture, manufacturing or anything else.

- Publicise African exporting and importing companies and their products, through trade fairs;

- Reduce the cost of transactions and operations;

- Promote and improve regional trade agreements, foster interregional trade liberalisation, and harmonise rules of origin, tariffs and product standards;

- Reduce export taxes.

- At the international level:[312]

- Negotiate measures and agreements to facilitate market access for African products to the world market;

---

312. Contrasting Nepad and the real interests of African countries in relation to international trade rules is a worthy topic with which to close this commentary. In the paragraphs that follow, Nepad requests a more liberalised international trade regime. The apotheosis of that approach was unveiled in April 2002 when the European Union's secret 'hit list' of requests for trade concessions under the General Agreement on Trade in Services was leaked to the *Guardian* newspaper. Especially evident in the leaked reports was the arrogance with which EU negotiators aim to open all aspects of daily life to commodification by European firms, especially with respect to middle-income countries like South Africa (other African countries aren't worth wasting time with, it appears).

The problem, in sum, is that Pretoria essentially sides with international trade liberalisers, against those in Africa who want to retain sovereignty, dignity and the possibility of building an economy based upon human need, not profit. Several African trade negotiators have positioned themselves far to the left of South African trade minister Erwin, and until November 2001 they foiled his attempts to impose a South African-centric African economy based upon the investment and trade ambitions of Johannesburg corporations. The divisive role of Erwin in the Doha ministerial conference in November 2001 (*Mail & Guardian*, 9 and 16 November 2001) followed his setback at the Seattle summit in December 1999, when Pretoria adopted a position entirely distinct from that of the Organisation for African Unity. (The angry OAU delegates were the main reason that the Seattle WTO summit failed, although Erwin took great pains to criticise the workers, environmentalists and other protesters who objected to the WTO's attack on democracy).

In contrast to Erwin, there were important African voices amongst those in the so-called 'Like-Minded Group' - Egypt, Uganda, Zimbabwe, India, Pakistan, Indonesia and the Dominican Republic - which, joined by Cuba, Haiti, India, Kenya, Peru and Venezuela, called for radical changes to international trading rules just as Nepad was being drafted:

Developing countries have clearly not received the benefits they thought they would. Developed countries continue to be heavily regulated in the form of maintaining trade barriers especially in several sectors of interest to developing countries. For example, technical standards and licensing in certain professional services, is used to effectively restrict entry by developing countries into the industry...

The regulatory initiatives taken by developing countries would already seem to be having a negative impact on them since many developing countries have adopted regulations that have turned out to be more suited to the needs and level of development of services industries of the developed countries...

There is the danger that re-regulation, as promoted in Article VI, could in fact become deregulation [and that this] could be fundamentally incompatible with the requirement or the desire of many governments to provide basic public services for their people, especially since certain sections of their population may not be able to afford to pay market prices for these services...

Many services markets are dominated by only a few large firms from developed countries and a number of small players. The top 20 service exporters are mainly from developed countries...

Liberalisation under these circumstances of unequal competition has aggravated the alarming divide in supply capacity between developed and developing countries...

Developing countries' small suppliers are also disadvantaged in other ways, such as through discriminatory access to information channels and distribution networks...

Under conditions of liberalisation, privatisation of services could very easily happen since foreign corporations which are more competitive are likely to enter the new market and take over from the local company. This could have consequences on access to basic services for those who may not be able to afford these commercial prices of services.

In addition, investments, when they come in, have often not been in sectors that could most benefit the host countries...

For the rural sectors in many developing countries, these basic services may not even be provided by the state, but by communities and local authorities which use currently common resources, such as water, minerals, fuels...

Through marketisation, previously available public goods are put out of reach of many when these are commodified in the process of privatisation. The experience of several developing countries with structural adjustment already shows that large segments of the population are having serious difficulties gaining access to basic commodities and services at prices they can afford. (Cuba, Dominican Republic, Haiti, India, Kenya, Pakistan, Peru, Uganda, Venezuela and Zimbabwe (2001), 'Assessment of Trade

- Encourage foreign direct investment;

- Assist in capacity-building in the private sector, as well as strengthening country and sub-regional capacity in trade negotiations, implementing the rules and regulations of the WTO, and identifying and exploiting new trading opportunities that emerge from the evolving multilateral trading system;

- The African heads of state must ensure active participation in the world trading system, which has been managed under the auspices of the WTO since 1995. If a new round of multilateral trade negotiations is started, it must recognise and provide for the African continent's special concerns, needs and interests in future WTO rules.

170. Participation in the world trading system must enhance:

- Open, predictable and geographically diversified market access for exports from Africa;

- The provision of a forum in which developing countries can collectively put up their demand call for structural adjustment by developed countries in those industries in which the natural competitive advantage now lies with the developing world;

- Transparency and predictability as preconditions for increased investment in return for boosting supply capacity and enhancing the gains from existing market access;

- Technical assistance and support to enhance institutional capacity of African States to use the WTO and to engage in multilateral trade negotiations.

171. In addition to broad-based support for the WTO, African heads of state must identify strategic areas of intervention and, together with the international community, strengthen the contribution of trade to the continent's recovery. The strategic areas include:

---

in Services,' Special Communication to the World Trade Organisation, 9 October.)

These very valid concerns conflict explicitly with Nepad, which *welcomes* the foreign investors whose privatisation agenda invariably limits access to services to those who have resources. While Nepad talks of the need for partnership, it asks for practically nothing. The critique of Gats offered by Kenya, Uganda and Zimbabwe, among others, is penetrating and rigorous. Nepad pales in comparison.

- The identification of key areas in export production in which supply-side impediments exist;

- The diversification of production and exports especially in existing and potential areas of competitive advantage, and bearing in mind the need to move towards higher value-added production;

- An assessment of the scope for further liberalisation in manufacturing, given the concentration of access in low value-added sectors, and its restrictiveness in high value-added activities with the greatest economic and growth potential;

- Renewed political action by African countries to intensify and deepen the various integration initiatives on the continent. To this end, consideration needs to be given to: (1) a discretionary preferential trade system for intra-African trade; (2) the alignment of domestic and regional trade and industrial policy objectives, thereby increasing the potential for intra-regional trade critical to the sustainability of regional economic arrangements.

172. Heads of State must act to: (1) secure and stabilise preferential treatment by key developed country partners, e.g. the Generalised System of Preferences (GSP), the Cotonou Agreement, the 'Everything But Arms' (EBA) initiative, and the Africa Growth and Opportunity Act (AGOA); (2) ensure that further multilateral liberalisation does not erode the preferential gains of these arrangements; (3) identify and address deficiencies in their design and application.

(viii) Removal of non-tariff barriers

173. African leaders believe that improved access to the markets of industrialised countries for products in which Africa has a comparative advantage is crucial. Although there have been significant improvements in terms of lowered tariffs in recent years, there remain significant exceptions on tariffs while non-tariff barriers also constitute major impediments. Progress on this issue would greatly enhance economic growth and diversification of African production and exports. Dependence on ODA would decline and infrastructure projects would become more viable as a result of increased economic activity.

VI. A NEW GLOBAL PARTNERSHIP

174. Africa recognises the centuries-old historical injustice and the need to correct it. The central injunction of the new partnership is, however, for combined efforts to improve the quality of life of Africa's people as rapidly as possible.[313] In this, there are shared responsibilities and mutual benefits for Africa and her partners.

175. The global technological revolution needs an expanding base of resources, a widening sphere of markets, new frontiers of scientific endeavour, the collective capacity of human wisdom, and a well-managed ecological system. We are aware that much of Africa's mineral and other material resources are critical inputs into production processes in developed countries.[314]

176. In addition to its indispensable resource base, Africa offers a vast and growing market for producers across the world.[315] A developing Africa, with increased numbers of employed and skilled workers and a burgeoning middle class, would constitute an expanding market for world manufactured products, intermediate goods and services.[316]

---

313. The term 'however' suggests that there is a contradiction between 'correcting' the 'centuries-old historical injustice' and the need to 'improve the quality of life of Africa's people as rapidly as possible.' There is no such contradiction, especially if full debt cancellation occurs immediately and if reparations are provided on the basis of well-constructed arguments and analysis, and are provided in forms not associated with the current regime of neo-liberalism and aid dependency.

314. 'We are aware' suggests a coy threatening tone, as does the statement that Africa's exports are 'critical inputs into production processes' in the North. But Nepad fails to back up either sentiment, by documenting the (imagined) 'critical' reliance of the North upon Africa or by sketching conditions for withdrawal of the inputs so as to make the threat real. For this reason, the term 'sophisticated begging bowl' has come to characterise Nepad.

315. The African market is neither vast nor growing; it is tiny and stagnant.

316. More appropriately, Nepad should condemn the importation of Northern junk culture and luxury goods, when scarce hard currency should instead be used for import-substitution of basic-needs goods and importation of those vital requirements, such as some medicines and high-tech goods, that cannot be produced in Africa in the immediate future.

177. At the same time, Africa provides a great opportunity for investment. The *New Partnership for Africa's Development* creates opportunities for joint international efforts in the development of infrastructure, especially in ICT and transportation.[317]

178. Africa also provides prospects for creative partnerships between the public and private sectors in beneficiation, agro-industries, tourism, human resource development and in tackling the challenges of urban renewal and rural development.[318]

179. Furthermore, Africa's biodiversity – including its rich flora and fauna and the rain forests – is an important global resource in combating the environmental degradation posed by the depletion of the ozone layer and climate change, as well as the pollution of air and water by industrial emissions and toxic effluents.[319]

180. The expansion of educational and other opportunities in Africa would enhance the continent's contribution to world science, technology and culture, to the benefit of all humankind. After all, modern science recognises Africa as the cradle of humanity. Fossils, artefacts, artistic works and the versions of ancient human settlements are to be found throughout

---

To speak of Africa as a consumer for Northern commodities in such an uncritical manner, is merely to add to the world's problems.

317. As noted above, these Public Private Partnership incentives are socially and ecologically dubious. Just as importantly, as the South African case shows, even the wealthier countries cannot really attract investors who have seen numerous failing post-apartheid precedents of privatised infrastructure.

318. Aside from the PPP investment areas which are debunked above, Nepad has failed to spell out any instances where such investment is genuinely profitable.

319. The role of Africa as a 'sink' for Northern pollution has been discussed above, as have the problems of South African global warming gasses and of biopiracy. This would be the place to mention the massive ecological debt that the North owes the South for so grotesquely polluting the planet. Nepad is too impotent a document to mention such a debt, much less to follow it up as a means of unlocking more resources from the North.

Africa, providing material evidence of the emergence of *Homo sapiens* and the progression of humanity.[320]

181. A part of the process of the reconstruction of the identity and self-confidence of the peoples of Africa, it is necessary that this be understood and valued by Africans themselves.[321] In the same vein, Africa's status as the birthplace of humanity should be cherished by the whole world as the origin of all its peoples.

182. Africa's rich cultural legacy is reflected in its artefacts of the past, its literature, philosophies, art and music. These should serve both as a means of consolidating the pride of Africans in their own humanity and of confirming the common humanity of the peoples of the world.[322]

183. The *New Partnership for Africa's Development* has, as one of its foundations, the expansion of democratic frontiers and the deepening of the culture of human rights. A democratic Africa will become one of the pillars of world democracy, human rights and tolerance.[323] The resources of the world

---

320. What Nepad should also state, at this stage in the Partnership proposition, is that Northern museums and private collections include precious art and artefacts that have been forcibly removed from Africa during periods of slavery, colonialism and neo-colonialism - and that these must be returned to their heirs as a matter of moral urgency.

321. The need to establish African dignity is obvious given that most of the current and recent African ruling classes have prostrated themselves to the West. However, the conception of dignity is terribly limited if it can be restored, even 'partially,' through mere reference to fossils. In living memory, Western colonialists, financial/development agencies and corporations - in conjunction with African *comprador* leaders - have looted Africa, and genuine dignity requires that those relationships be broken and that reparations be paid. Nepad's failure to raise these issues forcefully ensures that African elites will continue to be subservient, and that dignity will be gained for Africa only through their replacement.

322. As mentioned repeatedly, Nepad would be more convincing in its celebration of African cultural legacies if it more systematically identified the past, present and future negations of African culture, and set out to rectify these. To the extent that Nepad turns to the West for investment, trade, loans and aid, it runs the danger that the negations of African culture will only intensify.

323. On the contrary, Nepad leaders Mbeki and Obsanjo demonstrated in March 2002, in the wake of the Zimbabwean election, that they prefer to see the African pillars of world democracy, human rights and tolerance

currently dedicated to resolving civil and interstate conflict could therefore be freed for more rewarding endeavours.

184. The converse of such an initiative, that is the collapse of more African states, poses a threat not only to Africans, but also to global peace and security. For industrialised countries, development in Africa will reduce the levels of global social exclusion and mitigate a major potential source of global social instability.[324]

---

crumble. As Wade of Senegal argued, the heads of state, ministers and parliamentarians in South Africa, SADC and other African countries who endorsed the stolen election formed a 'trade union' of leaders defending each other no matter how much Mugabe rejected democracy, human rights and tolerance.

324. The problem of 'exclusion' of Africa has not really bothered the West, even in the post-Cold War era. There are no serious challenges to 'global security' from Africa. On the contrary, the most durable benefits of African underdevelopment to the West - e.g., continued export of ever-cheaper raw materials, and repayment of illegitimate debt - are occasionally threatened by popular uprisings ('IMF Riots'), yet the global economic system's exploitative relationships have become ever more burdensome for Africa. Recent initiatives in the WTO (trade) and IMF/WB (debt) have only enhanced the power relations and structural economic processes that leave Africa more 'marginalised,' the more exposed that the continent becomes to globalisation.

The lack of Western concern is especially evident in post-Cold War geopolitical trends. In Somalia during the early 1990s, Western (especially US and Belgian) atrocities were matched to only a tiny extent by a backlash and punishment for the 'peacekeepers' - but the lesson to the West was unmistakable: African civil wars cause blowback. In Rwanda, the West basically ignored the inclement genocide, and indeed the World Bank not only exacerbated matters through its early 1990s imposition of structural adjustment, but also funded the import of hundreds of thousands of machetes through a fast-disbursing structural adjustment loan just prior to the 1994 mass murders. In Sudan, Bill Clinton attempted to distract attention from his debilitating sex scandal by bombing a crucial pharmaceutical plant in the name of combating terrorism, despite the lack of proof. In other cases of failed states, such as Liberia, the West looked on passively and expected West African troops to keep the peace. (Sierra Leone was the only exception to this rule, but even there the West resisted demands to boycott the 'blood diamonds' trade through which South Africa's DeBeers empire has made billions of dollars in profit.) In Angola, US oil and diamond importers did not object to the destruction of the state from the mid-1970s to the present, and indeed the US government funded Unita's terrorism, because it made the corrupt government in Luanda more dependent upon transnational capital.

185. Africa is committed to the development and strengthening of South-South partnerships.[325]

• Establishing a new relationship with industrialised countries and multilateral organisations

186. A critical dimension of Africans taking responsibility for the continent's destiny is the need to negotiate a new relationship with their development partners. The manner in which development assistance is delivered in itself creates serious problems for developing countries. The need to negotiate and account separately to donors supporting the same sector or programme is both cumbersome and inefficient. Also, the tying of development assistance generates further inefficiencies.[326] The appeal is for a new relationship that takes the country programmes as a point of departure. The new relationship should set out mutually agreed performance targets and standards for both donor and recipient.[327] There are many cases that clearly show that the failure of projects is not caused only by the poor performance of recipients, but also by bad advice given by donors.

As noted above, the more genuine 'threat' to the West would not come from dark hints about 'global instability' due to 'marginalisation.' It would come, instead, when a continent's leadership and grassroots/shopfloor activists unite against the West's geopolitical and economic exploitation. Since Nepad invites more of both, the idea of an African threat via the present leadership is farcical.

325. There may be many Africans with such a commitment. But as the debates over the Doha Round demonstrated, South Africa is one of the least committed countries in the South, in relation to joining other Southerners in coalitions against corporate-dominated 'free trade.'

326. Omitted from this list of problems with donor aid is one of the most important: the *compradorism* that compels African leaders to follow policy advice from Northern donors. Nepad is itself a reflection of this problem, insofar as it tells Western donors what they want to hear, no matter how inconsistent that message and its implications are for African realities.

327. There is very little or nothing here that represents anything 'new,' given that donor responsibilities are typically spelled out in their budgetary allocations and recipients are bombarded by conditionalities. The important issue for African aid relationships is not whether donors perform badly - of course they do - but whether aid should be used to cancel debts and cease being used for discrete projects, so as to instead form the genesis of a further-reaching, more consistent reparations programme.

187. The various partnerships between Africa and the industrialised countries on the one hand, and multilateral institutions on the other, will be maintained. The partnerships in question include, among others: the United Nations New Agenda for the Development of Africa in the 1990s; the Africa-Europe Summit's Cairo Plan of Action; the World Bank-led Strategic Partnership with Africa; the International Monetary Fund-led Poverty Reduction Strategy Papers; the Japan-led Tokyo Agenda for Action; the Africa Growth and Opportunity Act of the United States; and the Economic Commission on Africa-led Global Compact with Africa. The objective will be to rationalise these partnerships and to ensure that real benefits to Africa flow from them.[328]

188. The African leaders envisage the following responsibilities and obligations of the developed countries and multilateral institutions:

- To support materially mechanisms for and processes of conflict prevention, management and resolution in Africa, as well as peacekeeping initiatives;[329]

- To accelerate debt reduction for heavily indebted African countries, in conjunction with more effective poverty reduction programmes, of which the Strategic Partnership with Africa and the PRSP initiatives are an important starting point;[330]

---

328. Nepad does not mention the ideological strings attached here, mainly associated with expansion of the Washington Consensus through removal of barriers to Western investment, trade and finance. But there are two interesting admissions implicit in this paragraph: firstly, that the 'partnerships' have a fragmenting effect, and secondly that at present, 'real benefits to Africa' do *not* 'flow from them.' Yet if these are serious problems, Nepad again shows its frailty by asking that these partnerships be 'maintained.'

329. If recent and ongoing experiences with African peacekeeping were not so flawed, if the UN Security Council were run in a more democratic manner, if UN troops were not generally understood as an appendage of the West's interests, and if the West's own record of troop deployment in Africa were not so abysmal, this would make sense.

330. The critique of the ongoing application of the Washington Consensus, via HIPC debt relief and PRSPs, is discussed above. Nepad's endorsement of the renamed structural adjustment programmes (PRSPs), its promotion of failed debt-relief plans that have extremist neo-liberal conditions attached, and the failure of South Africa's own homegrown adjustment

- To improve debt relief strategies for middle-income countries;[331]

- To reverse the decline in ODA flows to Africa and to meet the target level of ODA flows equivalent to 0.7 per cent of each developed country's gross national product (GNP) within an agreed period. Increased aid flows will be used to complement funds released by debt reduction for accelerating the fight against poverty;[332]

- To translate into concrete commitments the international strategies adopted in the fields of education and health;[333]

- To facilitate the development of a partnership between countries, international pharmaceutical corporations and civil

---

programme (*Growth, Employment and Redistribution*), together have provided justification for Nepad's nickname in South Africa: *'the Africanisation of Gear.'*

331. Since there are no debt-reduction strategies for middle-income countries, any improvement would be welcome. But the most hopeful sign for middle-income countries escaping the debt trap is Olesegun Obasanjo's recent rejection of new IMF loans and conditions – albeit so that he is able to run a populist reelection campaign. Amongst the few African middle-income countries that provide the least hope for debt reduction, is South Africa, because Pretoria refused to challenge the inherited apartheid debt and instead is taking on more foreign loans – including from the World Bank – without reducing unnecessary foreign imports (luxury goods or manufactured products which should be manufactured locally), or forcing those financiers responsible for the Reserve Bank's forex-denominated forward-cover book to pay more of the costs.

332. As noted above, there is nothing in Nepad to suggest that the new aid will be used for anything new and different than the old project-based aid, which is so replete with neo-liberal conditionalities as to ensure defeat in 'the fight against poverty.' When aid was used as a threat in the Doha Round to ensure that African countries signed a deal not in their interests, and when the EU's Gats negotiating strategy now includes forcing open Africa's water, electricity, healthcare and other services for capture by European corporations (in a context in which most European donor agencies peddle privatisation), it should be clear that an increase in ODA flows via existing channels may do more harm than good.

333. The most important such international strategy emerged in an October 2000 law from the US Congress, which prohibits the Bretton Woods institutions from imposing cost-recovery on health and education programmes. Nepad ignores this major breakthrough.

society organisations to urgently secure access to existing drugs for Africans suffering from infectious diseases;[334]

- To admit goods into markets of the developed countries through bilateral initiatives, and to negotiate more equitable terms of trade for African countries within the WTO multilateral framework;[335]

- To work with African leaders to encourage investment in Africa by the private sector in developed countries, including the establishment of insurance schemes and financial instruments that will help lower risk premiums on investments in Africa;[336]

---

334. Such partnerships have already sprung up as a result of massive social protest against Big Pharma's profiteering from 1999-2001, and in spite of the role of Pretoria - especially President Mbeki - in denying Aids as a problem that can be addressed by anti-retroviral drugs from 2000-02. If this is true, then to strengthen this partnership provision will require two simple ways forward: more protest and less Pretoria.

335. This paragraph implicitly concedes the failure of the WTO as a site for increasing Africa's market access (especially in view of EU agricultural subsidies), but Nepad has not shown that increased access will translate into a better deal for Africa. It is just as likely that an expansion of the world's agricultural and mineral trade will exacerbate glutted markets, falling prices and control by multinational corporate middle-men. Likewise, efforts within the WTO to improve terms of trade cut against the essential problem of global capitalism: declining terms of trade for the South the more that export-led growth ensures all countries attempt to grow.

In an April 2002 report by the UN Conference on Trade and Development, this problem was finally permitted to surface in international debate, when economist Richard Kozul-Wright conceded, 'We have seen a decoupling of the trade engine from the growth engine in developing countries over the last two decades.'

336. Such schemes have existed for many years, e.g. in the World Bank's MIGA and the US OPIC deals. Merely adding a small Western-taxpayer subsidy to the investment calculus has done very little, thus far, to offset the broader problem of Africa's systematic looting, which in turn is responsible for the worsening standards of living and effective demand across the continent.

- To raise consumer protection standards for exports from developed countries to developing countries as applicable to the domestic markets in the developed countries;[337]

- To ensure that the World Bank and other multilateral development finance institutions participate as investors in the key economic infrastructure projects, in order to facilitate and the secure private sector participation;[338]

---

337. This is a good suggestion, but ignores the sweatshop role of Southern countries - especially in East Asia - which produce cheap manufactured exports to Africa with horrendous social, labour and environmental inputs. Changing those conditions cannot occur through the 'Social Clause' strategy once favoured by South African minister Erwin, but can only happen through the self-activity of exploited workers (especially women) and liberation movements which take seriously the problems associated with their countries' insertion into the world economy. Very few African countries can claim movements, much less states, that have developed such a consciousness, so in the meantime it is crucial to raise the issue of production conditions associated with imported goods, and raise the profile of those trade unions and social movements which are struggling for social justice in the global assembly line.

338. The record of these institutions' investments is extremely poor, and systematic project flaws should be reversed and compensation paid for prior mistakes as a prerequisite to any further investments. These mistakes include:

- the systematic propping up of undemocratic African rulers during and even after the Cold War;
- the construction of colonial- and apartheid-era infrastructure whose beneficiaries were limited to *white* consumers and corporations;
- ongoing environmental damage associated with Washington-designed infrastructure (e.g., the Bujagali and Mohale dams, and the Chad-Cameroon pipeline); and
- ongoing corruption problems associated with transnational construction corporations funded by the multilateral institutions (e.g. the documented bribery of a key Lesotho dam official, which the World Bank recently announced it would neither continue to help prosecute nor engage in 'barring' measures against the implicated companies).

The alternative strategy in relation to the World Bank and other multilateral financiers like the IMF and African Development Bank was spelled out in the final 'sentence' of the April 2002 International People's Tribunal on Debt (chaired by South African judged Dumisa Ntsebeza).

The International makes the following declarations:

- To provide technical support to accelerate the implementation of the programme of action, including strengthening Africa's capacity in planning and development management, financial and infrastructure regulation, accounting and auditing, and development, construction and management of infrastructure;[339]

---

1. All external debt being illegitimate should be immediately repudiated and cancelled.
2. In return for the wealth illegitimately transferred to the North from the South, the countries of the South should be provided reasonable compensation, to determine the magnitude and manner of payment of which a Global Commission on Debt should be constituted.
3. Since unnatural power is related to unwarranted size and reach, the banks, financial institutions, industrial corporations, landed interests and other economic agents who control assets which give them such power should be broken down and their power curtailed, so that the recurrence of the process of growth of illegitimate debt is foreclosed.
4. International institutions which serve as agents to coordinate, oversee and guarantee debt flows, such as the IMF and the World Bank, should be decommissioned and any residual useful role served by them should be handed over to more democratically-managed international institutions.
5. Neo-liberal policy regimes that are designed to sustain and worsen debt and obfuscate the resulting process of economic aggrandizement at one pole and social deprivation at the other should be dismantled, to be replaced by more pro-people and pro-poor policies of development.
6. Besides social mobilisation to pressurise governments in the North and the South to implement these recommendations, the Tribunal calls on people to use supplementary legal procedures such as petitions in the International Court of Justice at the Hague to bring individual instances of violation of individual social and human rights to trial and force governments to implement these recommendations. (http: //www.jubilee.net)

339. Such capacity building is crucial, but South Africa provides good examples of where US and British aid agencies have self-interestedly prioritised their work: in promoting municipal privatisation on behalf of transnational corporate capital; and in strengthening the ability of customs officials to intercept counterfeit East Asian imports of patented products.

- To support governance reforms of multilateral financial institutions to better cater for the needs and concerns of countries in Africa;[340]

- To set up co-ordinated mechanisms to combat corruption effectively, as well as commit themselves to the return of monies (proceeds) of such practices to Africa.[341]

---

340. This provision apparently refers to the ability of the US government to veto any decisions of the IMF and World Bank with merely 17.8% of the voting shares, as a result of terribly unequal power relations that prevailed when the Bretton Woods articles of association were drawn up and later amended. But the most important question to ask is whether in the event that, for example, Africa's largest shareholder in the IMF/WB (South Africa) had a higher voting share, *would that make any difference to Bretton Woods policies?* Given the SA representatives' consistent votes on behalf of Bretton Woods policies, programmes and projects that undermine Africa, as well as the homegrown nature of Pretoria's own austerity programme, the answer is by no means clear.

341. The demand for the return of monies stolen from Africa by elites is welcome, given that such funding far exceeds the continent's outstanding debts, according to reliable research. In Nigeria, president Obasanjo has indeed asked that money stolen by military regimes – especially Abacha's – that received Bretton Woods loans should be returned, and that the debt should be cancelled. The Bretton Woods institutions' refusal of that request (leading in part to Obasanjo's break with the IMF in March 2002) and the well-documented ability of London's banks to lie to the Chancellor of the Exchequer about their dirty-money hordes, together suggest that much tougher action must be taken against the institutions that fuel African corruption.

Sadly, as noted above, Pretoria lacks either capacity or political will to take leadership in this crucial area, as judged by evidence such as:

- the most extreme contemporary case of Odious Debt – $25 billion of apartheid-era foreign loans – which Nelson Mandela agreed to repay in 1994, and which president Mbeki subsequently endorsed in Davos in 2001, at a time when church leaders were demanding cancellation and reparations;
- the decision by then deputy-president Mbeki, then-trade minister Manuel and then-deputy finance minister Erwin to allow the demise of the financial rand exchange control and relaxation of foreign investment regulations by local financial institutions in 1995-96, which allowed hundreds of billions of apartheid-era funds to be permanently shifted abroad; and
- the decision by finance minister Manuel to allow the offshore listing of the largest South African companies in 1998-2000, which led to a

VII. IMPLEMENTATION OF THE NEW PARTNERSHIP FOR AFRICA'S DEVELOPMENT[342]

189. Recognising the need to sequence and prioritise, the initiating Presidents propose that the following programmes be fast-tracked, in collaboration with development partners: (a) Communicable diseases – HIV/Aids, malaria and tuberculosis; (b) Information and Communications Technology; (c) Debt reduction; (d) Market access.

190. Work has already been done on all these programmes by a variety of international partnerships and institutions. However, Africa's participation and leadership need to be strengthened for better delivery. We believe that addressing these issues could fast-track the renewal of the continent. (Detailed proposals on each programme are available as annexes.)

• Projects

191. Much as the promoters of the *New Partnership for Africa's Development* appreciate the dangers of a project approach to development, they are proposing a number of projects that are crucial to an integrated regional development, as conceived by the *New Partnership for Africa's Development.* Not only will these projects strengthen country and regional development programmes, but they will also go a long way in kick-starting the regeneration of the continent.

---

temporary inflow of foreign exchange but a permanent outflow of profits and dividends which will far outstrip the inflows and which contributed to South Africa's 2000-01 60% currency crash.

This record of allowing apartheid-era loot to flow out of South Africa at a time when massive investments could have been made in overcoming the apartheid infrastructural, housing and industrial legacy, suggests that this paragraph cannot be taken seriously if Pretoria retains leadership of Nepad.

342. Any critique of Section VII would be premature, for several reasons:

- 'projects presented below are for illustrative purposes only,' are relatively meagre in scope, and are incapable of capturing the ambitious nature of Nepad's claims for a genuine 'partnership';
- the 'assessment of sub-regional sectoral needs' is still incomplete; and
- the Heads of State Implementation Committee and the Nepad Secretariat are still being formed and gaining capacity.

192. The projects presented below are for illustrative purposes only. A detailed list of projects can be found on the web site of the *New Partnership for Africa's Development* (www.mapstrategy.com).

(i) Agriculture

193. Expand the ambit and operation of the integrated land and water management action plan for Africa. The project addresses the maintenance and upgrading of Africa's fragile agricultural natural resources base. Many African governments are already implementing these initiatives as part of this programme. Partners include the Global Environment Facility (GEF), the World Bank, ADB the FAO and other bilateral donor agencies.

194. Strengthen and refocus the capacity of Africa's agricultural research and extension systems. The project addresses the issue of upgrading of the physical and institutional infrastructure that supports Africa's agriculture. Technological innovation and technology diffusion hold enormous potential for accelerating agricultural output and productivity, but the continent lacks the research capacity that is necessary for major breakthroughs. Major players include the Forum for Agricultural Research in Africa (FARA), the World Bank, the FAO and the Consultative Group on International Agricultural Research (CGIAR).

(ii) Promotion of the Private Sector

195. International experience suggests that one of the best practices in promoting enterprises in highly innovative areas is through the establishment of business incubators. This project will formulate required guidelines and policies for the establishment of such incubators at the national level, drawing on international experience and established best practice, tailored to African needs and conditions.

(iii) Infrastructure and Regional Integration

196. The *New Partnership for Africa's Development* process has identified many energy, transport, telecommunications and water projects that are crucial to Africa's integrated development. The projects are at various stages of development and require funding. The next step is to accelerate their continued development in collaboration with

the African Development Bank, the World Bank and other multilateral institutions.

197. The view of the initiating Presidents is that, unless the issue of infrastructure development is addressed on a planned basis – that is, linked to regional integrated development – the renewal process of the continent will not take off.

Therefore, the international community is urged to support Africa in accelerating the development of infrastructure. Detailed infrastructure projects can be found on the web site of the *New Partnership for Africa's Development* (www.mapstrategy.com).

- **Needs assessment**

198. As part of assessing the required action in the priority sectors, a needs assessment will be undertaken, progressing from the national level, to the subregional and sub-regional levels. The aim is to assess the needs in the five priority sectors in terms of structures and staff.

199. The assessment of sub-regional sectoral needs will start from the national needs assessment. The proposal is that the experts and ministers in each sub-sector meet in one of the sub-regional capitals. For each sector, national data would have been aggregated and used to elaborate a sub-regional sectoral plan. Once sub-regional sectoral needs are assessed in the five sectors, they can be aggregated to formulate over all regional plan.

200. It should be stressed that sub-regional sectoral needs are not to be simply added up – the starting point is a sub-regional perspective leading to at least two new elements:

- Specific needs of the sub-region perceived as a single space for all states in the sub-region. For instance, roads and railroads will not be conceived from a national perspective but from a sub-regional one;

- Needs that should be rationalised on a sub-regional basis. For instance, the universities should be distributed according to a sub-regional territorial rationale;

- Finally, the continent's needs will be assessed in the five sectors considered as priority sectors in the light of the global sub-regional plans. The details can be found on the web site of the *New Partnership for Africa's Development* (www.mapstrategy.com).

• Management mechanism of the New Partnership for Africa's Development

The Heads of State promoting the New Partnership for Africa's Development will advise OAU on an appropriate mechanism for its implementation.

201. There will be a need for core technical support for the implementing mechanism in the areas of research and policy formulation.

Heads of State Implementation Committee

202. A Heads of State Implementation Committee composed of the five Heads of State, promoters of the *New Partnership for Africa's Development* and ten others, (2 from each region) will be appointed for the implementation.

203. The functions of the Implementation Committee will consist of:

- Identifying strategic issues that need to be researched, planned and managed at the continental level;

- Setting up mechanisms for reviewing progress in the achievement of mutually agreed targets and compliance with mutually agreed standards;

- Reviewing progress in the implementation of past decisions and taking appropriate steps to address problems and delays;

VIII. CONCLUSION

204. The objective of the *New Partnership for Africa's Development* is to consolidate democracy and sound economic management on the continent. Through the programme, African leaders are making a commitment to the African people and the world to work together in rebuilding the continent. It is a pledge to promote peace and stability, democracy, sound economic management and people-centred development and to hold each other accountable in terms of the agreements outlined in the programme.[343]

343. The ambitions are impressive, but the process is flawed (no civil society participation), the commitment questionable (as witnessed by debacles in

205. In proposing the partnership, Africa recognises that it holds the key to its own development.[344] We affirm that the *New Partnership for Africa's Development* offers an historic opportunity for the developed countries of the world to enter into a genuine partnership with Africa, based on mutual interest, shared commitments and binding agreements.

206. The adoption of a development strategy as set out in the broad approach outlined above, together with a detailed programme of action, will mark the beginning of a new phase in the partnership and co-operation between Africa and the developed world.[345]

207. In fulfilling its promise, this agenda must give hope to the emaciated African child that the 21st century is indeed Africa's century.

ABUJA, NIGERIA OCTOBER 2001

Zimbabwe and other countries), and the conflation of democracy and 'sound economic management' (via Washington Consensus policies) incongruous. Most importantly, as this annotated critique has documented, the inability of the Nepad leader, Pretoria, to implement its ambitions at home, under far better conditions than exist elsewhere in Africa, is ominous.

344. Nepad earlier admits that 'the bulk of the needed resources [US$64 billion] will have to be obtained from outside the continent' (paragraph 147) as lubricant in the keyhole of international economics. The alternative to such a begging bowl (for aid) or red carpet (for irresponsible transnational corporate investors) would be genuine self-reliance, consisting of: debt repudiation, demands for reparations and return of looted wealth, imposition of exchange controls, mobilisation of domestic resources through prescribed assets and other modes of financial regulation, nationalisation of banking systems that have become corrupt and/or instable, promotion of import-substitution, discouragement of luxury-goods imports, proactive state industrial policies and directed investments, regional coordination based on linkages not competition, and the international solidarity required – as in the case of anti-retroviral drugs and anti-apartheid sanctions – to make genuine self-reliance and liberation possible.

345. Much of Nepad is, in reality, merely an extension of existing relations, but with Pretoria setting up the conditions for South Africa to play a more explicitly subimperialist role.

Afterword

Introduction

The pages above provided the initial English-language reactions to Nepad, especially by critics whose arguments emanated from traditional Left standpoints of social justice, democracy, internationalism, African self-reliance, gender equity, ecological sustainability and the like. Now, two and a half years later, it is fair to ponder whether Nepad is worth taking seriously in any respect.[1] The programme was, after all, soon termed 'philosophically spot-on' by the Bush regime's lead Africa official, Walter Kansteiner,[2] and endorsed by the World Bank and IMF, while on the other hand, more than 20,000 protesters demonstrated against Nepad in August 2002 at the World Summit for Sustainable Development in Johannesburg.

We will contemplate two crucial, interrelated problems especially evident from 2002-04: Africa's worsening political economic prospects and geopolitical entanglements, especially in relation to imperialism; and Nepad's record to date on governance and African democratisation. Addressing the first, we must continue to query whether Nepad is merely a subimperialist gambit by

1. This Afterword draws upon arguments presented at greater length in the following 2004 publications: *Talk Left, Walk Right: South Africa's Frustrated Global Reforms,* Pietermaritzburg, University of KwaZulu-Natal Press; 'South Africa tackles Global Apartheid: Is the Reform Strategy Working?', *South Atlantic Quarterly*, 103, 4; 'From Racial to Class Apartheid: South Africa's Frustrating Decade of Freedom', *Monthly Review*, 55, 10; 'Bankrupt Africa: Imperialism, Subimperialism and Financial Politics', *Historical Materialism;* 'The ANC's "Left Turn" and South African Subimperialism: Ideology, Geopolitics and Capital Accumulation', *Review of African Political Economy,* 31; and 'Talk Left, Walk Right: Rhetoric and Reality in the New South Africa', *Global Dialogue*, 6, 4.

2. Gopinath, D. (2003), 'Doubt of Africa,' *Institutional Investor Magazine*, May.

Pretoria, to lubricate neoliberalism and western political interests, for the sake, largely, of South African capital's improved standing in the system, and perhaps also Pretoria politicians' own power and prestige. The evidence is not fully conclusive yet, it must be conceded, because large-scale capital – whether from Johannesburg or from London, New York, Paris, Tokyo, Frankfurt or even Houston – is not apparently interested in the specific projects Nepad has on offer, even if business elites welcome the overall mood-change associated with the programme.

Likewise there is confusion on governance, given prevailing power relations. Consider how Nepad's credibility was thrown into question by Pretoria's then trade minister Alec Erwin, just as Robert Mugabe was stealing a presidential election in Zimbabwe in early 2002: 'The West should not hold the Nepad hostage because of mistakes in Zimbabwe. If Nepad is not owned and implemented by Africa it will fail, we cannot be held hostage to the political whims of the G8 or any other groups.'[3] Ownership and implementation looked like low priorities to many Africans. When just seven African presidents showed up at the 2003 Heads of State Implementation Committee meeting, Thabo Mbeki complained to a World Economic Forum regional summit: 'We must insist that our fellow heads of state attend the meetings.'[4] (Not only would they not attend meetings, fewer than half Africa's governments agreed to sign up for the Nepad Peer Review Mechanism – itself a dubious exercise with no teeth - a year after it was launched, a fact that SA finance minister Trevor Manuel termed 'shameful'.)[5]

At the next gathering, in Maputo, in July 2003, the pro-Mbeki *Sunday Times* headlined, 'The George Dubya of Africa: Even as he relinquishes the reins of the African Union, Thabo Mbeki is regarded with suspicion by other African leaders.' According to the article, Mbeki is 'viewed by other African leaders as too powerful, and they privately accuse him of wanting to impose his will on others ... In the corridors they call him the George Bush of Africa, leading the most powerful nation in the neighbourhood and using his financial and military muscle to further his own agenda.'[6]

3. Cited in Taylor, I. (2002), 'Obstacles to change in Africa: Nepad, Zimbabwe, and Elites,' Foreign Policy in Focus Commentary, http://www.fpif.org/outside/commentary/2002/0204Nepad.html.

4. SA Institute of International Affairs (2003), 'Nepad and WEF,' *eAfrica*, July, p.11.

5. *Business Day*, 16 September 2004.

6. *Sunday Times*, 13 July 2003.

That muscle was especially in the realm of international and regional commerce, where Pretoria's free-trade strategy radically diverged from most African countries. Ideological backing for corporate-oriented subimperialism can usually be found within the South African Institute for International Affairs (SAIIA) at Johannesburg's University of the Witwatersrand. Yet because SAIIA heartily supports Nepad, its writers have the space to speak a certain kind of truth to corporate power. In 2001, a SAIIA researcher warned that Erwin's trade strategy 'might signify to the Africa group of countries that South Africa, a prominent leader of the continent, does not have their best interests at heart.'[7] In 2003, a colleague issued a technical report on trade which conceded that African governments viewed Erwin 'with some degree of suspicion' because of his promotion of the WTO. Indeed, at Seattle and Cancun Erwin stood in direct opposition to the bulk of the lowest-income countries, whose beleaguered trade ministers were responsible for derailing both summits.[8]

In these two regards, perhaps Nepad 'isn't working', because it can't work, because indeed the contradictions have already become overwhelming. Generally, mainstream opinion judges Nepad as a valid programme, consistent with what Chris Alden and Garth le Pere term Pretoria's 'loftier aims to play a key role in reshaping current international norms, institutions and process to further global justice for Africa and the South.'[9] The reality, however, is far less wholesome. To undergird this argument, we begin with economic and geopolitical dimensions of South African subimperialism, and then consider broader difficulties faced by Nepad's sponsors in terms of domestic politics and 'governance'.

Nepad as subimperialism

Leadership roles in Africa, the Third World and the entire international community were Pretoria's for the taking in the early 2000s. It was, hence a surprise, but not an aberration, when former president Nelson Mandela remarked in January 2003, just prior to the US/UK invasion of Iraq, 'If there is a country which has committed

7. *Mail & Guardian*, 16 November 2001.

8. *Business Day*, 2 June 2003.

9. Alden, C. and G. le Pere (2004), 'South Africa's Post-apartheid Foreign Policy: From Reconciliation to Ambiguity?,' *Review of African Political Economy*, 100, pp.104,106. In the same spirit, see Sidiropoulos, E. (Ed)(2004), *Apartheid Past, Renaissance Future: South Africa's Foreign Policy 1994-2004*, Johannesburg South African Institute of International Affairs. For more skeptical views, see Nel, P. and J. van der Westhuizen (Eds)(2004), *Democratizing Foreign Policy? Lessons from South Africa*, Lanham, Lexington Books.

unspeakable atrocities, it is the United States of America.'[10] Nor was it a surprise, or aberration, for him to conclusively retract that comment in May 2004: 'The United States is the most powerful state in the world, and it is not good to remain in tension with the most powerful state.'[11] As SAIIA's Greg Mills explained, 'I think there was a bluster by the South African government, or those associated near or around it, prior to the American invasion of Iraq in March last year, but that was toned down fairly quickly by the South African government and most notably, president Mbeki.'[12]

In an environment we can label 'talk left, walk right,' sorting out the dynamics of US-SA ties is not easy. As one University of Fort Hare academic alleged (in an attack on your author), 'I can't think of an instance when South Africa has supported the US unless the international community was already on board the issue. On Zimbabwe, the Democratic Republic of Congo, Sudan, Iraq, Haiti and Equatorial Guinea, South Africa has flat-out opposed US policies.'[13] But there is convincing, contrary evidence from those particular sites, and from international politics more generally.

On Zimbabwe, Mbeki was anointed 'point man' (*sic*) by Bush during his July 2002 visit, resulting in absolutely no further visible pressure from Washington on Mugabe. At the 2004 G8 Summit in Sea Island, Zimbabwe's semi-dictatorship was not even raised during the imperialist leaders' talks with Mbeki and other Africans. Aside from the occasional silly embarrassment, such as British foreign minister Jack Straw's September 2004 handshake with Mugabe (the former did not recognise the latter until he was pulled into a darkened corner of the United Nations, he claimed) and the trivial exclusion of Zimbabwe from the Commonwealth's Abuja summit in 2003, the imperial powers fear the race-related backlash associated with pressure on Zimbabwe, and appear willing to let Mbeki dominate Southern African regional politics because so little real wealth and power are at stake.[14]

---

10. CBS News (2003), 'Mandela Slams Bush On Iraq', 30 January.

11. CNN.com (2004), 'Mandela Extends Conciliatory Hand to United States,' 24 May.

12. Williams, L. (2004), 'SA to Export Arms?', *Business Day*, 21 July.

13. Blatchford, M. (2004), 'Walking Left, Writing Drivel', *Mail & Guardian*, 17 September.

14. For details, see Bond, P. and M.Manyanya (2003), *Zimbabwe's Plunge: Exhausted Nationalism, Neoliberalism and the Search for Social Justice*, London, Merlin Press and Pietermaritzburg, University of KwaZulu-Natal Press; and Bond, *Talk Left, Walk Right*, Chapter Five.

In the DRC, Africa's greatest mineral riches alter the equation. Pretoria and Washington back different corporations engaged in extraction and exploitation, to be sure, but are agreed on the general framework for regional geopolitics, and for enslaving Kinshasa via the multilateral agencies and the DRC's repayment of Mobuto-era 'odious debt.' In the latter case, it was Mbeki's Cabinet in mid-2002 that arranged an emergency 75 million Special Drawings Rights loan (then translated to R760 million), so as to clear some IMF arrears and permit a new round of World Bank and IMF missions, backed by the US Treasury. This overlap of interests extends into the chaotic peace/ war process, where Mbeki's mediation strategy gave relatively free reign to the pro-US factions, especially Kagame in Rwanda and Museveni in Uganda. Recall that it was Zimbabwe, Namibia and Angola which in 1998 committed military resources to tackle the US-backed Rwandan and Ugandan invasions of the DRC, in protection of their own militarised accumulation agendas, while South Africa refused to countenance a SADC-wide intervention to stabilise the faltering regime of Kabila, Sr. Finally, like Washington, Pretoria has refused to address its responsibility for the egregious behaviour of its multinational corporation. Both countries' illegal corporate extractions of DRC wealth during the late 1990s were noted by the UN Security Council in a damning 2002 report, but the corporations involved were rewarded with a blind eye in both capitals.[15]

In the Sudan, neither did much to pressure Khartoum to halt the Darfour genocide, aside from *jawboning* about sanctions and offering very small-scale peacekeeping troop deployments.

In Iraq, Pretoria certainly talked left about the war, but when it came to two crucial tests - the $250 million in Denel (parastatal) arms sales to the belligerents in Washington/London, and recognising the Iraqi government imposed by Bush in mid-2004 - the reality was tacit acceptance of the illegal war and occupation.

In Haiti, again, Mbeki certainly talked left, admirably so in early 2004 when he used the country's bicentenary to remind a very few listeners of the importance of that period's only successful slave rebellion, and likewise of the durable racial hierarchy in global political economy. Yet much more could have been done to confront the Washington/Paris state militarists for their eviction of Jean-Bertrand Aristide less than two months later, including active solidarity - via concrete punitive actions taken in the African

15. For details, see Bond and Manyanya, *Zimbabwe's Plunge,* Afterword and Bond, P. (2002), *Unsustainable South Africa: Environment, Development and Social Protest,* London, Merlin Press and Pietermaritzburg, University of KwaZulu-Natal Press, Introduction.

Union, the Non-Aligned Movement and other bodies – with the Caribbean island states which protested the coup d'etat. Washington ultimately had its way in Haiti. The regular reminder of that fact, through Aristide's exile in Pretoria and his regular appearances at public events, is consistent with Bush's agenda of signaling 'rogue regimes' – like nearby Venezuela's and Cuba's – that US-supported anti-government forces and the deployment of marines together pose an ongoing threat. Is Washington irritated by Aristide's exile in South Africa? There is no indication, and indeed the public reminder indeed evokes regular concern across the Third World, including in ruling South African circles. To illustrate, in a public debate at Wits University in August 2004, former Limpopo Province premier Ngoako Ramathlodi announced that 'South Africa cannot contest our foreign apartheid debt. Look what happened to Aristide when he asked France for reparations!' [16]

In Equatorial Guinea, there appears no mid- or long-term conflict with the US over that country's classical banana republic function, other than the predictable contestation over whether US or South African firms are the primary vehicles for oil extraction and distribution. But Pretoria seems to accommodate the overall context of corruption and violence practiced through venal dictatorial rule in US-backed petrol baronies (stretching from Latin America through West Africa through the Middle East out to Central Asia), with revenues flowing from multinational corporations to the elites' offshore accounts. The merits of the model to Pretoria were evident not only in the mid-2004 red-carpet visit by Equatorial Guinea's leader Teodoro Obiang Nguema M'Basogo and cooperation in his prosecution of early-2004 coup plotters (possibly including Margaret Thatcher's son Mark). Mbeki announced Pretoria's hope for a special binational commission – an unusual sign of cooperation – and a new South African diplomatic mission in the capital Malabo.

In addition to growing ties with West Africa's most notorious dictatorship, the rerouting of oil revenues out of Africa, to the Cayman Islands in particular, was apparently endorsed by Mbeki in 1999, according to a *Mail & Guardian* investigation. Beneficiaries from the Cayman-registered 'South African Oil Company', 75% owned by a Nigerian-American, included the wives of Provincial and Local Government Minister Sydney Mufamadi and of Ramathlodi, ANC senior official Zwelibanzi Nzama and the brother-in-law of the then-Eastern Cape premier Makhenkesi Stofile. Mbeki had helped set the

16. Plenary session at the University of the Witwatersrand Centre for Urban and Built Environment Studies Matthew Goniwe Lecture Series, Johannesburg, 4 August 2004.

deal up in 1999 and was unapologetic, even though the newspaper described it as a fraud against citizens of both Nigeria and South Africa.[17] Such a model is similar to those established by the US to channel both petrol and petrodollars in a manner hostile to the interests of local residents, dating back many decades.

In all these respects, US-SA relations can be compared to occasionally hostile brothers scrapping over their patches of Africa, but nevertheless siblings in a family enterprise not dissimilar to mafia control of a neighbourhood or city. Decades-long supplies of oil and minerals are the prizes, and though Washington and Pretoria contest certain particular sites, they seem together convinced that multinational corporate interests should lead the process of 'development', that African debt peonage should continue, that national governments' financial and trade restrictions should be dropped (hence making African countries ever more vulnerable to markets in the imperial and subimperial centres), and that geopolitical maneuvres should be conducted - with military backup in the nearly inevitable event of failure - in a manner consistent with South Africa's own elite political-economic transition.

It is, of course, worthwhile to flag the broader petro-military trajectory Washington is pursuing. An expert at the US Naval War College recently drew up 'The Pentagon's New Map,' highlighting countries now considered danger zones for imperialism. In Africa, these included Angola, Burundi, the Democratic Republic of the Congo (DRC), Rwanda, Somalia and even South Africa, sites which could not only 'incubate the next generation of global terrorists', but also host interminable poverty, disease and routine mass murder.[18] Benign - or malign - neglect would no longer be sufficient. The period during the 1990s after the failed Somali intervention, when Washington's armchair warriors let Africa slide out of view, may have come to an end with September 11. Army General Charles Wald, who controls the Africa Programme of the European Command, told the BBC in early 2004 that he aims to have five brigades with 15,000 men working in cooperation with regional partners including South Africa, Kenya, Nigeria and two others still to be chosen.[19] NATO's Supreme Allied Commander for Europe, General James Jones, confirmed the US geographical strategy in May 2003: 'The carrier battle groups of the

17. *Mail & Guardian*, 30 May 2003 and 6 June 2003

18. Barnett, T. (2003), 'The Pentagon's New Map', United States Naval War College, http://www.nwc.navy.mil/newrules/ ThePentagonsNewMap.htm.

19. Plaut, M. (2004), 'US to Increase African Military Presence,' http://www.bbc.co.uk, 23 March.

future and the expeditionary strike groups of the future may not spend six months in the Mediterranean Sea but I'll bet they'll spend half the time down the West Coast of Africa.'[20] Within weeks, 3000 US troops had been deployed off the coast of Liberia (and went briefly ashore to stabilize the country after Charles Taylor departed). Potential US bases were suggested for Ghana, Senegal and Mali, as well as the North African countries of Algeria, Morocco and Tunisia.[21] Another base was occupied by 1,500 US troops in the small Horn country of Djibouti. Botswana and Mozambique were also part of the Pentagon's strategy, and South Africa would remain a crucial partner.

Central and eastern Africa remains a problem area, and not merely because of traditional French and Belgian neocolonial competition with British and US interests.[22] President Bill Clinton's refusal to cite Rwanda's situation as formal genocide in 1994 was an infamous failure of nerve in terms of the emerging doctrine of 'humanitarian' imperialism - in contrast to intervention in the (white-populated) Balkans. With an estimated three million dead in Central African wars, partly due to struggles over access to coltan and other mineral riches, conflicts worsened between and within the Uganda/Rwanda bloc, vis-à-vis the revised alliance of Laurent Kabila's DRC, Zimbabwe, Angola and Namibia. Only with Kabila's assassination in 2001 and Pretoria's management of peace deals in the DRC and Burundi, did matters settle, however briefly, into a fragile peace combining neoliberalism with opportunities for minerals extraction. However, as turmoil resumed in mid-2004, it was clear that coups and outbreaks of strife would be a constant threat, demonstrating how precarious Pretoria's elite deals are when deeper tensions remain unresolved. Another particularly difficult site is Sudan, where US Delta Force troops have been sighted in informal operations, perhaps because although China showed some interest in oil exploration there during the country's civil war chaos, US oil firms have subsequently arrived. On the west coast, the major petro prize remains the Gulf of Guinea. With oil shipment from Africa to Louisiana refineries taking many fewer weeks than from the Persian Gulf, the world's shortage of supertankers is eased by direct sourcing from West Africa's offshore oil fields.

In this context, it is not surprising that of $700 million destined to develop a 75,000-strong UN peace-keeping force in coming years,

---

20. http://www.allAfrica.com, 2 May 2003.

21. *Ghana News*, 11 June 2003.

22. Taylor, I. (2003), 'Conflict in Central Africa: Clandestine Networks and Regional/Global Configurations,' *Review of African Political Economy*, 95, p.49.

$480 million is dedicated to African soldiers.[23] But Africa is also a site for the recruitment of private mercenaries, as an estimated 1,500 South Africans - including half of Mbeki's own 100 personal security force - joined firms such as South Africa's Executive Outcomes and British-based Erinys to provide more than 10% of the bodyguard services in occupied Iraq.[24] Some African countries, including Eritrea, Ethiopia and Rwanda, joined the 'Coalition of the Willing' against Iraq in 2003, although temporary UN Security Council members Cameroon, Guinea and the Republic of the Congo opposed the war, in spite of Washington's bullying. The Central African Republic proved reliable during the reconciliation of Jacques Chirac and the Bush regime in March 2004, when Aristide was kidnapped and temporarily dumped there. Africa is also an important site for Washington's campaigns against militant Islamic networks, especially in Algeria and Nigeria in the northwest, Tanzania and Kenya in the east, and South Africa. Control of African immigration to the US and Europe is crucial, in part through the expansion of US-style incarceration via private sector firms like Wackenhut, which has invested in South African privatized prison management, along with the notorious Lindela extradition camp for 'illegal immigrants,' part of a highly racialised global detention and identification system.

Within this broadly accepted context, in which Pretoria is increasingly seen as a reliable deputy sheriff, there is naturally room for disagreement on details. For example, in mid-2004, the US House of Representatives extended a year-old ban on military assistance to 32 countries - including South Africa (allegedly costing Pretoria roughly $7.6 million in 2003) - which agreed to cooperate in future with the International Criminal Court against alleged US war criminals. Nevertheless, Washington's ambassador to Pretoria, Cameron Hume, quickly announced that several bilateral military deals would go ahead in any case. According to Peter McIntosh of *African Armed Forces* journal, the US 'had simply re-routed military funding for South Africa through its European Command in Stuttgart.' Hume reported the Pentagon's desire 'to train and equip two additional battalions to expand the number of forces the [SA National Defense Force] have available for peacekeeping in Africa.' South African newspaper *ThisDay* commented, in the wake of two

23. The major dilemma, here, appears to be the very high level of HIV-positive members of the armed forces in key countries. See Elbe, S. (2003), *Strategic Implications of HIV/AIDS*, Adelphi Paper 357, International Institute for Strategic Studies, Oxford: Oxford University Press, pp.23-44.

24. *Vancouver Sun*, 11 May 2004.

successful joint US/SA military maneuvres in 2003-04: 'Operations such as Medflag and Flintlock clearly have applications other than humanitarian aid, and as the US interventions in Somalia and Liberia have shown, humanitarian aid often requires forceful protection.'[25]

The two countries' military relations were fully 'normalised' by July 2004, in the words of SA deputy minister Aziz Pahad. In partnership with General Dynamics Land Systems, State-owned Denel immediately began marketing 105 mm artillery alongside a turret and light armoured vehicle hull, in support of innovative Stryker Brigade Combat Teams ('a 3500-personnel formation that puts infantry, armour and artillery in different versions of the same 8x8 light armoured vehicle'). According to one report, 'The turret and gun is entirely proprietary to Denel, using only South African technology. At sea level, it can fire projectiles as far as 36 km.'[26] This followed a period of serious problems for the SA arms firm and others like it (Armscor and Fuchs), which were also allowed full access to the US market in July 2004 after paying fines for apartheid-era sanctions-busting.[27] Given Pretoria's 1998 decision to invest US$6 billion in mainly offensive weaponry such as fighter jets and submarines, there are growing fears that peacekeeping is a cover for a more expansive agenda, and that Mbeki is tacitly permitting a far stronger US role in Africa – from the oil rich Gulf of Guinea and Horn of Africa, to training bases in the South and North – than is necessary.[28]

The way forward appears to be more of the same, although contradictions do occasionally slow progress. US ambassador to Pretoria Jendayi Frazer argued in September 2004 that the relationship was mutually constitutive: 'America needs South Africa. The US is the most economically and politically powerful country in the world, while South Africa is the most economically and politically powerful country in sub-Saharan Africa. The US economy represents about 30% of the world's output, and South Africa's GDP is about 38% of sub-Saharan Africa's output.' The mutual interests 'will grow stronger as our commercial ties are strengthened. There is a mutual benefit from this strong relationship that will shape Africa and the

25. Schmidt, M. (2004), 'US offers to Train and Equip Battalions,' *ThisDay*, 19 July.

26. South African Press Association (2004), 'Denel to Benefit from US Defence Trade', 21 July.

27. See Batchelor, P. and S. Willett (1998), *Disarmament and Defence Industrial Adjustment in South Africa*, Oxford: Oxford University Press; Crawford-Browne, T. (2004), 'The Arms Deal Scandal,' *Review of African Political Economy*, 31, pp.329-342.

28. Black, D. (2004), 'Democracy, Development, Security and South Africa's "Arms Deal"', in Philip Nel and Janis van der Westhuizen (Eds), *Democratizing Foreign Policy? Lessons from South Africa*, Lanham, MD: Lexington Books.

world at large. As South Africa develops as a key global economic player, it can do this better by expanding its ties with the US, more so than with any other country or regional grouping.' Washington, too, believes that 'we must expand our ties to South Africa more so than any other country in Africa. In many ways, South Africa's role in sub-Saharan Africa is analogous to the role of the US in the world. Our two countries are in a historic moment where deepening our relationship and our commercial ties will positively shape global affairs.' Hence intensified trade interrelationships are vital: 'For the first time, we are negotiating a free trade agreement (FTA) in sub-Saharan Africa with the Southern Africa Customs Union (SACU), signaling a recognition of Africa's central role in the global economy and its strategic importance to the US.'[29]

Ironically, just as Frazer was publicising this intent, US-SACU FTA negotiations actually broke down. According to one report,

> South Africa's chief negotiator, Xavier Carim, tried to put on a brave face this week, saying that due to the complex nature of trade negotiations, periods of difficulty in which the process slowed down could be expected... But the US-SACU negotiators have so far failed to resolve fundamental differences on a number of key issues in which SACU negotiators believe US demands run counter to the region's development agenda. These include intellectual property and investment rules – US demands are said to conflict with key SA development concerns, such as the provision of health services and black economic empowerment. Carim said US standards on intellectual property were high and 'may not be appropriate for a developing country'. The issue also came up in the US's recent agreement with Australia, where the US pushed for higher prices on generic medicines to protect the intellectual property of US drug makers. This is likely to be even more important for those SACU economies that are struggling to contain an HIV/Aids epidemic and need to source cheap drugs to extend treatment. Other sources of disagreement are believed to include government procurement, where equitable access for foreign firms could have serious consequences for the government's black economic empowerment initiatives and other policies.[30]

29. Frazer, J. (2004), Why SA and the US Need each Other', *Sunday Times,* 19 September.

30. Mnyanda, L. (2004), 'Trade Talks Grind to a Halt,' *Sunday Times,* 19 September.

In a recent survey, Robert Biel identified two central contradictions in US imperialism vis-à-vis Africa: 'First, central accumulation always tends to siphon away the value which could form the basis of state-building, bringing with it the risk of "state failure", leading to direct intervention. Second, the international system becomes increasingly complex, characterised by a range of new actors and processes and direct penetration of local societies in a way which bypasses the state-centric dimension.' Because of the complexity of indirect rule, and the difficulty of co-opting all relevant actors, Biel continues, 'A reversion to the deployment of pure power is always latent, and the post-September 11th climate has brought it directly to the fore. This is a significant weakness of international capitalism.'[31] And it explains why Pretoria is so desirable as Washington's ally.

However, because South Africa has its own material interests, which occasionally conflict with those of the imperialist bloc, leading to rare breakdowns in negotiations such as US-SACU, it is useful to more closely consider whether the economic motor of South African organic subimperialism in Africa can be found in Johannesburg boardrooms. As intimated, the contradictions in central and subimperial accumulation mean that siphoning value is not always as easy as Pretoria desires.

SOUTH AFRICAN INVESTMENT PATTERNS, THEN AND NOW

Nelson Mandela may have been diplomatic - or disturbingly frank - when in mid-2003 he launched the Mandela Rhodes Foundation at Rhodes House in Cape Town, the former De Beers corporate headquarters. De Beers was, at the time, a high-profile defendant in Jubilee South Africa and apartheid victim lawsuits to reclaim apartheid profits. Mandela not only condemned the suits, but his speech contained a positive reference to the company founder's subimperial role: 'I am sure that Cecil John Rhodes would have given his approval to this effort to make the South African economy of the early 21st century appropriate and fit for its time.'[32]

What kind of precedent did Rhodes set? In Southern and Central Africa, the consolidation of settler colonialism was feasible in large part thanks to the 1880-90s entrepreneurship and geopolitical leadership of Rhodes, a financier who graduated from diamond merchant cartelisation in Kimberley, where the DeBeers monopoly

31. Biel, R. (2003) 'Imperialism and International Governance: The Case of US Policy towards Africa', *Review of African Political Economy*, 95, p.87.

32. South African Press Association (2003), 'Mandela Criticises Apartheid Lawsuits,' 25 August.

was born, to become governor of the Cape Colony. Rhodes received permission from Queen Victoria to plunder what are now called Gauteng Province (greater Johannesburg) once gold was discovered in 1886, and then Zimbabwe, Zambia and Malawi; his ambition was to paint the map British imperial red, stretching along the route from the Cape to Cairo. Rhodes' two main vehicles were the British army, which invented the concentration camp and in the process killed 25,000 Afrikaner women and children and 14,000 black people during the 1899-1902 Anglo Boer South African War, and the British South Africa Company (BSAC), a for-profit firm which in 1890 began its drive from Cape Town north of the Limpopo River by sponsoring the 'Pioneer Column'. That settler initiative soon founded present-day Harare while massacring thousands of Shona and Ndebele people who had established pockets of resistance from 1893-96. London imperialists assumed that competition would continue beyond Berlin's 'Scramble for Africa', and that only BSAC-style expansion, at relatively little cost to Britain's taxpayers, would ensure geographical dominance over the interior of the continent in the face of hostile German, Portuguese, French, Belgian and Boer forces. Such a strategy was critical, they posited, to the protection of even the Nile Valley, which in turn represented the life-line to the prize of India.[33]

As is the case today, however, a crucial economic dynamic was playing out in Europe, above and beyond the never-ending search for gold, which helped explain the resource flows behind Rhodes' conquests: chronic overaccumulation of capital, especially in the London and Paris financial markets. Moreover, the push of capital was joined by the pull of white settlers from the colonising powers, as a result of growing social, ethnic and nascent class unrest across Southern Africa, itself a logical consequence of the establishment of systemic migrant labour systems. This dynamic fit the general thesis concerning financial control, capital-export, sub-imperial settler sites, and the advanced capitalist countries' 'labour aristocracy' advanced by, among others, Hobson, Hilferding and Lenin.[34]

Likewise, the easy availability of foreign portfolio funding for nascent Southern African stock markets in Johannesburg

33. Loney, M. (1975), *Rhodesia: White Racism and Imperial Response,* Harmondsworth, Penguin, pp. 31-32.

34. Lenin illustrated *Imperialism* with a quote Rhodes uttered in 1895: 'In order to save the 40,000,000 inhabitants of the United Kingdom from a bloody civil war, we colonial statesmen must acquire new lands to settle the surplus population, to provide new markets for the goods produced in the factories and mines. The Empire, as I have always said, is a bread and butter question. If you want to avoid civil war, you must become imperialists.' (Lenin, V. [1986](1917), *Imperialism*, Moscow, Progress Publishers, p.87.)

and Bulawayo stemmed from a lengthy international economic depression, chronic excess financial liquidity (a symptom of general overaccumulation), and the global hegemony enjoyed by City of London financiers. Surplus capital was still concentrated in the London stock market in the early 1890s, and flowed easily not only to other European countries and the New World, but also to the high-profile, well-tested initiatives of Rhodes, supported by the likes of the then journalist, Winston Churchill.

In sum, it was a period, Ian Phimister contends, of increasing geopolitical turbulence across Africa emanating from 'capitalism's uneven development during the last third of the nineteenth century, particularly the City of London's crucial role in mediating the development of a world economic system.' As Britain faced industrial decline during the 1870s in both absolute and relative terms, manufacturers unable to compete in European markets joined ascendant London financial and commercial interests in promoting Free Trade philosophy, in contrast to the protectionism of other Europeans and the United States.[35]

A central function of Rhodes' role in the region was, in the course of searching for gold, to ameliorate the contradictions of global capitalism by channeling financial surpluses into new infrastructural investments, such as the telegraph, railroad and surveying that tamed and commodified the lands immediately north of South Africa. Even if these did not immediately pay off for the BSAC, they did succeed in extracting resources and assuring political allegiance to South African corporate power, a power that was generally in harmonious unity with the evolving British-run states of the region. We return to this point shortly, because regional economic domination – through liberalism backed by the forces of colonial power then, and today, through neoliberalism with military capabilities not yet fully tested – has also become the objective of the contemporary South African ruling class.

Today, the most important ways that South African corporate investments in the region foster economic relations in the tradition of Rhodes are through retail trade, mining, agricultural technology and the Nepad private infrastructure investment strategy.[36] The terrain is terribly uneven, with Nepad in particular so far failing to attract

35. Phimister, I. (1992), 'Unscrambling the Scramble: Africa's Partition Reconsidered,' Paper presented to the African Studies Institute, University of the Witwatersrand, Johannesburg, 17 August, pp.11-15.

36. Miller, D. (2004), 'South African Multinational Corporations, Nepad and Competing Claims on Post-Apartheid Southern Africa,' Institute for Global Dialogue Occasional Paper 40, Johannesburg.

the desired privatisation ('public-private partnership') resources. Still, a common criticism, that South African businesses are 'new imperialists', became a matter of 'great concern' by 2004, according to a leading member of Mbeki's cabinet, Jeff Radebe: 'There are strong perceptions that many South African companies working elsewhere in Africa come across as arrogant, disrespectful, aloof and careless in their attitude towards local business communities, work seekers and even governments.'[37]

For example, Johannesburg retailers are deindustrialising many African countries by sourcing their goods from South Africa instead of local producers, so as to take advantage of economies of scale.[38] As noted above, Johannesburg mining firms became an embarrassment in part because of the DRC looting allegations, and in part because of the role the DeBeers diamond conglomerate and its Botswana government and World Bank allies played in the displacement of the Basarwa/San bushmen in 2003-04.[39]

It may well be, however, that the longer-term implications of South African subimperialism can best be observed in the agricultural sector. While the governments of Zimbabwe, Zambia and Angola all attempted to resist genetically modified organisms in food crops, in part because that would shut down their European export potentials, South Africa became the gateway to infecting African agriculture. 'Despite comprehensive objections raised by the African Centre for Biosafety and Biowatch South Africa,' according to the *Mail & Guardian* in July 2004, Pretoria 'approved a United States funded project that will soon see genetically engineered potatoes sprouting in six secret locations in African soil. Similar potatoes were first grown in the United States but were withdrawn from the market due to consumer resistance.' Biowatch South Africa requested a delay in the decision until a High Court ruling on the secret proliferation of genetically engineered organisms, but was initially unsuccessful.[40]

Surprisingly, perhaps the most significant *potential* factor in South African corporate subimperialism, Nepad, was apparently still-born as an operative investment framework. 'In three years not a

37. Sapa, 30 March 2004.

38. Miller, D. (2003), 'SA Multinational Corporations in Africa: Whose African Renaissance?,' International Labour Research and Information Group Occasional Paper, Cape Town.

39. Taylor, I. and G.Mokhawa (2003), 'Not Forever: Botswana, Conflict Diamonds and the Bushmen,' *African Affairs*, 102.

40. *Mail & Guardian* (2004), 'SA Biosafety Regulators in Bed with Industry on GM Potatoes?,' 27 July; http://www.biosafetyafrica.net; http://www.biowatch.org.za.

single company has invested in plan's 20 high-profile infrastructure development projects (roads, energy, water, telecommunications, ports), according to *Business Day* in mid-2004. 'The private sector's reluctance to get involved threatens to derail Nepad's ambitions.' In contrast, a 2002 World Economic Forum meeting in Durban provided Nepad with endorsements from 187 major companies, including Anglo American, BHP Billiton, Absa Bank and Microsoft. According to the programme's chief economist, Mohammed Jahed, 'Nepad is reliant upon the success of these infrastructure projects, so we need to rethink how we will get the private sector involved, because clearly they have not played the role we expected.'[41]

Johannesburg capital is indeed moving rapidly into the region, but the problem seems to be a disconnect between longer-term, public-oriented investments within the Nepad portfolio, and the short-termist self-interest of corporations. John Daniel, Varusha Naidoo and Sanusha Naidu of Pretoria's Human Sciences Research Council documented Johannesburg capital's march up-continent in a useful survey. However, they concluded, 'A distinction needs to be drawn between the behaviour of South Africa's corporates and its government… it is not possible for Africa's politicians to make the same charge ['they bulldoze their way around', according to a Kenyan MP on Johannesburg business leaders in 2001] against those who represent South Africa's political interests in Africa... Here there has been a sea-change from the past... non-hegemonic co-operation has in fact, been the option embraced by the post-apartheid South African state.'[42]

The reality, as even journalists have surmised, is different. In August 2003, the *Sunday Times* remarked on SADC delegates' sentiments at a Dar es Salaam regional summit: 'Pretoria was "too defensive and protective" in trade negotiations [and] is being accused of offering too much support for domestic production "such as duty rebates on exports" which is killing off other economies in the region.'[43] One key problem is that actions taken by Pretoria bureaucrats, including the Department of Trade and Industry, don't

41. Rose, R. (2004), 'Companies "Shirking" their Nepad Obligations', *Business Day*, 24 May.

42. Daniel, J., V.Naidoo and S.Naidu (2003), 'The South Africans have Arrived: Post-Apartheid Corporate Expansion into Africa,' in J.Daniel, A.Habib and R.Southall (Eds), *State of the Nation: South Africa 2003-04*, Pretoria, HSRC, pp.388-389. For an update, see Daniel, J., J.Lutchman and S.Naidu (2004), 'Post-apartheid South Africa's Corporate Expansion into Africa,' *Review of African Political Economy*, 31, pp.343-348.

43. Munusamy, R. (2003), 'SADC wants to Raise SA's Trade Tariffs', *Sunday Times*, 24 August.

necessarily correspond to the integrative investment strategies proposed by the Nepad secretariat.

Hence Nepad's function has *not* been, so far, to boost profits for South African and allied businesses in the 20 major projects. Instead, it is probably more accurate to describe Nepad as subimperialist because of the way it revitalises the bankrupt philosophy of neoliberalism in Africa.

Neoliberal Nepad

Washington and the rest of the West had no problems with Nepad's economic foundations. *Institutional Investor* magazine quoted the Bush administration's chief Africa bureaucrat, Walter Kansteiner: 'The US will focus on those emerging markets doing the right thing in terms of private sector development, economic freedom and liberty.'[44] An IMF *Working Paper on the New Partnership for Africa's Development* termed Nepad 'visionary', and promoted 'the active selling of reforms' through national marketing and advice centres, such as the African Regional Technical Assistance Centre in Dar es Salaam. African governments should 'use Poverty Reduction Strategy Papers (PRSPs) to translate Nepad's framework into operational blueprints.'[45]

If PRSPs were the model, Nepad's operational blueprints would be no different than the standard Washington Consensus approach to economic development: export-led growth, fiscal and monetary discipline, and trade/financial liberalisation. That approach considers as a central premise that deeper integration into the world economy will benefit the continent. Yet Africa's *share* of world trade declined over the past quarter century, while the *volume* of exports increased. 'Marginalisation' of Africa occurred not because of *lack* of integration, but because other areas of the world, especially East Asia, moved to the export of manufactured goods. Africa's industrial potential declined thanks to excessive deregulation associated with structural adjustment.[46]

Moreover, Africa's debt crisis worsened as globalisation intensified. From 1980-2000, Sub-Saharan Africa's total foreign debt rose from $60 billion to $206 billion, and the ratio of debt to GDP rose from 23% to 66%. Africa now repays more than it receives. In 1980,

44. Gopinath, 'Doubt of Africa.'

45. http://www.brettonwoodsproject.org, May 2003.

46. Arrighi, G. (2002), 'The African Crisis: World Systemic and Regional Aspects,' *New Left Review* 2, 15; Saul, J. and C.Leys (1999), 'Sub-Saharan Africa in Global Capitalism,' *Monthly Review*, July.

loan inflows of $9.6 billion were higher than the debt repayment outflow of $3.2 billion. By 2000, only $3.2 billion came in, and $9.8 billion was repaid, leaving a net financial flows deficit of $6.2 billion.[47] Meanwhile, donor aid was down 40% from 1990 levels. There is convincing documentation that the tearing of safety nets under structural adjustment worsens the vulnerability of women, children, the elderly and disabled people. They are expected to survive with less social subsidy and greater pressure on the fabric of the family during economic crisis, which makes women more vulnerable to sexual pressures and, therefore, HIV/AIDS.[48]

The other source of outflows that must be reversed, if Africa is to overcome its systematic underdevelopment within the circuits of international finance, is capital flight. James Boyce and Léonce Ndikumana argue that a core group of subSaharan African countries with a joint foreign debt of $178 billion, suffered a quarter century of capital flight by elites that totaled more than $285 billion, including imputed interest earnings. 'Taking capital flight as a measure of private external assets, and calculating net external assets as private external assets, minus public external debts, sub-Saharan Africa appears to be a net creditor vis-à-vis the rest of the world.'[49] Capital flight by African elites is not taken seriously in Nepad. A crackdown would conflict with South African finance minister Trevor Manuel's commitment to further financial liberalisation on a 'fast-track' basis, which promised he would pursue during a 2002 talk to the Commonwealth Business Forum.[50]

Subsequently, the danger of free-flowing finance rose to new levels. Two years later, Manuel's director general Lesetja Kganyago announced a new 'Financial Centre for Africa' project to amplify

47. World Bank (2002), *Global Finance Tables*, Washington.

48. See, e.g., Elson, D. (1991), 'The Impact of Structural Adjustment on Women: Concepts and Issues,' in B.Onimode (ed), *The IMF, the World Bank and the African Debt*, London, Zed Books; Longwe, S. (1991), 'The Evaporation of Policies for Women's Advancement,' in N.Heyzer et al (Eds), *A Commitment to the Worlds Women*, New York, UNIFEM; Mahmoud, F. (1996), 'Building a Pan-African Women's Movement', in T.Abdul-Raheem (Ed), Pan-Africanism: Politics, Economy and Social Change in the 21st Century, Trenton, Africa World Press; and Tskikata, D. and J. Kerr (Eds)(2002), *Demanding Dignity: Women Confronting Economic Reforms in Africa*, Ottawa, The North-South Institute and Accra, Third World Network-Africa..

49. Boyce, J. and L. Ndikumana (2000), 'Is Africa a Net Creditor? New Estimates of Capital Flight from Severely Indebted Sub-Saharan African Countries, 1970-1996', Occasional Paper, University of Massachusetts/Amherst Political Economy Research Institute.

50. Manuel, T. (2002), 'Mobilizing International Investment Flows: The New Global Outlook,' Speech to the Commonwealth Business Council, 24 September.

the financialisation tendencies already evident in Johannesburg's exclusive new Sandton central business district: 'Over the five years to 2002, the financial sector grew at a real rate of 7.7% per year, more than twice as fast as the economy as a whole.' Responsible for a full quarter of post-apartheid South African GDP growth, the sector required further room to expand. According to Kganyago, 'What is needed is a financial hub especially focused on the needs and circumstances of the region, much in the same way that Singapore and Hong Kong cater for the capital needs of the Asian continent... International financial centres tend to have a foundation in common. Elements include political stability, free markets, and what is best described as the rule of commercial law.' Pretoria's specific aims included 'opening South Africa's markets to African and global issuers; global lowest trading costs and trading risk; global leadership in investor protection; and a global hub for financial business process outsourcing.' Concluded Kganyago, 'Africa's economies cannot wait the slow maturing of national financial markets to provide the necessary channel for large-scale foreign capital flows for development. Only a regional financial centre will be in a position to provide these services in the foreseeable future.'[51]

Much the same attitude of regional dominance, no matter how infirm the basis, was evident in the sphere of geopolitics.

Political Nepad

At first blush, the most hopeful political intervention from the African Union and Nepad was a set of peace-keeping efforts in West African hotspots and the Great Lakes region. However, the particularly difficult Burundi and DRC terrains of war were riven with deep-seated rivalries and socio-economic desperation, which Pretoria did not comprehend much less resolve. In 2003, prominent South African officials (Mandela – who was chief mediator in Burundi, Mbeki, foreign minister Nkosazana Dlamini-Zuma and deputy president Jacob Zuma) facilitated two power-sharing peace deals in these countries, but left the underlying contradictions intact.

The papering-over efforts did not halt the massacre of hundreds in the northeast of the DRC the day of the celebrated Sun City peace deal. Nor did it succeed in bringing key Burundian rebel leaders to the table for many months. By year-end 2003, reported Jean-Jacques Cornish in the *Mail & Guardian*, 'war-weary Burundians continue to

51. Kganyago, L. (2004), 'South Africa as a Financial Centre for Africa,' Speech to the Reuters Economist of the Year Award Ceremony, Johannesburg, 11 August.

be denied their peace dividend,' because the National Liberation Front was not included in Pretoria's deal. This left 1 500 South African troops in that war zone along with 2 000 other African peace-keepers. The UN Security Council expressed unease at the lack of reform and disarmament in the DRC.[52]

Millions have died in the DRC, and hundreds of thousands in Burundi. On the surface, Pretoria's senior conflict mediation in central Africa during 2003 appeared positive. However, closer to the ground, the agreements more closely resemble the style of elite deals which lock in place 'low-intensity democracy' and neoliberal economic regimes. Moreover, because some of the belligerent forces were explicitly left out, the subsequent weeks and months after declarations of peace witnessed periodic massacres of civilians in both countries and a near-coup in the DRC.

By mid-2004, the highly-regarded intellectual and leader of the Rassemblement Congolais la Democratic, Ernest Wamba dia Wamba, was publicly critical of Pretoria's interference, arguing that Mbeki and his colleagues set the process off 'on a wrong footing'. He complained, 'Some feel like South Africa has actively put us in the situation we are in. They had a lot of leverage to make sure that certain structural problems were anticipated and solutions proposed. They seem to have fallen in the Western logic of thinking that mediocrity is a less evil for Congolese, if it stops the war. They also have a lot of leverage to get a clear on-going commitment to resolve the contradictory fears of both the DRC and Rwanda; they do not seem to use it.'[53]

One can only hope that Pretoria's peace deals will stick. Yet the interventions were characterised by top-down decisions from the presidency, and apparently neglected consultation with the SA National Defence Force or Foreign Affairs, much less African parliaments and societies. Trying to police the global capitalist periphery required more common sense in relation to the root causes of conflict, because without making provision for total debt cancellation in Burundi, for example, the massive drain on that country's resources is a recipe for conflict. In 1998, as strife became endemic, Burundi spent nearly 40% of its export earnings on debt repayment – in the same league as only two other countries, Brazil and Zimbabwe. In Brazil, the people's anger at the economic oppression associated with this level of debt repayment saw the Workers' Party assume political power five years later. In Zimbabwe,

52. *Mail & Guardian,* 19 December 2003.

53. Majavu, M. (2004), 'Interview with Ernest Wamba dia Wamba,' http://www.zmag.org, 22 June.

the state turned to brutal repression. Burundi, meanwhile, was led, slowly and painfully, first by Julius Nyerere and then Mandela, toward a power-sharing deal that was meant to sort out ethnic divisions, but that could exacerbate the crisis because of the lack of root-cause problem solving.

There was, nevertheless, hope that the good-governance rhetoric in the Nepad base document might do some good: 'With Nepad, Africa undertakes to respect the global standards of democracy, which core components include ... fair, open, free and democratic elections periodically organised to enable the populace choose their leaders freely.'[54]

While South Africa under Mbeki's rule permits free and fair elections (after all, the ANC wins easily), the other main Nepad leader, Nigeria's Obasanjo, does not. This was apparent during the April 2003 presidential poll, which resulted in what a United Nations press agency termed, 'the threshold of total one-party dominance' by the ruling People's Democratic Party. As one example, according to official records, a near 100% turnout occurred in the southern Rivers State, with 2.1 million of 2.2 million registered voters supporting president Obasanjo. Yet electoral observers reported a low turnout.[55] In Obasanjo's home state of Ogun, the president won 1 360 170 votes against his main opponent's 680. The number of votes cast in a simultaneous race in the same geographical area was just 747 296. Obasanjo's explanation, by way of denigrating European Union electoral observers, was that, 'certain communities in this country make up their minds to act as one in political matters... They probably don't have that kind of culture in most European countries.' International observers found 'serious irregularities throughout the country and fraud in at least 11 of 36 states.'[56]

According to Chima Ubani of the Civil Liberties Organisation, 'it's not the actual wish of the electorate but some machinery that has churned out unbelievable outcomes. We've seen a landslide that does not seem sufficiently explained by any available factor.' The opposition All Nigeria People's Party called the vote, 'the most flagrantly rigged in Nigeria's history.' Complaints also came from the Transition Monitoring Group and the Catholic Church's Justice Development and Peace Commission, which together had 40 000 monitors documenting abuse.[57] In contrast, Mbeki's weekly ANC

54. Nepad, paragraph 79.

55. IRIN news service, 12 May 2003.

56. *Mail & Guardian*, 26 April 2003.

57. IRIN news service, 12 May 2003.

internet *ANC Today* letter proclaimed, 'Nigeria has just completed a series of elections, culminating in the re-election of president Olusegun Obasanjo into his second and last term. Naturally, we have already sent our congratulations to him.' Mbeki registered, but then dismissed, the obvious: 'It is clear that there were instances of irregularities in some parts of the country. However, it also seems clear that by and large the elections were well conducted.'[58]

NEPAD'S ZIMBABWE TEST

A similar lack of respect for democracy was evident in Zimbabwe.[59] Ironically, after opposing Nepad at the AU meeting in Durban, Mugabe and foreign minister Stan Mudenge were visited by a humble Dlamini-Zuma in October 2002. A few days later, finance minister Herbert Murerwa used his budget speech to parliament to proclaim that it was, 'critical that Zimbabwe remains part of this [Nepad] process.'[60] An increasingly cozy relationship between Pretoria and Harare alienated Zimabwe's democratic opposition. Morgan Tsvangirai, leader of the Movement for Democratic Change, concluded that Mbeki had, 'embarked on an international safari to campaign for Mugabe's regime. Pretoria is free to pursue its own agenda. But it must realise that Zimbabweans can never be fooled anymore.'[61] Tsvangirai was framed on a ludicrous treason charge in early 2002, which two years later continued dragging on in the courts.

According to Tsvangirai, the February 2003 gambit by Mbeki and Obasanjo to readmit Zimbabwe to the Commonwealth represented

> the disreputable end game of a long-term Obasanjo-Mbeki strategy designed to infiltrate and subvert not only the Commonwealth effort but, all other international efforts intended to rein in Mugabe's violent and illegitimate regime. Through this diabolical act of fellowship and solidarity with a murderous dictatorship, General Obasanjo and Mr Mbeki have now openly joined Mugabe as he continues to wage

58. http://www.anc.org.za, 25 April 2003.

59. The story of Pretoria's bizarre relationship with the Zanu-PF regime is told in Bond, P. and M.Manyanya (2003), *Zimbabwe's Plunge.*

60. Murerwa, H. (2002), 'The 2003 National Budget Statement,' Parliament, Harare, 14 November.

61. Tsvangirai, M. (2002), 'President of the MDC's Speech to MDC Parliamentarians,' Harare, 18 December.

> a relentless war against the people of Zimbabwe. They are now self-confessed fellow travelers on a road littered with violence, destruction and death.[62]

Most in Zimbabwean civil society shared that cynicism. In a foreword to a 2003 booklet subtitled, *Why the New Partnership for Africa's Development is Already Failing*, Zimbabwe Coalition on Debt and Development chairperson Jonah Gokova wrote of the

> profound rejection of Nepad by Zimbabweans from important social movements, trade unions and NGOs within our increasingly vibrant civil society... we now call on Africans to rally around an African People's Consensus, inspired by a vision of the development of the continent that reflects more genuine African thinking, instead of Nepad, that 'homegrown' rehashing of the Washington Consensus augmented by transparently false promises of good governance and democracy.[63]

Did Mbeki and Obasanjo deserve the derision? They termed Zimbabwe's 2002 presidential election 'legitimate,' and repeatedly opposed punishment of that regime by the Commonwealth and UN Human Rights Commission. In February 2003, Dlamini-Zuma stated, 'We will never criticise Zimbabwe.' The Nepad secretariat's Dave Malcomson, responsible for international liaison and co-ordination, admitted to a reporter, 'Wherever we go, Zimbabwe is thrown at us as the reason why Nepad's a joke.'[64]

Later in 2003, the Zimbabwe issue emerged as an international scandal once again. Mbeki had failed in his March 2003 attempt to have Zimbabwe readmitted to the Commonwealth, following the March 2002 election-related suspension. He then tried to ensure Mugabe would be invited to the December 2003, Abuja meeting of the Commonwealth, hosted by Obasanjo. But the Nigerian was under pressure from London, Canberra and Ottawa, and his fact-

---

62. Cited in Manyanya, M. (Ed)(2003), *NEPAD's Zimbabwe Test: Why the New Partnership for Africa's Development is Already Failing*, Harare, Zimbabwe Coalition on Debt and Development, Foreword. For reasons that are unclear, Tsvangirai, in December 2003, 'encouraged' Mbeki's constructive engagement. At the time, the MDC was hoping to gain admittance to the Socialist International whose other main African member was the ANC.

63. Manyanya, *NEPAD's Zimbabwe Test*, Foreword.

64. *Business Day*, 28 March 2003.

finding mission to Harare a few weeks before the Commonwealth summit did not give him sufficient logical ammunition to persuade Commonwealth powerbrokers that political freedom now existed in Zimbabwe.

With Obasanjo refusing to invite Mugabe, Mbeki reportedly decided to punish the Commonwealth secretary-general, New Zealander Don McKinnon, who, according to Pretoria, had bent Commonwealth rules. McKinnon's secret 2002-03 consultations concluded a majority of members wanted the Zimbabwe issue decided in December 2003, and not March of that year. Apparently in revenge, Pretoria proposed replacing McKinnon with former Sri Lankan foreign minister Lakshma Kadirgamar. But Mbeki's candidate lost the election by 40-11. The news agency Zwnews.com opined that Botswana, Cameroon, The Gambia, Ghana, Kenya, Malawi, Mauritius and Sierra Leone voted for McKinnon.

At the Abuja summit, Zimbabwe was suspended indefinitely. Mugabe immediately announced at a ZANU(PF) congress that Zimbabwe would leave the organisation. The real loser, however, was Mbeki, for as University of Pretoria politics professor Hussein Solomon remarked, 'Mbeki has no credibility as a leader. He is not prepared to stand by the principles espoused in terms of the African renaissance.'[65]

Clearly bitter upon his return home, Mbeki helped craft a statement issued by the Southern African Development Community plus Uganda, complaining that unnamed Commonwealth members were, 'dismissive, intolerant and rigid.' Mbeki's next ANC website letter condemned the original March 2002 justification for suspending Zimbabwe, noting that the electoral observation mission Pretoria had reported back with these lines: 'The Mission is, therefore, of the view that the outcome of the elections represents the legitimate voice of the people of Zimbabwe.'

Mbeki then rubbished Zimbabwean democrats:

> In his book Diplomacy, Dr Henry Kissinger discusses the place of the issue of human rights in the East-West struggle during the Cold War. He writes that: 'Reagan and his advisers invoked (human rights) to try to undermine the Soviet system.' ... It is clear that some within Zimbabwe and elsewhere in the world, including our country, are following the example set by 'Reagan and his advisers', to 'treat human rights as

65. *Business Day*, 9 December 2003.

a tool' for overthrowing the government of Zimbabwe and rebuilding Zimbabwe as they wish. In modern parlance, this is called regime change.[66]

Zimbabwe Lawyers for Human Rights director, Arnold Tsunga, commented that Mbeki created 'a real danger of human rights defenders being attacked or clamped down upon... These remarks are likely to have far reaching and grave consequences on the operating environment of human rights defenders in Zimbabwe.'[67]

To top it off, the next week, Mbeki visited Mugabe and saw Tsvangirai for 25 minutes. The Zimbabwean president once again failed to agree to liberalise the political environment. Mbeki then attempted a diplomatic nicety: 'President Mugabe can assist us to confront the problems we have in South Africa, so that we can assist you to solve the problems that face Zimbabwe.' The comment caused a sudden decline in the rand's value, and so *Sunday Independent* political writer John Battersby, a loyal transmission belt for Pretoria, quoted a 'senior government spokesperson' that the comment was 'to ensure that the Zimbabweans continue listening to us.'[68] But would anyone else?

German chancellor Gerhard Schroeder had a chance in January 2004 during a state visit, when Mbeki announced: 'I'm happy to say that they [ZANU(PF) and the MDC] have agreed now that they will go into formal negotiations.' In reality, Tsvangirai was back in court on the treason frame-up that same week and the MDC's Harare office was raided by police – hardly auspicious signs. The last formal 'talks about talks' had occurred seven months earlier. MDC secretary-general Welshman Ncube replied to Mbeki, 'We have heard it all before.' Mugabe's justice minister, Patrick Chinamasa, leader of the government's negotiating team, confirmed that he was 'not aware of any new developments.'[69]

Similar episodes occurred throughout 2004. And the spurning of democrats in Zimbabwe followed the pattern already established in

66. Mbeki, T. (2003), 'We Will Resist the Upside-Down View of Africa,' *ANC Today* 49, http://www.anc.org.za, 12 December. Notably, Mbeki failed to use the Commonwealth as a venue to criticise the illegal invasion and occupation of Iraq by Britain and Australia.

67. Tsunga, A. (2003), 'The Legal Profession and the Judiciary as Human Rights Defenders in Zimbabwe,' Mutare, 24 December, p.1.

68. *Sunday Independent,* 21 December 2003.

69. *London Times,* 23 January 2004.

relation to civil society more generally: ignoring the opposition, until the point at which (half-hearted) co-option was required.

NEPAD AND CIVIL SOCIETY

Notwithstanding the fact that until April 2002, there was *no* involvement by organised civil society in the construction of the Nepad base document or consultation about its implementation, it was not surprising that a flurry of activity occurred once the programme began to be better publicised as Africa's governance blueprint in mid-2002. For example, at the World Economic Forum (WEF) Southern Africa regional meeting in June 2002, Nepad's commitment to participation was unveiled as meaningless. Ashwin Desai reports how, at the Durban International Convention Centre,

> police arrived with a massive show of force and drove protesters away from the building with batons and charging horses. One of the organisers of the WEF was approached by an incredulous member of the foreign media and asked about the right to protest in the 'new South Africa.' The organiser pulled out the programme and, with a wry smile, pointed to an upcoming session entitled, 'Taking Nepad to the People.' He said he could not understand the protests because the 'people' have been accommodated.[70]

As for African intellectuals, not only had a tough critique already been launched by the Council for the Development of Social Science Research in Africa, as recorded in Part 2, above, but other impressive radical analyses continued to emerge.[71] By the time of the July 2002,

70. Desai, A. (2003), 'Neoliberalism and Resistance in South Africa,' *Monthly Review*, January.

71. They were not available for inclusion in the first edition, but the most rigorous studies in 2002 were conducted by experienced political economists: Adedeji, A. (2002), 'From the Lagos Plan of Action to the New Partnership for Africa's Development, and from the Final Act of Lagos to the Constitutive Act: Whither Africa?' Keynote Address for the African Forum for Envisioning Africa, Nairobi, 26-29 April; Adesina, J. (2002), 'Development and the Challenge of Poverty: Nepad, Post-Washington Consensus and Beyond', Paper presented to the Codesria/TWN Conference on Africa and the Challenge of the 21st Century, Accra, 23-26 April; Anyang'Nyong'o, P. et al (Eds)(2002), *NEPAD: A New Path?*, Nairobi, Heinrich Böll Foundation; Nabudere, D. (2002), 'Nepad: Historical Background and its Prospects,' in P.Anyang'Nyong'o, et al (Eds), *NEPAD: A New Path?* Nairobi, Heinrich Böll Foundation; Olukoshi, A. (2002), 'Governing the African Political Space for Sustainable Development: A Reflection on Nepad,' Paper for the African Forum for Envisioning Africa, Nairobi, 26-29 April.

Durban launch of the African Union, more than 200 opponents of Nepad in human rights, debt and trade advocacy groups from the Democratic Republic of Congo, Kenya, South Africa, Tanzania and Zimbabwe were sufficiently organised to hold a militant demonstration at the opening ceremony.[72]

Reacting to the growing pressure from the political left, Mbeki began holding civil society consultations, with the assistance of a loyalist faction of the SA Council of Churches and the Africa Institute, although not without controversy.[73] *Business Day's* Jonathan Katzenellenbogen and Vuyo Mvoko reported that 'Nepad is under fire from African experts':

> The group, which met in Pretoria recently and was addressed by Mbeki, panned several aspects of the blueprint for Africa's economic recovery, referring to Mbeki and members of Nepad's steering committee as 'a small group of political elites' and saying the nature of Nepad would... 'perpetuate and reinforce the subjugation of Africa in the international global system, the enclavity of African economies and the marginalisation of Africa's people.' Responding to the criticism, Mbeki's spokesman, Bheki Khumalo, said: 'Ideology and slogans don't feed people. That has been the problem in the past.'[74]

In an unconvincing letter to the editor, Africa Institute director Eddie Maloka replied to the reporters' alleged 'serious distortion and sensationalisation'. He wrote: 'Your article is based on a selective citation of our report to support your afropessimistic negativity and alarmist reporting of the Group of Eight's meeting with African leaders.'[75]

Nepad's defenders did eventually locate some civil society allies. At the Durban AU African summit, trade unions met with Mbeki and repeated the criticism that Nepad, as a 'paradigm and model,

72. *Business Day,* 9 July 2002.

73. Several churchpeople told me how upset they were that, in spite of efforts by some in the SACC to circulate a powerful critique of Nepad, the presence of Mbeki in the room seemed to shake the more conservative forces into a patriotic pro-Nepad fervor.

74. *Business Day,* 27 June 2002.

75. *Business Day,* 4 July 2002. Revealing the weakness of his case, Maloka could merely cite the intellectuals' agreement on an 'all-Africa academy of arts and sciences' to advance 'intra-African academic partnership as a civil society component of Nepad.'

does not depart fundamentally from previous programmes designed by the World Bank and the International Monetary Fund.' Mbeki offered union leaders resources to establish a corporatist structure that would allow ruling parties, 'to hold formal talks with African trade unions and business about Nepad.' Cosatu suggested that this structure 'could possibly be along the lines of the National Economic Development and Labour Council of South Africa,' the very organisation which repeatedly failed to persuade Erwin to honour the tripartite Social Clause agreement in trade negotiations.[76]

In Nigeria, a similarly corporatist faction of civil society was organised by an NGO, the Shelter Rights Initiative, in October 2002 to take advantage of Nepad. The group denounced the lack of activity by Mbeki's main Nepad co-promoter, Obasanjo: 'There appears to be no high-ranking, middle-level or articulate support staff or bureaucracy to support their work. The situation creates doubt as to whether Nepad will outlive the present government.'[77]

NEPAD'S 'PEERS'

Suspicion towards Nepad from democratic, progressive forces across Africa appeared validated when, in October 2002, political-governance peer review was nearly excised from the programme. *Business Day's* Katzenellenbogen described how Nepad 'had fallen victim to the realities of African politics... Diplomats said that there were indications that SA had succumbed to pressure from other African countries, including Libya and Nigeria, to confine peer review to economic and corporate governance matters.' But, as Katzenellenbogen offhandedly remarked, 'With reports done by the International Monetary Fund, World Bank, African Development Bank, and United Nations Economic Commission for Africa it is unlikely that a great deal of value can be added.'[78]

Canadian prime minister Jean Chretien reportedly called Mbeki to insist that peer review be restored, even though Nepad's approach was voluntary and, hence, toothless. Mbeki failed to do damage control on 'the stream of contradictory statements [from Pretoria] since deputy foreign minister Aziz Pahad's bombshell [about peer review being dropped] to the press at the Union Buildings,' Katzenellenbogen wrote.[79] Journalists and diplomats sensed that the fiasco was grounded in *realpolitik*, despite Mbeki's insistence that he stood by Nepad's

76. *Business Day*, 3 July 2002.

77. *Business Day*, 23 October 2002.

78. *Business Day*, 31 October 2002.

79. *Business Day*, 31 October 2002.

democratic rhetoric. African elites didn't want that sort of donor aid-gatekeeping leverage located in Pretoria or anywhere else.

Thus, the March 2002 decision by AU leaders in Abuja to adopt the peer review mechanism, was only actioned fourteen months later, when a panel of six 'Eminent Persons' was named, just three days before the Evian G8 meeting. The five from outside South Africa were Mozambican Graca Machel, UN children's advocate and wife of former president Mandela; former Kenyan diplomat, Bethuel Kiplegat, a Renamo supporter during that group's mass murder of Mozambicans; Keynesian-oriented Nigerian economist Adebayo Adedeji; Senegal's former UN development official Marie-Angelique Savane; and Dorothy Njeuma from Cameroon.

The South African peer was Chris Stals, the former Reserve Bank governor whose African credentials included concern stated in late 1993 about the 'huge burden' the subregion presented South Africa.[80] *Mail & Guardian* columnist Richard Calland commented, 'Nepad's Declaration on Democracy, Political, Economic and Corporate Governance says precious little about development and poverty, and even less about socio-economic rights. Given that he must now oversee compliance, it is hard to know whether to laugh or cry at the fact that the declaration is full of the language that Stals will understand and has very little of that which he would not.'[81] During the 1990s, Stals had been embroiled in several serious governance controversies that should have disqualified him from being a 'peer' to any but the most greedy dictators:

- as a member of the exclusive, racist Afrikaner Broederbond, he participated in venal National Party apartheid politics from 1974;
- he lost R33 billion in SA's hard currency reserves one weekend in mid-1998 trying to defend the Rand, during one of its periodic crashes and won winning criticism from the IMF for incompetence, a few weeks later;
- he shifted Reserve Bank monetary policy to a tight-money, deregulatory financial regime, which put real interest rates on SA government bonds at more than 10% by the mid-1990s, compared to less than 5% in Britain and Germany, and approximately 3% in the US, Japan and Australia;

80. Bond, P. (1993), 'If and When the New South Africa Looks North,' *Financial Gazette*, 22 November.

81. *Mail & Guardian*, 27 June 2003.

- assisted with the National Party project of making the Reserve Bank 'independent' in the 1993 Constitution, so that his job would not be subject to influence from parliament or any democratic forum;
- Reserve Bank governor during several bank failure scandals, including the 1992 Cape Investment Bank and Commuter Corporation pension fund bankruptcies, and the 1993 Masterbond crash, as well as other bank closures in which depositors lost their savings, with no Reserve Bank deposit insurance as proposed by consumer advocates;
- he bailed out failing large Afrikaans banks, subsequently merged as ABSA, in the early 1990s with an extremely generous low-interest loan, which cost taxpayers more than a billion rand;
- his reign as Reserve Bank governor included the early 1990s onset of bank redlining against black neighbourhoods and the dramatic 1993 relaxation of the Usury Act which increased interest rates to loan-shark levels for small borrowers.

How, then, was Stals chosen? A similar question was asked in 1994, when Mandela reappointed him Reserve Bank governor, until his retirement in 1999, when he was succeeded by Tito Mboweni. The terms of a December 1993 IMF loan to South Africa, kept secret until leaked to the press in March 1994, included intense pressure on the ANC to reappoint both apartheid finance minister Derek Keys and Stals. A visit by IMF managing director Michel Camdessus in early 1994 sealed the arrangement, and was publicly resented by Mboweni.[82]

Before the 2003 Evian summit, in time to influence the Abuja peer review selection process, Camdessus was named G8-host France's 'Africa personal representative,' and he enthusiastically endorsed the 'speed' at which the Nepad peer reviewers were chosen. Just prior to the Evian summit, Camdessus explained Nepad's attraction in the following way: 'The African heads of state came to us with the conception that globalization was not a curse for them, as some had said, but rather the opposite, from which something positive could be derived... You can't believe how much of a difference this makes.'[83]

---

82. Reported in the *Cape Times*, 5 May 1994; *Business Day*, 24 January and 24 March 1994.
83. http://www.g7.utoronto.ca/summit/2003evian/briefing_apr030601.html

The G8 and Africa

The result was, perhaps ironically, a cautious and also disdainful G8 attitude toward Africa. When Pretoria's delegation flew to the Kananaskis, Canada summit in June 2002, expectations had been high, not least because of a front-page *Time* feature on 'Mbeki's mission: 'He has finally faced up to the AIDS crisis and is now leading the charge for a new African development plan.'[84]

However, as *Institutional Investor* magazine reported, the G8's 'misleadingly named' Africa Action Plan represented merely 'grudging' support, for the main donor countries with 'only an additional $1 billion for debt relief. (The G8) failed altogether to reduce their domestic agricultural subsidies (which hurt African farm exports) and – most disappointing of all to the Africans – neglected to provide any further aid to the continent.'[85] South Africa's *Sunday Times* confirmed that 'the leaders of the world's richest nations refused to play ball.' Mbeki's comment was thus surprising: 'I think they have addressed adequately all the matters that were put to them.' Kananaskis, he said, was 'a defining moment in the ... evolution of Africa and the birth of a more equitable system of international relations... it signifies the end of the epoch of colonialism and neocolonialism.'[86]

The epoch of neocolonialism continued. At the January 2003 World Economic Forum in Davos, Manuel angrily told journalists, 'Africa didn't really shine here. There is a complete dearth of panels on Africa.' A wire service report revealed, 'Among the many snubs Africa received here was the decision by former US president Bill Clinton to cancel his presence at a press conference on Africa today to discuss Nepad. Forum officials said Clinton did not give reasons for not attending.'[87]

By the time of the 2003, G8 meeting in Evian, France, world elites were aware of Nepad's lack of street credibility. *Institutional Investor* captured the tone: 'Like other far-reaching African initiatives made over the years, this one promptly rolled off the track and into the ditch... Almost two years after Nepad's launch, it has little to show in aid or investment. Only a handful of projects have fallen within the plan's framework.'[88]

---

84. *Time*, 10 June 2002.

85. Gopinath, 'Doubt of Africa.'

86. *Sunday Times*, 30 June 2002; *Business Day*, 28 June 2002.

87. Interpress Service, 28 January 2003.

88. Gopinath, 'Doubt of Africa.'

Evian provided paltry concessions on the UN Global Fund for health, as well as what the *Financial Times* termed, 'year-old pledges to provide an extra $6 billion a year in aid to Africa,' a fraction of the amount spent on the Iraq war a few weeks earlier.[89] An estimated 120 000 activists protested the G8 in the Swiss cities of Geneva and Lausanne. Civil society leaders from six African social movements meeting nearby were scathing: 'The outcome of the 2003 Summit of the G8 reveals that the political will of the eight most powerful nations to meet their obligations to Africa has simply dried up... One or two drops of aid out of Evian amounts to a small patch for the haemorrhaging economies of Africa.'[90]

Mbeki had, a few weeks earlier, offered a righteous condemnation of the protesters, especially Jubilee Africa and the Africa Trade Network:

> What is happening at the precise moment when our continent is taking bold steps to determine its future. I am told that there are some Africans who describe themselves as members of African civil society, who have decided to fly to Evian in France to demonstrate against Nepad…
>
> Strange to say, Africans will fly to France to demand that nothing should be done to help our continent to move forward on these matters, on the basis of programmes conceived and elaborated by us as Africans. I think the most sensible thing for these Africans to do, if they were inspired to oppose African liberation and development, would have been to demonstrate at the headquarters of the African Union in Addis Ababa, rather than at a place in France closely associated with the high cost that France imposed on the Algerian people as they fought for their independence.[91]

Northern NGOs were also surprised at the lack of progress at Evian. Oxfam complained: 'Not only are there no firm commitments, even their rhetoric is watered down compared with last year.' The health advocacy group, Medicins sans Frontiers, put the G8's failure

---

89. *Financial Times*, 2 June 2003. According to Reuters (2 June 2003), 'Ismaila Usman, an executive director of the IMF and former Nigerian finance minister, said late on Saturday some creditors are obstructing debt-relief efforts by selling poor countries' debts to litigious third parties rather than forgiving them.'

90. African Womens Communication and Development Network et al, 'Joint Statement.'

91. Mbeki, T. (2003), 'Address at the SA National Editors Forum Conference on the Media, the AU and Democracy,' Johannesburg, 12 April..

in geopolitical terms: 'To get a pat on the back from Bush, Chirac has sacrificed the right for millions of people to have access to medicines they need to survive. He abandoned his widely publicised commitment to improving access to life-saving medicines, and the rest of the G8 are merrily going along for the ride.'[92]

Mbeki's response was to spindoctor the supposed gains from Evian: 'I think we have bitten off more than we can chew. If we had tried to take a bigger bite... we would not have been able to absorb it... we would produce disappointments. With all these resources committed, [people would ask] what are these Africans doing now? They are not using it.'[93] But the game was given away by Africa's finance ministers, who issued a joint statement after Evian expressing 'deep concern that negotiations on the key elements of the Doha development round have achieved little.'[94]

Another Evian visitor, Brazilian president Lula da Silva, declared that the G8's 'Incoherence between words and acts cannot but breed skepticism and distrust.'[95] Notwithstanding his subsequent desire for an alliance with Mbeki, Lula remarked, 'I noted that the presidents of the poorer countries spend their whole time complaining that the United States does not give us that to which we think we have a right... It does not help to keep crying to the European Union for it to reduce the subsidies it pays to its agriculturalists. No one respects a negotiator who cries or who walks around with his head low.'[96]

As global justice movement strategist Dennis Brutus wrote, Mbeki and his African colleagues were 'apparently intent on selling out the continent under the rubric of a plan crafted by the same technocrats who wrote Pretoria's failed Growth, Employment and Redistribution economic programme, under the guidance of Washington and the corporate leaders of Davos... It is past time for us to insist that President Thabo Mbeki rise off his kneepad and assume the dignity of an African leader, or face ridicule.'[97]

But if Mbeki rose, in which direction would he turn?

---

92. *Guardian*, 4 June 2003.

93. *Business Day*, 4 June 2003.

94. *Business Report*, 8 June 2003.

95. *Le Figaro*, 4 June 2003.

96. Agencia Folha, Alto Araguaia (translation T.Oppermann), 7 June 2003.

97. Brutus, D. (2002), 'Global Agendas are Set by the Usual Suspects,' *Business Day*, 27 June.

MIGHT PRETORIA SPIN LEFT?

In June 2004, according to *Business Day* newspaper, 'President Thabo Mbeki set the seal yesterday on a decisive broad policy shift to the left for his final term in office, lashing out at what he called the "new conservatism" sweeping the world, which enshrined the individual and denigrated the state in a way which could never bring a better life for SA's millions.'[98]

The 'full-frontal attack on free-market economics' was interpreted by *The Economist* in these terms: 'Since attaining power, Mbeki has governed in a reasonably market-friendly manner. But he has recently started to veer back to the left, in word if not yet in deed... Two years ago he fought trade unionists and communists, who are formally allied with the ruling party, the African National Congress, when they ,threatened to strike against privatisation. He beat them down, but he fears they may bounce back.'[99]

Mbeki's 2004 recourse to anti-market rhetoric was to some extent a reversion to an analysis learned within the exiled ANC and at the Lenin Institute in Moscow, and it deeply worried Peter Bruce, editor of *Business Day*: 'Has President Thabo Mbeki lost his mind? Has he lost his temper? His patience? Or has he just lost his faith?'[100] (Just a year earlier, in mid-2003, Bruce was more confident: 'The government is utterly seduced by big business, and cannot see beyond its immediate interests.')[101]

But would talking left be accompanied, still, by walking right? Following from such analysis, the way forward from colonialism and neo-colonialism to a fairer world economy and better-balanced geopolitical system would not pass through Washington, London, Geneva, Brussels or the G8 meeting-ground resorts, which is where Mbeki and his two key allies - Manuel and Erwin - have mainly chosen to promote reforms. Were Mbeki genuinely serious about challenging 'global apartheid' (his preferred term for imperialism), he would have addressed international power relations rather differently. The analysis, strategies, tactics and alliances adopted by Pretoria reveal a *subimperial* location in terms of both geopolitics and capital accumulation, instead of an approach based upon Mbeki's occasionally counter-hegemonic rhetoric.

98. Hartley, W. and P. Bruce (2004), 'Mbeki signals Policy Shift to the Left with fiery Defence of State', *Business Day*, 24 June.

99. *The Economist* (2004), 'South Africa's Economy: Tack to the Left,' 1 July.

100. Bruce, P. (2004), 'Mbeki Shifts to the Left', *Business Day*, 25 June.

101. Bruce, P. (2003), 'SA Needs a Market Economy that Works for All People', *Business Day*, 4 June.

As noted at the outset of Chapter One, the problem was not lack of access to sites of potential reform. Pretoria's lead politicians were allowed, during the late 1990s, to preside over the UN Security Council, the board of governors of the IMF and Bank, the United Nations Conference on Trade and Development, the Commonwealth, the World Commission on Dams and many other important global and continental bodies. Simultaneously taking Third World leadership, Pretoria also headed the Non-Aligned Movement, the Organization of African Unity and the Southern African Development Community.[102] Then, during a frenetic two-year period beginning in September 2001, Mbeki and his colleagues hosted, led, or played instrumental roles at the following dozen major international conferences or events: the World Conference Against Racism in Durban (September 2001); the launch of NEPAD in Abuja, Nigeria (October 2001); the Doha, Qatar ministerial summit of the World Trade Organization (November 2001); the UN's Financing for Development conference in Monterrey, Mexico (March 2002); the G8 summits in Genoa, Italy (July 2001) and Kananaskis, Canada (June 2002); the African Union launch in Durban (July 2002); the World Summit on Sustainable Development (WSSD) in Johannesburg (August-September 2002); the Davos World Economic Forum (January 2003); the Evian G8 Summit (June 2003); George W. Bush's first trip to Africa (July 2003); the Cancun WTO ministerial (September 2003); and the World Bank/IMF annual meeting in Dubai (September 2003).

However, virtually nothing was actually accomplished through these opportunities. At the UN racism conference, Mbeki colluded with the EU to reject the demand of NGOs and African leaders for slavery/colonialism/apartheid reparations. By all accounts, NEPAD provided merely a homegrown version of the Washington Consensus. At Doha, Erwin split the African delegation so as to prevent a repeat of the denial of consensus that had foiled the Seattle ministerial in December 1999. In Monterrey, Manuel was summit co-

102. During this period, Pretoria can claim one intervention worthy of its human rights rhetoric: leadership of the 1997 movement to ban landmines (and hence a major mine-clearing role for South African businesses which had helped lay the mines in the first place). At the same time, however, Mandela's government sold arms to governments which practised mass domestic violence, such as Algeria, Colombia, Peru and Turkey; recognised the Myanmar military junta as a legitimate government in 1994; gave the country's highest official award to Indonesian dictator Suharto three months before his 1998 demise (in the process extracting $25 million in donations for the ANC); and invaded neighbouring Lesotho in 1998, at great social and political cost, mainly so as to secure Johannesburg's water supply.

leader (with Michel Camdessus and disgraced Mexican ex-president Ernesto Zedillo), but his role was merely to legitimize ongoing IMF/WB strategies, including debt relief gimmicks. From Kananaskis, Mbeki departed with only an additional $1 billion commitment for Africa (aside from funds already pledged at Monterrey). The African Union supported both NEPAD and the repressive Zimbabwean regime of president Robert Mugabe. At the Johannesburg WSSD, Mbeki undermined UN democratic procedure, facilitated the privatization of nature, and did nothing to address the plight of the world's poor majority. In Davos, global elites ignored Africa and from Evian, Mbeki returned with nothing. For hosting a leg of Bush's Africa trip, Mbeki became the US 'point man' on Zimbabwe (as Bush pronounced), and avoided any conflict over Iraq. In Cancun, the collapse of trade negotiations left Erwin 'disappointed', because he and his G20 colleagues hoped for a deal, no matter how contrary it would be to ACP country interests. At Dubai, with Manuel leading the Development Committee, there was no Bretton Woods democratization, no new debt relief and no 'Post-Washington' policy reform. This was evident in March 2004 when a new IMF managing director was chosen, amidst Third World elite consternation about the job's reserved 'European-only' designation. Nothing else, aside from the peace-keeping funding and a minor extension of the ineffectual HIPC, was provided at Sea Island, while in contrast, Iraq won debt cancellation worth $87 billion.

Consider a few hypothetical questions in relation to Pretoria's strategy and alignments.[103] Instead of selling the US$250 million worth of arms to the Iraq War aggressors - the US and UK - and warmly welcoming George W. Bush a few weeks after his illegal occupation of Baghdad, what if Mbeki had taken the lead of Mandela (before his 2004 retraction) and explicitly punished Bush with a snub, and strengthened anti-war resistance and even US/UK boycotts in venues like the Non-Aligned Movement and African Union?

Instead of rejecting reparations struggles to punish international financiers, corporations and the Bretton Woods Institutions for supporting apartheid, what if Mbeki and his colleagues had nurtured the anti-racism cause, for the sake of both repairing apartheid's racial and socio-economic damage and warning big capital off future relations with odious regimes?

103. The following cases are chapters from Bond, *Talk Left, Walk Right*. See also Bond, P. (2005)[2000], *Elite Transition: From Apartheid to Neoliberalism in South Africa,* London, Pluto Press and Pietermaritzburg, University of KwaZulu-Natal Press, for more on global/domestic disjunctures.

Instead of battling the global justice movement and African trade officials from Seattle through Doha to Cancun, what if trade minister Erwin had tried uniting the continent and its allies behind a counterhegemonic trade agenda so as to meet popular needs, not those of global capital?

Instead of rejecting debt cancellation as a strategy, what if Manuel had joined the Jubilee movement, denounced bogus World Bank and IMF plans for crumbs of relief in the midst of amplified neoliberalism, and helped to organise a debtors' cartel?

Instead of exacerbating the World Summit on Sustainable Development's orientation to commodification, not to mention repressing legitimate dissent, what if the ANC leaders had tried to harmonise and genuinely implement the agendas of poverty-eradication and environment? Instead of promoting water commercialisation and large dams, what if South Africa helped establish sound principles of decommodification and respect for nature, both in water catchments at home and in international talk-shops?

And instead of a New Partnership for Africa's Development considered, simultaneously, 'philosophically spot-on' by the Bush regime and ridiculous by Zimbabweans, Swazis and many other Africans hoping for pro-democracy pressure, what if Pretoria had helped establish a bottom-up African programme for recovery based upon partnerships between Africans themselves?

The reality is not only persistence in neoliberal policies, with two very minor exceptions: privatisation has only slowed not halted (mainly due to popular resistance and adverse market conditions), and the tight post-apartheid fiscal straightjacket has been loosened very slightly. In addition, the climate for debate between the centre-left ruling party and its Alliance partners - the SACP and Cosatu - on the one hand, and the independent left on the other, is still chilly. The latter still allege that the ANC adopted and continues to implement neoliberal macroeconomic and microdevelopment policies, as orthodox monetary policy is maintained, liberalisation of trade and finance proceeds apace, corporatisation of state enterprises speeds up,[104] and the ongoing attack by state service providers against low-income people continues.

---

104. One of the highest-profile cases is transport. Transnet chief executive Dolly Mokgatle told the AfricaRail 2004 conference in June to 'get out from under the aura of State-owned enterprises... The days of "tunnel vision" are over. We have customers who want to catch up; some are competing with China's vibrant and growing economy... We need to look for public-private partnerships and strategic equity partners as we look for growth.' (*Creamer's Engineering News*, (2004), 'Railways should Strengthen Nation's "competitiveness"', 24 June.)

To illustrate, in June 2004, Cosatu expressing confidence in the new minister of public enterprises, Alec Erwin: 'We welcome the fact that the minister has, like the president, placed the issue of employment creation at the centre of the restructuring of the State-Owned Enterprises.' But by September, the only logical reply was or unions to threaten 'the worst strike in Spoornet's history if the railway company went ahead with plans to retrench 946 employees in the next two months,' in the immediate wake of parent parastatal firm Transnet's R6.3 billion pretax loss. According to Chris de Vos, secretary-general of the Spoornet union Utatu, at his first meeting with labour in July, 'Erwin had said Spoornet as a state-owned company had the responsibility of creating jobs, not shedding them.' By the end of August, Erwin had changed position, 'saying state-owned companies were not employment agencies and that managers had to do everything possible to make businesses profitable, including cutting jobs.'[105]

Moreover, there are ongoing reports of state repression and judicial harassment against social movements which resist. *Mail & Guardian* editor Ferial Haffajee initially ridiculed as 'melodrama' the observations of Naomi Klein, who wrote of South Africa:

> There's a huge amount of struggle going on in this country. There are movements exploding. They are resisting privatisation of water and electricity, resisting eviction and demanding land reform. They are reacting against all the broken promises of the ANC. This is a security state. It spends three times as much on private security as it does on affordable housing – just to keep the rich from the poor.[106]

A month later, Haffajee's paper revealed:

> The killing of a 19-year-old boy in Phoenix, Durban, two weeks ago by city council security guards has again cast a spotlight on the measures state authorities use against impoverished communities in protest. Marcel King was shot dead on Thursday June 24 by a member of a security company hired by the Durban council to disconnect electricity that had

105. Faniso, M. (2004), 'Unions plan major strike if Spoornet continues axing jobs,' Business Report, 3 September.

106. Cited in Haffajee, F. (2004), 'Fact, Fiction and the New Left', *Mail & Guardian*, 11 June.

> apparently been illegally reconnected in the impoverished Durban suburb...
>
> This incident is one of many recent clashes between state security, social movement activists and community members in suburbs in Gauteng, the Western Cape and KwaZulu-Natal. Marchers and protests are a regular feature of political life and are governed by a series of regulations governing gatherings. Most occur without incident. But several have gotten ugly recently.
>
> On election day this year (14 April 2004) three Landless People's Movement activists were arrested and were detained and allegedly tortured. On Freedom Day (21 March 2004) police fired on a group of Anti-Privatisation Forum members protesting outside the Constitutional Court in Johannesburg against electricity cut-offs.[107]

There are many more such cases, of course.[108] Moreover, if we project Pretoria's style of governance to the regional scale, it is easy to comprehend the processes of domination and exclusion that allow the South African government to exploit its semi-peripheral position within imperialism. For example, in spite of promoting the globalisation of *capital*, Pretoria is opposed to the globalisation and regionalisation of *people*, according to a recent Refugees International (RI) report:

> South Africa is denying access to political asylum to thousands of Zimbabweans seeking to escape persecution. Of the 5,000 applications for political asylum filed by Zimbabweans to date, fewer than 20 Zimbabweans have actually received political asylum in South Africa. But more troubling still is the fact that few Zimbabweans are able even to apply for political asylum...
>
> RI interviewed people who told of being asked for a bribe merely to receive a letter giving them an appointment to present their asylum claim. Police officers ask for bribes to look the other way when rounding up undocumented asylum seekers or those whose temporary permit of stay has expired.

107. Robinson, V. (2004), 'Concern at Government Violence against Protesters,' *Mail & Guardian*, 12 July.

108. Updates on independent left struggles and state repression can be found at http://southafrica.indymedia.org, http://www.ukzn.ac.za/ccs, http://www.apf.org.za, http://www.khanya.org.za, http://www.aidc.org.za, http://red.org.za and in some of the newspapers that have township coverage, though not URL links.

> One Zimbabwean told us, 'I was stopped while walking down the street. The policeman asked for my papers but told me that for 200 Rand [U$33] he would not deport me.' At the Lindela detention center, bribes are demanded for release, while deportees can also pay to jump from the 'deportation train' on the way back to Zimbabwe...
>
> Police and Army in the border regions rely on spurious methods to identify Zimbabweans, such as asking questions in a South African language or checking which arm bears a smallpox scar. According to an NGO working in Musina, 'The police have no training. Some people are being deported because [Zimbabweans] are darker.'[109]

The best explanation for Pretoria's increasing repression of poor and working-class people both locally and regionally is growing desperation. As conceded even by Joel Netshitenzhe (government's leading ideologue) in a review of post-apartheid accomplishments, 'The advances made in the First Decade by far supersede the weaknesses. Yet, if all indicators were to continue along the same trajectory, especially in respect of the dynamic of economic inclusion and exclusion, we could soon reach a point where the negatives start to overwhelm the positives.'[110]

The negatives are formidable, and in mid-2004 took various forms combining social deprivation, economic austerity and financial vulnerability. According to Nenad Pacek of The Economist Corporate Network, 'Portfolio investments accounted for a massive 24% of South Africa's gross domestic product, and 65% of the rand's trading took place offshore.'[111] Given the strength of the currency – a July 2004 high of R5.8/US$ – that logically resulted from vast financial capital inflows beginning in late 2001, when the rand hit a low of R13.8/US$, South Africa's cumulative trade balance fell spectacularly from a US$2 billion surplus in 2003 to a deficit of US$290 million during the first half of 2004.[112]

Meanwhile, in the real productive sectors, job shedding continued unabated, notwithstanding the rise of unemployment

109. Refugees International (2004), 'Zimbabweans in South Africa: Denied Access to Political Asylum,' Washington, 14 June.

110. The Presidency (2003), *Towards a Ten Year Review*, Pretoria, South African Government Communication and Information Service, October.

111. Stones, L. (2004), 'Volatile Rand, Aids Deter Foreign Investors,' *Business Day*, 19 July.

112. South African Press Association (2004), 'Warship, Strong Rand help Widen Trade Deficit,' 1 August.

from 15% in 1994 to 32% in 2003 (43% when frustrated jobseekers are added).[113] In spite of a minor uptick of domestic fixed investment – at 15% of GDP in late 2003, still far below the 25% required for 5% GDP growth – the official statistical agency reported that formal sector (non-agricultural) employment fell by another 41,000 in the first quarter of 2004.[114] The contrast between the economy's 'slow rotting' (in the words of frequent government consultant Stephen Gelb)[115] and the vast speculative inflow was explained by Michael Power (a Keynesian economist who writes regularly for *Business Day*):

> Take a look at the emerging market rankings in The Economist. First where we 'lead': currency strength, 1/25; lowest inflation, 3/25. Yet we lag in: gross domestic product growth, 25/25; foreign exchange reserves, 25/25; industrial production, 21/25; current account, 20/25. A little digging reveals our real interest rates, cost of capital and unemployment is among the highest; our foreign direct investment inflow is among the lowest.[116]

It is here that the core concession made by the ANC during the early 1990s transition deal is apparent, namely in the desire by white businesses to escape the economic stagnation and declining profits born of a classical organic capitalist crisis, in the context of a sanctions-induced laager, and amplified by the 1970s-80s rise of black militancy in workplaces and communities.

The deal represented simply this: black nationalists got the state, while white people and corporations could remove the bulk of their capital from the country, and simultaneously remain domiciled in South Africa with, thanks to economic liberalisation, still more privileges. Trade, credit, cultural and sports sanctions ended; exchange controls were mainly lifted; luxury imports flooded in; white people's incomes rose by 15% during the late 1990s; taxes were cut dramatically; and the corporate pre-tax profit share soared during the late 1990s, back to 1960s-era levels associated with apartheid's heyday.

113. Statistics South Africa (2001), *South Africa in Transition*, Pretoria, for 1995, and Statistics South Africa (2003), *Labour Force Survey, September 2002*, Pretoria, p.iii for 2002.

114. Webb, B. (2004), 'SA Investment Appears to be on Track,' South African Press Association, 16 July.

115. Gelb, S. (2003), 'Inequality in South Africa: Nature, Causes and Responses,' DfID Policy Initiative on Addressing Inequality in Middle-income Countries, Johannesburg, The EDGE Institute, November.

116. Power, M. (2004), 'Strong Rand is Stairway to Ruin,' *Business Day*, 16 July.

Hence inequality soared during ANC rule, even state statistics show. Black 'African' South Africans suffered an income crash of 19% from 1995-2000, with every indication of further degeneration in subsequent years. The ANC rebuttal is that when state spending is accounted for, the divergence is reversed. Yet notwithstanding deeper poverty, the state raised water and electricity prices, to the point that by 2002 they consumed 30% of the income of those households earning less than $70 per month.[117] An estimated 10 million people had their water cut off, according to two national government surveys, and 10 million were also victims of electricity disconnections. In June 2004, even the director-general of the water department admitted, '275,000 of all households attributed interruptions to cut-offs for non-payment last year,' a shocking record in view of the ANC's 2000 local government election promises of 'free basic services' covering water and sanitation, electricity and other municipal functions.[118] The higher cost of services reflects the permanent contradiction between big-business advocates of essentially neoliberal development policies, and well-mobilised activists.

CONCLUSION: STORMY DAYS AHEAD

There is no South African model to lift Africa out of its socio-economic doldrums, and no heroic Nkrumahist figure to coordinate other elites into a progressive, good-governance mode of political behaviour. Frustrated Zimbabwean democrats know this best, but so do the tens of thousands of South Africans who periodically mobilise in dramatic protest against Pretoria's policies.

In sum, it should be clear that Mbeki's agenda is not that of the majority of Africans or South Africans. If the largely parasitical – not development-oriented – Johannesburg corporations profit from Nepad's legitimation of neoliberalism and lubrication of capital flows out of African countries, these flows mainly end up in London, where Anglo American Corporation, DeBeers, Old Mutual insurance, South African Breweries and others of South Africa's largest firms re-listed their financial headquarters during the late 1990s. And if Mbeki and his colleagues are benefiting from the high profile provided by Nepad and a variety of other global-managerial functions, the real winners are those in Washington and other imperial centres who, increasingly, require a subimperial South African frontman for the ongoing superexploitation and militarisation of Africa.

117. Statistics South Africa (2002), 'Database on Expenditure and Income, 2000', Pretoria.
118. Muller, M. (2004), 'Keeping the Taps Open,' *Mail & Guardian*, 25 June.

So it is to the activists that we must again turn, in conclusion. Since the first edition was completed in June 2002, there have been more developments in the African Social Forum and other networks and coalitions, aiming at ultimately displacing neoliberal Nepad arguments and replacing them with social justice, ecological sensitivity, the reversal of patriarchy, and finally, genuine economic progress. The most spectacular manifestation of the conflict between the top-down and bottom-up approaches was probably the August 31, 2002 march of more than 20,000 activists from impoverished Alexandra Township to the Sandton Convention Centre. One of the two central slogans of the historic march was 'Phansi Nepad!'

But Nepad's core content also continues to be rejected in a myriad of ways, and alternatives are being established by the masses of Africans in the course of their struggles. For example, in 2004, activists in the Africa Trade Network soundly rejected the liberalisation agenda, especially Economic Partnership Agreements between Africa-Caribbean-Pacific (ACP) countries and the European Union, and instead called for trade cooperation that:

- is based on a principle of non-reciprocity, as instituted in General System of Preferences and special and differential treatment in the WTO;
- protects ACP producers domestic and regional markets;
- reverses the pressure for trade and investment liberalisation; and
- allows the necessary policy space and supports ACP countries to pursue their own development strategies.[119]

On financial matters, African resistance movements also regularly voice anger. One striking example was the February 2004 stayaway called by the Zambia Congress of Trade Unions, in which half a million workers rejected a civil service wage freeze promoted by the IMF, demanding instead a minimum wage and other budgetary concessions.[120]

More generally, a June 2004 Cape Town meeting of Jubilee Africa members from Angola, Cameroon, Cote d'Ivoire, the DRC, Kenya, Mozambique, South Africa, Swaziland, Zambia, Tanzania and Zimbabwe, and partners from Brazil, Argentina and the Philippines worked on a comprehensive Illegitimate Debt Audit. They 'expressed

119. http://www.mwengo.org/acp/statements/default

120. SouthScan (2004), 'Massive Strike Against Austerity Plan,' 24 February.

deep concern with South Africa's sub-imperialist role and its use of Nepad to promote the neoliberal paradigm to further dominate the rest of the African continent politically, economically, culturally and militarily, serving the interests of transnational corporations.' The groups demanded:

- full unconditional cancellation of Africa's total debt;
- reparations for damage caused by debt devastation;
- an immediate halt to HIPC and PRSPs and the disguised structural adjustment program through Nepad and any other agreements that do not address the fundamental interests of the impoverished majority and the building of a sustainable and sovereign Africa; and
- a comprehensive audit to determine the full extent and real nature of Africa's illegitimate debt, the total payments made to date and the amount owed to Africa.[121]

Not only do the left forces oppose Nepad, they also openly call for their finance ministers to default on the illegitimate foreign debt. They advocate not only kicking the World Bank and IMF out of their countries, but also international strategies for defunding and abolishing the Bretton Woods Institutions. US groups like Center for Economic Justice and Global Exchange work with Jubilee South Africa and Brazil's Movement of the Landless, amongst others, to promote the 'World Bank Bonds Boycott', asking of their Northern allies: is it ethical for socially-conscious people to invest in the Bank by buying its bonds (responsible for 80% of the institution's resources), and to receive dividends which represent the fruits of enormous suffering? Other examples of what is being termed 'deglobalization' include the successful effort to deny Trade-Related Intellectual Property Rights status to AIDS medicines, to keep GMOs out of several Southern African agricultural markets, and to reject French and British water privatisers. To these ends, the African Trade Network and the Gender and Trade Network in Africa put intense pressure on the continent's delegates to reject the WTO's Cancun proposals. And with the US and EU offering no concessions on matters of great importance to Africa, bilateral or regional trade deals are also resisted by both civil society groups and African governments.

121. http://www.aidc.org.za

There are many more such reflections of latent African anti-capitalism, which Frantz Fanon would celebrate.[122] On a more local level, inspiring examples of what might be termed 'decommodification' are underway in Africa, especially South Africa. There, independent left movements have struggled to turn basic needs into human rights: anti-retroviral medicines to fight AIDS and other health services; free water (50 liters/person/day); free electricity (1 kiloWatt hour/person/day); thorough-going land reform; prohibition on services disconnections and evictions; free education; and even a 'Basic Income Grant,' as advocated by churches and trade unions. The idea is that all such services should be provided to all as a human right, and to the degree that it is feasible, financed through imposition of much higher prices for luxury consumption.

Because the commodification of everything is still underway in South Africa, this could provide the basis for a unifying agenda for a widescale movement for fundamental social change, if linked to the demand to 'rescale' many political-economic responsibilities that are now handled by embryonic world-state institutions under the influence of neoliberal US administrations. The decommodification principle could become an enormous threat to imperial capitalist interests, in the form of a denial of private intellectual property (such as AIDS medicines), resistance to biopiracy, the exclusion of GM seeds from African agricultural systems, the nationalisation of industries and utilities, or the empowerment of African labour forces.

To make any progress, delinking from the most destructive circuits of global capital will also be necessary, combining local decommodification strategies and tactics with the call to close the World Bank, IMF and WTO. Beyond that, the challenge for Africa's progressive forces, as ever, is to establish the difference between 'reformist reforms' and reforms that advance a 'non-reformist' agenda. The latter would include generous social policies stressing decommodification, and capital controls and more inward-oriented industrial strategies allowing democratic control of finance and ultimately of production itself. These sorts of reforms would strengthen democratic movements, directly empower the producers, and, over time, open the door to the contestation of capitalism itself.

---

122. For more on the African left, see Fisher, J. (2002), 'Africa,' in E.Bircham and J.Charlton, eds., *Anti-Capitalism: A Guide to the Movement*, London, Bookmarks; Zeilig, L. (Ed)(2002), *Class Struggle and Resistance in Africa*, Cheltenham, New Clarion; Bond, *Talk Left, Walk Right*, Chapter Twelve; and Ngwane, T. (2003), 'Sparks in Soweto', *New Left Review*, 21.

Not only does imperialism stand in the way, however, so do Pretoria's various subimperial barriers. Notwithstanding occasionally leftist rhetoric and the world-historic damage inflicted by US empire, Mbeki and his colleagues are situating South Africa as the continent's leading bourgeois-aspirant country, parallel to what Frantz Fanon so poignantly described as the stunted 'national bourgeoisie' of a post-colonial African state, i.e., the modern equivalent of an old Bantustan, where the coopted elite prosper under conditions of global apartheid.

Fanon's warning about 'the pitfalls of national consciousness', with which we began this book, is also a conviction that the instincts of social justice amongst ordinary people cannot be repressed forever. In 1961, as Fanon wrote *The Wretched of the Earth,* the inexorable force of anti-colonial consciousness, and the relationship of material grievances to organisational energy, were aligned in a potentially revolutionary way. More than four decades later, it is too easy to be despondent about the failure to establish a unified Africa-wide strategy to combat imperialism, neoliberalism, patriarchy, ecological degradation and so many other problems. Nevertheless, Fanon's warning is also a promise to us all:

> The peoples of Africa have only recently come to know themselves. They have decided, in the name of the whole continent, to weigh in strongly against the colonial regime. Now the national bourgeoisies, who in region after region hasten to make their own fortunes and to set up a national system of exploitation, do their utmost to put obstacles in the path of this 'Utopia.' The national bourgeoisies, who are quite clear as to what their objectives are, have decided to bar the way to that unity, to that coordinated effort... to triumph over stupidity, hunger, and inhumanity at one and the same time. This is why we must understand that African unity can only be achieved through the upward thrust of the people, and under the leadership of the people, that is to say in defiance of the interests of the bourgeoisie...
>
> The former colonial power increases its demands, accumulates concessions and guarantees and takes fewer and fewer pains to mask the hold it has over the national government. The people stagnate deplorably in unbearable poverty; slowly the awaken to the unutterable treason of their leaders. This awakening is all the more acute because the

leaders are incapable of learning its lesson. The distribution of wealth that it effects is not spread out between a great many sectors; it is not ranged among different levels nor does it set up a hierarchy of half-tones. The new caste is an affront all the more disgusting in that the immense majority, nine-tenths of the population, continue to die of starvation. The scandalous enrichment, speedy and pitiless of this caste is accompanied by a decisive awakening on the part of the people, and a growing awareness that promises stormy days to come.[123]

123. Fanon, F. (1963)[1961], *The Wretched of the Earth,* New York, Grove Press, pp.164,166.